Storytime Action!

2,000+
Ideas
for
Making
500
Picture
Books
Interactive

JENNIFER BROMANN

NEAL-SCHUMAN PUBLISHERS, INC.
NEW YORK   LONDON

Published by Neal-Schuman Publishers, Inc.
100 Varick Street
New York, NY 10013

Library of Congress Cataloging-in-Publication Data

Bromann, Jennifer.
   Storytime action! 2,000+ ideas for making 500 picture books interactive /
Jennifer Bromann.
      p. cm.
   Includes bibliographical references and indexes.
   ISBN 1-55570-459-X (alk paper)
   1. Children's libraries—Activity programs—United States. 2. School
libraries—Activity programs—United States. 3. Storytelling—United
States. 4. Picture books for children—United States—Bibliography. I. Title.

Z718.2.U6 B76 2003
027.62'51—dc21
                                             2002031994

Contents

Preface

INTERACTIVE BOOKS AND STORYTIMES

Interactivity has always been a part of children's stories. Some types of books, such as search-and-find, pop-up, or lift-the-flap books, seem naturally interactive. More traditional books often feature animal sounds or children dancing. These naturally elicit interactive responses. *Storytime Action! 2,000+ Ideas for Making 500 Picture Books Interactive* features techniques I have used for making more than 500 books interactive. In addition, I show you how you can create your own simple songs, games, rhymes, plays, or other activities to complement any book you may want to share with children.

Essentially, my definition of *interactive* takes elements directly from the story and then turns them into an engaging activity for the children. Suppose you're teaching *Where the Wild Things Are* (Sendak, 1963). Rather than reading the book and then moving on to a related activity, why not make an activity out of the story itself? Let the kids stomp around as if they really *are* where the wild things are. When the boy arrives in the land of the wild things, the children can hold up their arms and make claw hands while stomping around pretending to be monstrous creatures. You can easily and organically lead children into songs, plays, games, rhymes—all using the plot, characters, or settings from the book. The imaginative world of the story comes alive for the children.

This book is for public librarians and educators who perform weekly storytimes and programs and for school media specialists who tell stories to children during their visits to the media center. Even parents can benefit from the suggestions offered in this book. I lead storytimes as a librarian and I can report amazing results from using interactive methods. I wanted to share this concept with others who might be struggling with the challenge of entertaining and motivating inattentive, overactive, and even, sometimes, unruly children. You will see a change in the way children follow the story. Whether you completely switch to this style or only use it occasionally, it's useful to have the option.

INCORPORATING INTERACTIVITY

Making books interactive may sound like extra work—lots of planning and pre-production—but it really needn't be at all. Hundreds of plans are ready-made for you here. You will find 500 children's picture books briefly summarized with suggestions on how the book can be used interactively. Use *Storytime Action!* as a ready reference whenever you'd like, and you will soon see how you can easily make any book—even those not listed here—just as much fun. You will soon be creating your own activities, and you can stop trying to contrive theme-based activities. You can stop piecing together elaborate plans from the suggested activities of various storytime manuals. The stories themselves will bring fun activities to mind. Children won't notice that you haven't tacked on any additional games to the session. They'll be too caught up in the world of the stories!

Another innovative proposition of *Storytime Action! 2,000+ Ideas for Making 500 Picture Books Interactive* is the notion of relying only on interactive stories in storytimes rather than focusing primarily on the various activities sandwiched in between stories. The use of props, storytelling, movement, questions, board stories, repetition, playacting, music, art, and games is encouraged here just as enthusiastically as in any storytime manual. The idea here is to use all of these dynamic techniques *within the context of the stories you read*, not for them to be fun to get to after stories are read.

The 500 examples listed here are designed to be especially user-friendly. For those times when you don't want active or loud children (such as bedtime or when the library needs to be quiet), there are many suggestions of books that naturally involve quieter activities. You may also find that the summaries and activity descriptions here will be detailed enough for you to recreate many of these stories without the book in hand and in your own words.

Please keep in mind that the interactive method can also be adapted for kids of all ages. Many of the summaries in this book suggest ways to teach different lessons, such as geography or poetry, for kids of varying levels. Although the focus here is on ideas best suited for ages three to five, by adjusting the interactions, you can use the same books with younger children. Because of the complexity of some of the activities suggested, they can also be used at least up to third grade.

The 500 books were chosen to illustrate that literally any book can be made a dynamic experience. They reflect a variety of publication dates, themes, degrees of literary merit, and so on. Some I have used interactively before, some were brand new to me, and some I even remember reading as a child. You will see some inferior books; that's intentional. The point of including them is that *you* can supply the quality by making the book fun—and you can do it quite easily. By following the top ten elements listed in Chapter 1, "How to Make Any Book Interactive," you will never be at a loss for creating your own activities.

Soon you will discover that every book you pull off the shelf will lend itself to interactivity. At the end of the first chapter, there is also a storytime checklist to use as an aid for generating your own ideas and presentation plans. Chapter 2, "How to Create Interactive Storytime," incorporates all of my suggestions for a successful experience. Chapter 3, "2,000+ Ideas for Making 500 Books Interactive," offers a wide variety of books, listed alphabetically by author, with my ideas for making them interactive. There are title and theme indexes at the back of the book to help you find what you need quickly.

INTERACTIVITY AND LEARNING

Interactivity can often make children's early experience of books become more vivid, more dimensional, and more stimulating. The thinking behind my method is that the entertaining bells and whistles of your storytime sessions serve a greater purpose than merely keeping the kids entertained; they actually amplify the meaningful engagement of reading and sharing books. Both experience and research have shown that making stories interactive helps to give kids concrete reasons for paying closer attention to stories all the way through to their endings. It also prepares them for success in school. As Lonigan pointed out:

> In the study "Reading to Pre-schoolers Exposed: Is the Emperor Really Naked?" (Lonigan, 1994) it was found that interaction during story time between a parent and a preschool child can be a predictor of future academic success. Parents were studied who not only read books to their children, but also went beyond the text to ask questions and make commentaries that led their children into more abstract thinking and linguistic expression. The children were asked how and why events took place in stories and were encouraged to make comments about unfolding events and relate them to past experiences in their lives. Unlike children who did not experience this interactive reading, these children not only successfully learned to read in the early elementary years, but were also successful in "reading to learn" in the middle elementary years ..." (Schaefer and DiGeronimo, 2000).

Let's look at some of the most commonly cited purposes of storytime sessions to further illustrate the effectiveness of making books interactive.

1. Storytime improves listening skills.
   Listening skills are greatly improved when children are focused on waiting for their turn in a story or waiting to repeat certain words. Storytimes may not be completely quiet, but they will have moments of silence and moments of activity.
2. Storytime increases vocabulary.
   If more stories are told and extra in-between activities are eliminated, there is a greater chance of introducing new vocabulary.
3. Storytime introduces a number of good books.
   More books with fewer unrelated activities equal more exposure to books for the children. If a typical storytime had three books and three activities, and an interactive storytime features six books, that is twice the exposure.
4. Storytime introduces the concept of being a member of a group.
   Children learn to participate even more in a group when they are asked to take roles in a story or wait their turn.
5. Storytime shows that the library or school can be a fun experience.
   Children will have much more fun with stories when every book is a game.
6. Storytime instills a love of books and reading.
   All of this in turn adds up to being a positive experience for children leading to a greater likelihood that children will become, and remain, readers.

A BREAK WITH TRADITION

Traditional storytime format discourages unnecessary interactivity. "We do not stop along the way to ask questions or to deliver small lectures or explanations" (Broderick, 1977). "Questions or comments during the story can be disruptive to the rest of the group. Responses should be kept short and children should be encouraged to wait until the end for any discussion. Avoid asking children questions during the story. After a story keep any discussion short. The purpose of the story hour is to share literature, and not to check comprehension" (Conner, 1990). *Storytime Action!* encourages a very different approach.

Making picture books interactive is not lecturing or testing. And it does not advocate making comments unrelated to the story. Many librarians have found that interactive questions can be an excellent way to hold attention. Many experts today also suggest that you ask children "What's happening here?" or similar questions, or turn the book into an "I spy" game (Mayes and Cohen, 2002). The moment you ask a question of a child who will feel intelligent knowing an answer, you have gained immediate attention. Questions are not the only way to prompt interaction, but many librarians vouch that they can be used without disrupting the storytime process.

Kids want to have fun at the library, and we librarians are always eager to encourage reading and storytime as fun activities. It is also a given that children today arrive for storytime accustomed to the rapid action of TV, movies, and pop music. In response, we use games, songs, crafts, and countless other tricks-of-the-trade to hold their attention. It is increasingly rare to just read stories to young children anymore without at least one of them getting fidgety, pulling hair, or wandering around the room. The experience of countless librarians shows that to reach today's youth, we need to entertain them actively. The result is that most of us are now in the habit of breaking up storytimes with all sorts of fun planned for in between reading books—even running the risk that the stories themselves are no longer the primary purpose of storytime. Making stories interactive is one innovative alternative to this growing trend.

REFERENCES

Broderick, Dorothy M. 1977. *Library Work with Children*. New York: H. W. Wilson Co.

Connor, Jane Gardner. 1990. *Children's Library Service Handbook*. Phoenix, Ariz.: Oryx.

Lonigan, Christopher J. 1994. "Reading to Preschoolers Exposed: Is the Emperor Really Naked?" *Developmental Review 14* (3): 303–323.

Mayes, Linda C., and Donald J. Cohen. 2002. *The Yale Child Study Center Guide to Understanding Your Child*. Boston: Little, Brown.

Moore, Vardine. 1966. *Pre-School Story Hour*. New York: Scarecrow.

Sendak, Maurice. 1963. *Where the Wild Things Are*. New York: HarperCollins.

Schaefer, Charles E., and Theresa Foy DiGeronimo. 2000. *Ages and States: A Parent's Guide to Normal Childhood Development*. New York: John Wiley & Sons.

Acknowledgments

Thanks must once again go to Mike Giometti for handling almost all of my interlibrary loan requests for researching this book as well as to the circulation staff of the Prairie Trails Public Library District in Burbank, Illinois, especially Marlene Gilbert, for checking in the hundreds of books I returned. Thanks also to my sister, Natalie Bromann, young adult librarian at Glenside Public Library, Glendale Heights, Illinois, who assisted with the index and located the names of the illustrators of the books, and to my mother, Barbara Bromann, kindergarten teacher at Corporate Childcare Consultant's Learning Center in Chicago, who read through all the activities to make sure they were understandable to educators.

Chapter 1

How to Make Any
Book Interactive

FIND THE ESSENTIAL INTERACTIVE ELEMENTS OF ANY BOOK

All interactive stories—whether you use some of my 500 suggestions or go to your shelf to create your own—share familiar elements. No doubt you've used these building blocks in some ways before. Now begin to think creatively about using these imaginative elements with all books. Soon you'll discover that you can make every book interactive.

INCORPORATE THE TOP TEN INTERACTIVE ELEMENTS

1. Props
   With a page full of words, a motionless picture is not always going to keep every child's attention—no matter how great a storyteller you are. Props are an effective way to place attention on an object so children who cannot focus on the book have another place to look. The children still hear the text, but will not have to focus on one page for very long.

2. Storytelling
   One of the best ways to get a child's attention is to shift from reading a book to telling a story. It is much easier to move about and make a story interactive without the book in hand. Also, that allows you to focus on the children and more easily tell when their attention is fading so you can draw them back in. Children can also become involved by acting out the story as you tell it or responding to your questions.

3. Movement

   Maintain a flow of movement while reading stories. If you employ action and movement in stories, children might not even notice they are listening to a story. Movement helps kids with short attention spans enjoy literature. Many books are set up to use this type of involvement, but you can make other books work this way as well. Perform the actions in the story. Move around to look at objects set up around the room. Pretend to see what is happening in the story. Dancing, exercise, and animal motions are often easily introduced.

4. Questions

   Asking questions is a trick that has been around forever. If the story has no repetition, no props seem suitable, you have no time to memorize, and no movement is involved, simply ask questions. Often there is an obvious problem or situation in a book that calls for questions. If not, then ask the children simple questions about what the characters should do or what they think happened or what will happen next. These are always good ways to keep kids attentive during a story.

5. Board Stories

   Children enjoy the occasional break of watching the story happen on the board rather than watching still pictures in the book. Just about every librarian has used board stories for storytime. Use prepared ones or make your own simple versions. They do not necessarily have to have flannel backing, Velcro, or magnets. They can be laminated or you can even just tape pictures onto any surface. They can always be colored and laminated later. To find pictures, use your coloring and pattern books or search for coloring sheets on the Internet, using search terms such as "pig and coloring sheet" to find pictures to copy. Use board stories if a book has small or unclear pictures but a good story. Cut apart old books to make flannel board stories. Use books specifically designed for flannel board stories.

6. Repetition

   One of the oldest—and easiest—ways to keep a child's attention is to use repetitive stories. Allow the children to repeat a key phrase. They will wait to say that sentence or that word instead of letting something else in the room draw their attention. Many classic children's stories use repetition, especially cumulative tales. Even if a book has no repetitive phrases, you can still ask the children to say a specific word like "ball" when you point to them. Ask them to shout out a word or perform an action when they hear you say a specific word. Their listening will improve if they have something to watch out for. They can mimic you or repeat on their own.

7. Playacting

Allow children to act out roles in the stories. Assign them specific parts, have them mimic the actions, or let them repeat the words of one or all the characters in a story. Playacting is best with fairy tales, sports stories, or books with many characters.

8. Music

Use music if you know of a song that goes with the book—perhaps sing along if you have a book written from the lyrics of a song or play a song that has been written to accompany the book. If you are really talented, you can write your own melody to the text or put it to the tune of a familiar song. If there is a simple beat or rhythm to poetic words, you can have children tap it out. Allow children to play any instruments or use noisemakers for any book about music.

9. Art

Many books allow children to make a craft, such as a steering wheel or clock, to help them through the story. Enhance other stories by drawing parts of the story on a board or paper. Allow children to color, draw on paper, or take turns coloring or drawing on a surface at the front of the room. This is effective when a series of things is added to a character, object, or scene in a story, for example, articles of clothing in a story about getting dressed.

10. Games

Invent a new game to keep children attentive. Play bingo to help children keep track of days, months, or objects in the story. Stand or hold something up when a word is called. Let children toss something when a word is read. Search and find objects in the room. Think of any popular games and see if they might be adapted to the book.

MAKE ANY BOOK INTERACTIVE

Use the checklist on page 6 to make any book interactive. It will help you record new interactive ideas about books or keep track of past successful interactive storytimes. Keep these pages in a notebook for quick reference or to share with your fellow storytellers. You only need to combine a few (especially those with similar themes) to create an entire storytime.

Use the top of the checklist to list the theme and record all the pertinent bibliographic information about the book. Write a summary to help you begin thinking of the essential elements of the story. In the second half of the checklist, examine your story for any of the top ten elements of interactivity. Then brainstorm for any possible ideas.

1. Props
   - Can puppets or stuffed animals represent the characters in the story?
   - Are there a variety of different objects, people, or animals added to or removed from the story?
   - Is dressing up or giving children something to hold an option?
2. Storytelling
   - Is the story easy to memorize?
   - Will parts of the story be a surprise if the story is told without pictures?
   - Would actions be restricted with a book in hand?
   - Do situations reoccur with only slight changes in the story?
   - Are new people or objects added?
3. Movement
   - Do the characters travel from place to place?
   - Are actions already present in the story?
4. Questions
   - Are there already questions in the story?
   - Is there something new discovered on the next page?
   - Is there something silly or unusual that the children might not expect?
   - Are there no other interactive elements you can use?
5. Board Stories
   - Are there simple characters or objects that are repeated?
   - Is something being removed or added on?
6. Repetition
   - Is it a cumulative story?
   - Is there a phrase or word that is repeated over and over again?
7. Playacting
   - Are there simple roles for kids to act?
   - Are there many roles so everyone can have a part?
   - Are there a few characters who repeat something or don't involve much action or dialogue?
8. Music
   - Do you know of a song that goes with the story?
   - Can you think of a popular song that fits the lyrics?
   - Is there a simple rhythm that lends itself to tapping or playing a simple instrument?
   - Are instruments used in the story?

9. Art
- Is drawing a part of the story?
- Are colors used?
- Is a person, animal, or object changing in appearance?

10. Games
- Is there a game in the story?
- Are there different objects to find?
- Are objects repeated?
- Are there colors, numbers, or letters?

Ask yourself these questions and match any possible interactive elements with the essentials of the story. If you were able to check one box, then you can make your book interactive. If only one column is used on the checklist, you know that this is how you will make the chosen book interactive. If you check more than one, determine which activity would work best or how you might creatively combine them.

Checklist for Making Any Book Interactive

		Theme & Book Information
Theme		
Title		
Author		
Location/Call number		
Summary		
	√	Ideas for Interactivity
Props		
Storytelling		
Movement		
Questions		

(continued on following page…)

(continued from previous page)

Board Stories		
Repetition		
Playacting		
Music		
Art		
Games		

Chapter 2

How to Create an Interactive Storytime

SELECT THE RIGHT BOOKS

Consider titles with possible interactivity when ordering books. Read the titles and descriptions and consider whether they sound as if they would work interactively. Does the title ask a question, express movement, or sound silly? Think about interactivity when looking through the books on your shelves. You may be able to uncover—just from reading the title—what activity you might use. A book about a plane brings the thought of circling the room with arms flapping. A book title using a question will indicate an opportunity to ask the questions in the book. A book featuring action in a zoo might indicate using puppets. A book with the numbers "one" or "ten" in the title should indicate a flannel board story or bringing children up to the front of the room to demonstrate counting.

Once you begin to imagine every book as interactive, you will soon be able to select the ones that will work best or that will be the easiest to adapt in a short amount of time. As you choose books, keep in mind that some of the best books to use interactively will be short; easily re-told; or have something repeated, whether action, number, words, the same character, or characters added on.

ADD CRAFTS

Of course, many interactive stories can be presented successfully without crafts. Certainly the ability to present an interactive storytime without a craft streamlines the planning process. Even so, I must admit that

I still prefer to use a simple craft at the end of each storytime. Sometimes elaborate, sometimes simple, crafts are often an eagerly expected part of storytime. Here is a list of simple crafts you can use for almost any theme or book when making books interactive. Feel free to supplement my ideas with your own.

1. Hat: Cut strips of construction paper and copy a picture from a pattern book. Color and place it on the center of the hat.
2. Magnet: Place any picture on cardstock or cardboard and attach a magnet to the back.
3. Bag puppet: Find a picture of an object and glue the whole thing (or cut it in half to place half on the flap and half below) on the bag's flap.
4. Bag: Decorate a brown lunch bag with pictures of the day's theme. Put objects or pictures inside it or attach a construction paper strap.
5. Wallet/Purse: Lick a business envelope closed. Cut it in half. Punch holes on both of the open sides on each half and attach a string to make a purse or wallet. Provide pictures of the theme to glue on the outside or a related picture to place inside.
6. Card: Fold paper in half to form a greeting card. Decorate with pictures or color. Why not add a poem or rhyme to fit the stories told?
7. Door hanger: Color a picture (or cut and paste pictures), then punch a hole in the top, tie a piece of yarn through it, and make it a door hanger. This works well with patterns where you can dress an animal or child or attach parts to a car.
8. Straws: Make a fancy straw decoration. Take any picture, cut two slits or punch two holes, then weave the straw through the holes. Let the children color the picture.
9. Cup: Glue pictures onto a paper or plastic cup or even a jar. Provide juice if you wish. Combine with straw project. You might provide candy, a pencil, or something else to put inside the cups.
10. Windsock: Make a windsock by forming a wide tube out of construction paper with flowing streamers from the bottom and a piece of yarn reaching over the top to form a handle. Place pictures relating to your theme on the outside.
11. Firecracker: This is similar to the windsock. Use a toilet paper tube and cover with pictures or a color and have streamers or ribbon hanging from the bottom. Instruct kids to throw them and pretend they are firecrackers.
12. Flying object: Make reverse pictures of an object or animal. Glue them together with a piece of string taped inside. Attach the other

end of the long string to a straw, craft stick, or pencil. Have children hold onto the stick and spin around letting the picture fly around them, or they can just spin the stick or pencil to make the picture fly.

13. Planter: Use a cup or baby food jar, decorate with pictures and place dirt and seeds inside. Suggest the children bring them back at the last storytime or at the end of the school year and measure the plants.

14. Picture frame: Cut the center out of a half sheet of construction paper. Glue various pictures around the edges. Attach a piece of yarn to two punched holes on the top. You can glue the frame onto a picture or glue it onto another piece of construction paper, leaving the top unglued so you can slide in a picture or photo.

15. Animal sound maker: Take a toilet paper tube. Beforehand cut rectangular pieces to wrap over the tube. Color the paper to look like the skin of an animal or instruct the children to do so. You can make cow or leopard spots or draw the fuzzy fur of a bear or dog. Cut a square of tissue paper and cover the top of the tube with it. Wrap the animal-skin decorated paper around the tube. The children hum the animal sound into the tube (the open end) so that it buzzes with the child's humming.

16. Bookmark: Use cardstock or pieces of felt. Glue things or pictures on it to fit the theme. Cotton balls work nicely to make snowmen or animals. Use letter or number noodles for an alphabet or number theme.

17. Bank: Make a piggy bank or a bank of any kind. Take two of the same picture. Cut a slit through the top piece. Glue edges of one and place the other piece over it. When the glue dries, give each child a penny to slide inside the slit of his or her new bank. Ideally, the bottom piece will be blank while the top piece has details or the words "Bank," "Cow Bank," or "Horse Bank," etc., typed on it.

18. Plant decoration: Cut out two of the same picture or two pictures of similar sizes. Have children color them and glue them together with a popsicle stick in between. They can place this in a planter. You may want to combine this with making a planter.

19. Clock: Cut out numbers to put on a paper plate or construction paper circle. Cut out 1 picture or 12 little pictures to fit your theme.

20. Notebook/Book/Journal: Fold several sheets of paper or use real notebooks and paste pictures on the cover or stamp the inside pages.

21. Noise makers/instruments: Glue two small cups or paper plates to-

gether and put objects inside to shake and make noise. Decorate to fit the theme or use with a musical or sound theme. You could also use 35mm film canisters.

22. Magic Wand: Cover any kind of stick or straw with aluminum foil. Cut two stars out of paper and glue them together over the top of the stick. Add ribbon if you like.

23. Pillow/Cloud: Cut out two pictures of any subject, glue the edges of one, put cotton balls or other stuffing inside the glued edges and glue the two pieces together.

24. Ornament: Take any picture and attach a string to it to make an ornament. This works better if the picture is glued onto cardstock or cardboard.

25. Lift-the-flap picture: Take a piece of plain paper, and cut a window with a flap. Provide pictures for children to color or attach to paper. Glue the paper so the flap is over the picture to make a lift-the-flap picture.

DECIDE THE THEME QUESTION

There are advantages to presenting an interactive storytime without a theme. It is certainly less complicated. There is no need to spend time contriving ways to make books or activities fit a theme or creating a theme to go along with a new book you want to use. Without a theme, you can always use ideas that interest you most and share the best books available. Without a theme, you can also be completely spontaneous. You can pull out your best ideas. You can draw on the best-remembered ideas and use stories or ideas that have had the most success with the children.

I have experimented and eliminated themes in my interactive storytimes. I wanted to see if kids were just as entertained when I did not use activities apart from the stories. The truth is that, again and again, my storytimes went extremely well. By incorporating activities into the story—activities relevant to the plot and characters—I saw clearly that the children paid close attention through an entire session. In my experience, involving the children with active participation in stories, whether by actions or words, increased their focus.

In a school, you may be required to use a theme because you are following the curriculum, planning a lesson to coincide with a teacher's unit or request, or simply prefer to use a theme. Choosing broad themes will make planning easier. Another quick tip? Use a theme index. (You can find one in this book on page 219.) You may also want to create your own. Constructing your own list is easy if you organize the checklists (found on page 6) by theme. If you want to plan a storytime on "the body" for example, look in the index under that theme; there is a list of books. If there are not enough books for that theme, or if you do not own all the books, try combining topics, such as "the body and clothing" or "hats and shoes." Even throwing in a book about clothing or hats in a theme about the body will not put off the children or parents. It is always best to use books your library owns in case children want to hear them again on their own to enhance the experience. However, interlibrary loaning a couple of books each time is still acceptable. If a child asks for the book, tell the parents how they can get it from another library or suggest that you can order it if it is popular with the children.

PLAN USING THE TIME ELEMENT

Compiling a list of books and activities that go well with interactive stories (much like the books and activities provided in this book) will allow you tremendous freedom for simple and quick planning. Planning storytimes can take several hours. Using the interactive approach, storytime planning can be cut to under an hour. Depending on your familiarity and comfort with the books chosen, it is possible to select books, read them, and set everything up in less than 30 minutes without compromising the quality of the program.

It is usually assumed that planning storytime must be extremely time consuming. "By their nature, story hours are labor-intensive activities, whether stories are told from memory or presented with a picture book. Every aspect must be planned ahead of time to allow the storyteller freedom to interact with the audience" (Benne, 1991, p. 101). Using interactivity offers an alternative to this classic interpretation of storytime. All agree that there are an increasing number of demands on a librarian's time. Quality activities can be planned and prepared quickly by reading a book just once. You will just spend less time searching for additional activities, games, songs, and fingerplays. Whether you use the 500 books listed in this book or create lists of your own favorites, you no longer need to spend time searching through storytime books to find activities or fingerplays to fit your theme or stories. That is where you streamline your planning the most.

Let the activities spring from the books, not from research and planning. Many of the stories in this book have several options for activities, some more time consuming than others. While some involve cutting and locating pictures or props, others involve simply repeating words or moving around. Know your time limits and choose activities that will work best for your time frame. There are quick and easy ways to entertain today's increasingly preoccupied children to make them more aware during storytime. The goal is to expose them to more stories while allowing them to discover how fun reading and the library can be.

REFERENCES

Benne, Mae. 1991. *Principles of Children's Services in Public Libraries*. Chicago: American Library Association, pp. 100–101.

Chapter 3

2,000+ Ideas for Making 500 Picture Books Interactive

Ackerman, Karen. 1988. *Song and Dance Man.* **Illus., Stephen Gamell. New York: Knopf.**

Summary:
A former vaudeville performer entertains his grandchildren when they visit.

Activity:
Put on a hat and tie and maybe even carry a cane. For a few minutes be Grandpa performing the vaudeville act. Let the kids in your storytime be the grandchildren, and give them hats whenever Grandpa lets his grandchildren be part of his show. Also allow them to be the audience of the vaudeville act and dance and clap along as the story unfolds.

Adoff, Arnold. 2001. *Daring Dog and Captain Cat.* **Illus., Joe Cepada. New York: Simon & Schuster.**

Summary:
Daring Dog and Captain Cat are obedient during the day but get adventurous at night.

Activity:
Divide your group of children into the cats and dogs. Whenever you read "Captain Cat" in the story, the cats stand up. Whenever you read "Daring Dog," the dogs stand up. You can give the children cat and dog

nametags with pictures of their animals as a reminder. Also, the children could bark and meow as they stand, or bark and meow instead of standing.

Agee, Jon. 2001. *Milo's Hat Trick*. New York: Hyperion.

Summary:
Milo will be fired if he doesn't learn a magic hat trick, and luckily he finds a bear that can help.

Activity:
Find a hat and pull a bear puppet or stuffed animal, or even a picture of a bear, out of it at the appropriate parts of the story. Make it funny by pulling other things out of the hat as well. When Milo puts himself into the hat, use a picture of a person or a humanlike puppet or toy. Alternatively, pretend a basket and blanket is a hat and climb inside. Ask the children what they think Milo did when the bear was too tired to perform anymore.

Ahlberg, Allan. 1986. *Tell Us a Story*. Illus., Colin McNaughton. Cambridge, Mass.: Candlewick.

Summary:
Dad keeps telling different funny short stories about animals to his children.

Activity:
When the end of the book asks, "Is that really the end?" say "no" instead of "yes" and give each child a turn to suggest an animal. Continue telling them silly animal stories that you either make up off the top of your head or have previously prepared. During the story you can keep asking the children, "Do you want to hear another story?" "Are you sure you want to hear another story? I'm getting tired."

Alarcon, Karen Beaumont. 1997. *Louella Mae, She's Run Away*. Illus., Rosanne Litzinger. New York: Holt.

Summary:
Louella Mae, a pig, is missing. The townsfolk gather together to search for her, and finally they find her in a tub with her newborn babies.

Activity:
Bring the children to the front of the room or to the center of a circle. Start calling the hound dog and horses to help to find Louella Mae. Walk around the room with the children behind you, searching for Louella Mae as the story unfolds. Let all the remaining children act as the kin so that everyone can walk around the room searching for Louella Mae. Keep asking if anyone sees her. Hide a pig puppet or a picture of a pig in a place the children won't immediately look or some place that is usually off limits so they finally find Louella Mae at the end. Add little pigs for the babies if you'd like.

Allard, Harry. 1977. *Miss Nelson Is Missing!* Illus., James Marshall. Boston: Houghton Mifflin.

Summary:
A teacher teaches her class a lesson by dressing as a mean witch teacher when they misbehave.

Activity:
Put on a witch hat when Miss Nelson pretends to be a new teacher. You can ask children throughout the story if they think the new teacher is mean. If the children point out that the witch is actually Miss Nelson, pretend that you do not believe them. Say, "Are you sure?" or "I don't think so."

Andrews, Sylvia. 2001. *Dancing in My Bones.* Illus., Ellen Mueller. New York: HarperCollins.

Summary:
Children dance in many ways.

Activity:
Get the kids up and moving. First you dance, then tap your feet, bounce your knees, sway your hips, snap your fingers, clap your hands, shake your shoulders, and sing. Each rhyme goes something like, "I've got dancing in my bones, in my bones. I've got dancing in my bones, in my bones. I've got hip-hopping, tip-topping, be-bopping, no-stopping dancing in my bones, in my bones." On each page the first two phrases change to a new movement while the next two lines remain the same. The children can repeat this as well.

Appelt, Kathi. 1996. *Bat Jamboree*. Illus., Melissa Sweet. New York: Morrow.

Summary:
A counting book in which bats put on a show.

Activity:
When a number, such as "five," is read, tap or call on five children and have them stand up and perform the action suggested in the story. For "8 bats flew," have eight children stand up and pretend to fly around the room. When the text says "4 bats tapped as they all 4 ascended," have four children tap their feet and sit down. You can model the actions for the children. If it is too difficult or time consuming to have them stand in groups of the correct number, just do the actions as a group and use a flannel board or pictures to represent the correct number of bats. You could even have ten bat pictures and cover them, uncovering another bat each time. Have the children count along with you or ask how many bats are present to reinforce the concept of numbers.

Apperley, Dawn. 2002. *Good Night, Sleep Tight, Little Bunnies*. New York: Scholastic.

Summary:
Animals and birds go to sleep.

Activity:
Each animal has a rhyme followed by the phrase, "Good night, sleep tight, little . . . ." As you read the rhyme, pause before you get to each animal's name and point to the picture. The children will know to shout out the animal in the picture. You could also instruct them to say the whole phrase. Point to them when it is time to name the new animal. End by going around the room tapping each child's head with your hand or a magic wand, repeating the phrase, inserting their names, and asking them to lie down and pretend to sleep after you do this.

Armstrong, Jennifer. 1996. *The Snowball*. Illus., Jean Pidgeon. New York: Random House.

Summary:
A snowball keeps rolling along picking up people and objects along the way.

Activity:
Give each child a plain piece of white paper. Crinkle up one piece of paper as a snowball and pass it to a child. The children will then continue passing it to each other and each child will wrap another piece of paper around it so that a bigger snowball is formed. Then toss the snowball until it breaks apart.

Arnold, Tedd. 1997. *Parts*. New York: Dial.

Summary:
A boy thinks something is wrong with him because things keep falling off his body, but he soon realizes it is a natural process.

Activity:
Use a doll or an enlarged drawing of a child and place things on it from the story, such as gum on the nose, fake fingernails at the toes, hair on a comb (use yarn or string), a cotton ball for the bellybutton fuzz, piece of paper for skin off toes, and picture of a tooth by the mouth for a loose tooth. Have the children remove the pieces, or remove them yourself, as the story is told. If you cannot find anything to truly resemble the body parts or pieces, draw pictures or find objects that look similar. In the end you might want to get some masking tape and tape up your doll or picture as in the story. Follow up with the sequel *More Parts* (New York: Dial Books for Young Readers, 2001) in which the boy thinks figures of speech will really happen, such as cracking up, stretching arms and legs, and giving his dad a hand.

Asch, Frank. 1998. *Barnyard Lullaby*. New York: Simon & Schuster.

Summary:
A human family can't sleep because the animals in the barnyard keep singing a lullaby—in their own animal sounds.

Activity:
When the story reads, "To the farmer in his bed her song sounded like so much cluck, cluck, clucking," pause and let the children make the clucking sounds. Continue as the story progresses with other animal sounds, including a cow mooing, horse neighing, pig oinking, sheep baaing, and a goose honking, ending with the cry of a baby. This is a popular and easy activity for all animal-sound books, particularly *Ani-*

mal Sounds, authored and illustrated by Aurelius Battaglia (New York: Golden, 1981).

———. 1979. *Popcorn: A Frank Asch Bear Story.* **New York: Parents Magazine.**

Summary:
Bear has a party to which everyone invited brings popcorn.

Activity:
Beforehand, crinkle up a bunch of white scrap paper a little larger than a piece of popcorn. If you are afraid of cleanup, make them the size of popcorn balls. You could also have volunteers do it, save the "peanuts" that sometimes come in packaging, or use shredded paper. In the story, when guests start arriving and bringing popcorn, slowly throw a few pieces out to the kids. When Bear and friends decide to make the popcorn, start throwing the paper popcorn out to the kids a little faster. Let them start throwing it as well. You could use real popcorn, but the kids may want to eat it.

Augarde, Steve. 2001. *Vroom! Vroom!: A Pop-up Race to the Finish!* Boston: Little, Brown.

Summary:
Two racecars race to the finish line in this pop-up book.

Activity:
Give the children paper-plate steering wheels that you make—just plain paper plates—and allow them to pretend to race as you tell the story. Plates can be cut with an X or Y in the center to resemble steering wheels, or lines can be drawn on them with a circle in the center to represent a horn. They could raise their arms up with hands folded into fists to replicate holding onto a steering wheel instead. Move the pull tabs in the book to reveal what is happening and ask children along the way who they think is winning, red racer or blue racer, especially in the end when it is finally revealed. Children can also make steering wheels as a craft to use with the story.

Axtell, David. 2000. *We're Going on a Lion Hunt.* New York: Holt.

Summary:
Two young girls travel over and under and around and through different places in search of a lion that they never find.

Activity:
Children line up behind you as you pretend to walk over, under, around, and through the places in the story. They can repeat the phrases, "We're going on a lion hunt. We're going to catch a big one. We're not scared. Been there before," along with you or after you. When you approach the name of a place from the story say, "Can't go over it. Can't go under it. Can't go around it. Can't go through it," just as in the story. The children will then swish through grass, splash through a lake, squish through a swamp, and tiptoe through a cave. This is a version of the longtime favorite *We're Going on a Bear Hunt* by Michael Rosen, illustrated by Helen Oxenbury (New York: Margaret K. McElderry, 1989), which can be used in the same way.

Aylesworth, Jim. 1996. *My Sister's Rusty Bike*. Illus., Richard Hull. New York: Atheneum.

Summary:
The narrator tells what he finds and sees in different states while riding his sister's rusty bike.

Activity:
This activity is more for older listeners, but also possible for younger children. Use a map puzzle of the U.S. or any U.S. map. If using a puzzle, give each child one state mentioned in the story. Tell them the names of their states, and explain that when you read the name of their state in the story that they should come up and put their state on the right place on the map. If you use a regular map, give them each a piece of paper with the name of the state written on it, even if they cannot read it. Tell them which states they have and tell them that when they hear the name of their state, they are to come up and tape the slip of paper on the map in the proper place. Of course, you will help them. This way the children can track the character's travels as well as listen in anticipation for their states. If there are not enough states to go around, give several children the same state or have them work in pairs. The states named in the story are Massachusetts, Pennsylvania, West Virginia, Indiana, Kentucky, Alabama, Mississippi, Louisiana, Oklahoma, Minnesota, Colorado, Arizona, and California. You could also cover the other states at the end of the story, pointing them out or giving kids extra state names to find on the map. Another activity is to give each child a map and crayon. On a large map, show them where each state is located and ask them to color that state on their maps as you point it out on the large map. Even preschoolers can do this with some help, and it makes a good

first introduction to geography. Do the same thing for Laurie Keller's *Scrambled States of America* (New York: Holt, 1998).

———. 1992. *Old Black Fly*. Illus., Stephen Gammell. New York: Holt.

Summary:
In this alphabet book, a fly interacts with things that start with the different letters of the alphabet.

Activity:
After each phrase that shows a fly is disturbing someone or something, there is the phrase, "Shoo fly! Shoo fly! Shooo." Have the children repeat this as you point to them, or say something like, "What do you say?" Make sure to swat the fly in the end.

———. 2001. *The Tale of Tricky Fox: A New England Trickster Tale*. Illus., Barbara McClintock. New York: Scholastic.

Summary:
Tricky Fox keeps pretending he has valuable items in his bag. He then convinces people to guard the bag, and when he tells them that his valuables are missing, they are forced to give him a more valuable item.

Activity:
Have a bag or pillowcase and get ready to pull out the different objects and animals suggested in the story, such as a log, loaf of bread, a chicken, and a pig. Kids can even perform the roles of the people the fox visits, and the librarian or teacher can wear a homemade fox mask. Use different objects if those mentioned in the story are not available. You can even try to teach them the rhyme the fox repeats, "I'm so clever-tee-hee-hee! Trick, trick, tricky! Yes, siree! Snap your fingers. Slap your knee. Human folks ain't smart like me." Children can snap their fingers and slap their knees.

Balian, Lorna. 1984. *Humbug Potion: An A-B-Cipher*. Nashville: Abingdon.

Summary:
A witch deciphers a secret code to make a beauty potion.

Activity:
Use with older children. Have children number their paper from 1–26 and write the alphabet in order with one letter next to each number. You could also provide them with these numbers on a poster, chalkboard, or printed sheets. As the story unfolds, and a code such as 5–7–7–19 is read, students can look up the letters on their paper that correspond with the numbers and try to spell the words. In this case it would be "eggs." Younger children can look at the pictures in the book to try and decide what is in the potion. They can be used in a puzzle or clue program as well. It is not necessary to do all the ciphers, but maybe one or a few.

———. 1988. *The Socksnatchers.* Nashville: Abingdon.

Summary:
The Socksnatcher family is upset because their son stole a pair of clean socks from the family upstairs when he was only supposed to "share" one smelly sock. Meanwhile the Perkins family above is distressed over so many missing socks.

Activity:
Bring in your clean sock drawer and have kids help match socks throughout the story, after the story, or every time a sock is missing. Otherwise, just color pictures of socks to match as pairs and have the children take turns finding a match after every few pages. You could also wait until the end of the story to let each child find a match to a pair you have colored or copied in different colors. If you wait until the end, to keep them anxious, keep pulling out one sock and hand it to a different child after every few pages during the story, saying things like "Where did this come from?" or "Why can't I find the match?" and "Maybe you can help me find it later," as you hand it to a child. Then let the children loose to find the matching socks hidden somewhere in the room.

———. 1976. *The Sweet Touch.* Nashville: Abingdon.

Summary:
Peggy gets a magic ring out of a gumball machine that conjures up a genie. She also gets a magic wish, and she wishes that everything she touches will turn into something sweet.

Activity:
When Peggy has to decide what to wish for, ask the kids what they would

wish for if they had one wish. When Peggy decides to wish for something sweet, give examples from the story and then ask the children what
candy or sweet they would wish for. When it is finally time to make the
wish, have all the children stand up and do the magic steps. First the
children repeat, "I wish that everything I touch would turn into something sweet!" Then they follow the ritual with you as you ask them to
rub their wings together, which they do by rubbing their elbows together
instead. (You will probably want to leave the part out about standing on
their heads.) Next ask the children to wiggle their toes by just shaking
their feet in the air one at a time, lick their fingers, and jump up and
down six times. Then pretend to whisper magic words in your hand and
place them in an imaginary or real pocket. When Oliver flies around
Peggy's head 73 times, just turn in circles a few times and tell the children they have done enough. When it is time to say the alphabet backwards, you may stop the children after a brief attempt. However, some
older children may actually be able to do this. You could also go over
the alphabet backwards with them, using a chart to cheat from unless
you have it memorized. Now that the magic ritual is over, pretend to
pull taffy and lift up your feet to find chocolate oozing from them. At
the end of the story when Oliver's mother comes to take away the magic
wish, they should do the steps of the magic spell in reverse. Now they
will rub their elbows behind their backs, lick the other sides of their fingers, jump down and up six times, empty out the magic words from their
imaginary pockets, and spin in circles an abbreviated 37 times, and finally say the alphabet forwards. This is an excellent book for storytelling.

**Ball, Duncan. 1991. *Jeremy's Tail*. Illus., Donna Rawlins. New
    York: Orchard.**

Summary:
When Jeremy is blindfolded for his turn to play "Pin the Tail on the Donkey" at a party, he loses his way and travels around the world.

Activity:
If the children are older, blindfold them and have them wander around
the room as they hear that Jeremy is traveling through a crowded bus,
on a metal beam across a body of water, on a cruise ship, through different countries, in a hot air balloon, to a carnival, in outer space, on a
bicycle, and back home. Of course this could be dangerous, so make sure
the blindfolds are sheer or loose, or just give each child one eye patch.
The story does not name these places, so you will have to name them if

the kids cannot see the pictures. Also make up some places for Jeremy to travel to. Afterwards, you could let the children pin a tail on the donkey. You could also just ask questions while reading, such as, "Where is Jeremy now?" The children will respond where they think he is by looking at the pictures. "Is he getting closer?" "Is he near the donkey?" you could continue asking them, as Jeremy asks similar questions to those he meets along the way.

Bang, Molly. 1999. *When Sophie Gets Angry—Really, Really Angry . . .* New York: Blue Sky.

Summary:
The story tells what Sophie does to cool down after something makes her angry.

Activity:
Begin the story of what happens to make Sophie get angry, which is a fight with her sister over a toy. Then, when you get to the page that just shows Sophie's head with the text, "Oh is Sophie ever angry now!" ask the children what they do when they get angry. Ask them what sounds they make when they get angry and have them make those sounds or act out what they do. Then have them help Sophie out by acting out the ways she gets angry and then calms down: kicking, screaming, roaring, running, crying, climbing, blowing in the wind, climbing again, and walking home. It may even help the children think of ways they can cool down the next time they get angry. You can also ask what makes them feel better when they are upset.

———. 1991. *Yellow Ball.* New York: Morrow.

Summary:
In this simple story, a ball is lost at the beach and carried far away.

Activity:
While reading this very short story, have the kids sit in a circle and pass a yellow ball around to one another until everyone has had a turn and they see how far it can go. As you read the story and show the pictures, ask the children to tell you where the ball is going.

Barber, Barbara E. 1996. *Allie's Basketball Dream.* **Illus., Darryl Ligasan. New York: Lee & Low.**

Summary:
Allie gets a basketball as a gift from her father, but no one will play with her because they don't think girls should play basketball.

Activity:
Use a ball of any size and let the children pass it around or roll it across to one another either while you are telling the story or during the parts when Allie is throwing the ball. You may want to pause the story for these moments. End with a game of basketball. If you do not own a mini-basketball hoop and ball, do as they do in the story and hold up a garbage can or hula hoop and let the kids take turns throwing a ball into it. You could also use a laundry basket or a box.

Barner, Bob. 1996. *Dem Bones.* **Illus., Bob Barnes. San Francisco: Chronicle.**

Summary:
Dem Bones tells a story by using the song that begins, "Toe bone connected to da foot bone . . . "

Activity:
Find a skeleton pattern, make one of your own, or purchase window clings or decorations at Halloween time. Give each child a piece of the skeleton and tell him or her which bone it is. Let each student come up at the appropriate point in the song and add his or her bone to create the skeleton. You can add more to the story, such as the arms and hands. This is a good non-scary Halloween story. Find a copy of the song to play along, as well. This can also work well to accompany a science lesson.

———. 2001. *Dinosaur Bones.* **San Francisco: Chronicle.**

Summary:
Dinosaur facts are accompanied by a dinosaur rhyme.

Activity:
Cut out pieces of white paper resembling dinosaur bones. When the dif-

ferent bone pieces are mentioned in the story, such as sockets, joints, jaws, hips, legs, and bones with points, either you or the children can put them up on a board to form a dinosaur. You could place a picture or poster of a dinosaur on a board and have children put the bones where they think they belong. They could also do this on a dinosaur coloring sheet, which could be used as a craft. The end of the book offers more opportunity for interaction. There is a chart of the heights of the dinosaurs mentioned in the book. Put up a measuring tape or a growth chart and measure the kids. Hand the children a piece of paper that reads, "You are as big as a _____," and insert a dinosaur's name. Do the math ahead of time so you know the ratio of child heights to dinosaur heights. The last pages in the book offer a "Dino-meter" with facts about the dinosaurs. You can use this as a quiz if you have shared the dinosaur facts from the story with the children. Follow with the game "Pin the Bone on the Dinosaur."

Barrett, Judi. 1998. *Things That Are Most in the World*. Illus., John Nickle. New York: Atheneum.

Summary:
Superlatives (words ending in "-est") are used to describe strange creatures and things.

Activity:
This can be a simple case of question and answer. For example, on the page that reads, "The oddest thing in the world is an ant windsurfing in a bowl of pea soup," you can ask the children if they think this is odd. Using props you can also design some of these scenarios yourself. For example, put a picture of an ant on a boat in a bowl and place it with other objects and animals from the book around the room. Continue asking if the situations are really so odd, or if they have ever seen anything like that. "Really?" you might reply when they answer "No," and point out to them that these combinations exist somewhere in the room. To continue the story, make up some of your own strange situations and find props or draw pictures to represent them.

Barton, Byron. 1973. *Buzz, Buzz, Buzz*. Illus., Byron Barton. New York: Macmillan.

Summary:
A bee that happens to sting a bull starts a chain of disruptions on the farm until it comes full circle.

Activity:
A flannel board would be perfect for this story. You can find pictures of the objects and animals in the story, such as a bull, cow, woman, milk, mule, barn, goat, goose, cat, bird, and bee. Substitute if necessary. Show the kids visually how the story develops and how it comes back to the bull in the end with the bee stinging it so hard. The children can see this in the book, but they will understand it better if they see the bull running around the board and the farmer's wife knocking the milk off the board. You could make up a similar story using any flannel board pieces or pictures you may have.

———. 2001. *My Car.* **Illus., Byron Barton. New York: Green-willow**

Summary:
This is a simple story in which Sam describes what he does with a real car.

Activity:
Unlike other books in which driving is the focus, *My Car* is not conducive to the children's pretending to drive as an activity. However, you can use this book to show the other things one can do with a car. For example, have children pretend to wash a car and fill the tank with gas, as Sam does in the story. Ask children to point out the different parts of Sam's car as he does. Open and close your hands to represent the lights on the car, and wave your arms back and forth in front of you to show the windshield wipers. These activities are also appropriate for other driving stories. Later in the story children can pretend to drive, stopping to obey traffic signs. You might want to hold up a stop-sign shape or the colors red, green, and yellow to see if they can obey the signs while pretending to drive. Don't forget to yell, "beep beep," at the end. Follow the car activities with this popular game. Ask the children to line up across one side of the room. Hold up a green, yellow, or red circle of paper. Instruct the children to walk towards you when you hold up green, stop when you hold up red, and walk slowly when you hold up yellow.

Base, Graeme. 2001. *The Water Hole*. New York: Abrams.

Summary:
This is a counting book in which more and more creatures keep drinking the water until there is no more.

Activity:
The book starts, "One Rhino drinking at the water hole." Instead of reading each of the numbers and animal names to the children, ask them to
help. "One what is drinking at the water hole?" "A rhino," they may respond. Provide the answer if no one guesses correctly. Alternatively, you
could say the name of the animal and ask the children to count how many
are on each page. They will catch on as it goes in numerical order. Animal sounds, such as "Grrrrr!" and "Prrrrrr," are also provided on each
page, and the children can repeat them.

**Bate, Lucy. 1989. *How Georgina Drove the Car Very Carefully
from Boston to New York*. Illus., Tamar Taylor. New York:
Crown.**

Summary:
Georgina pretends to take a trip in her imaginary car.

Activity:
Make steering wheels out of paper plates or just use plain paper plates;
give one to each child. They could also pretend they have steering wheels
by lifting their arms up and making fists. As the story continues, have
the children pretend to drive to the places mentioned, saying "hi" to
cows, waving to horses, and stopping at a red light, a stop sign, and for
a pig. You might make a basic stoplight and stop sign out of construction paper to hold up at appropriate times in the story.

**Bauer, Marion Dane. 2001. *If You Had a Nose Like an Elephant's
Trunk*. Illus., Susan Winter. New York: Holiday House.**

Summary:
A girl thinks about what she could do with body parts of other animals.

Activity:
Throughout the story, ask the children what they would do with the different body parts. "What would you do with wings like an eagle?" you
could ask. At the end of the story, ask the children what they can do
with the body parts they actually have. Children can also act out what
they would do with the animal parts. You could even draw or find pictures of the animal body parts and place them on yourself or on a child
to better demonstrate the actions as you ask questions.

Beaton, Clare. 1999. *One Moose, Twenty Mice*. Illus., Clare Beaton. Cambridge, Mass.: Barefoot.

Summary:
A cat is hiding on every page while different animals are used to show the progression of the numbers from 1 to 20 until the cat finally comes out of hiding to attack the 20 mice.

Activity:
Since the cat is hiding on every page, walk around the room and let a different child find the cat each time. Since there are 20 pictures, there should usually be enough for everyone to have a turn. Also, let the kids help you count the objects and name the creatures that are on each page before you start counting. Ask, "What are these?" as you point to the next animal or insect. Then follow with, "How many are there?" and, "But where's the cat?" You could even have a cat hiding in the room that they can search for, or copy cat pictures and hide them around the room so everyone can find a cat after the story.

Bernstein, Robin. 1998. *Terrible, Terrible!: A Folktale Retold*. Illus., Shauna Mooney Kawasaki. Rockville, Md.: Kar-Ben Copies.

Summary:
A rabbi gives advice to a girl who thinks her house is too crowded by having her add more to the chaos. Then, when she removes everything she has added, the house seems so much more spacious.

Activity:
This retold folk tale can also be told using the version where the family complains how noisy their home is, so the rabbi suggests that more and more animals and people enter the house. This is perfect for storytelling, and you can make up other things to be added to the mix or ask for suggestions from the children. You will start by telling them the rabbi suggested bringing the following items into the house: bicycles, the pets, and the cousins. Then tell, as the rabbi suggests, that the bicycles, animals, and cousins must be removed. Now the house seems to have so much more room.

Blackstone, Stella. 1999. *Bear on a Bike*. Illus., Debbie Harter. Brooklyn: Barefoot.

Summary:
A boy follows a bear around the world.

Activity:
Every other double-paged spread begins with telling what form of transportation the bear is using. The text then continues with a rhyme that is repeated throughout. For example, "Bear on a boat, As happy as can be, Where are you going, bear? Please wait for me!" When you begin the phrase, point to what the bear is on, say, "Bear on a . . . " and pause until the children say "boat." Instruct the children to keep repeating the phrase, which you may also teach them at the beginning or have them repeat after you. Then read the description of where the bear is going. You could also have them guess where the bear is going by showing the pictures and pointing to clues such as crowns on characters that are in a castle.

————. 1998. *Can You See the Red Balloon?* Illus., Debbie Harter. New York: Orchard.

Summary:
Each page asks readers to find a different object.

Activity:
This is best for smaller groups. Ask the children to help you find the object named on each page. Ask the others to name something else they see in the pictures so that everyone is involved and has a turn. You could even place more objects around the room or use the objects already in the room to follow up with further questions. If you have some of the objects pictured in the book in your library or home, you might place them around the room and ask the children if they see them somewhere besides in the book (such as the blue flower, white moon, red balloon, gray mouse, purple house, green sock, black clock, pink car, yellow star, and orange tower).

————. 2000. *Making Minestrone*. Illus., Nan Brooks. New York:
   Barefoot.

Summary:
A group of friends gather all the ingredients for minestrone soup.

Activity:
Gather the ingredients as listed in the cookbook, which a child holds at
the beginning of the story. Make sure you have a pot and pictures of
each ingredient, including green beans, carrots, onions, peas, potatoes,
zucchini, pasta, cooking oil, salt, pepper, and water. Don't forget the tomatoes, which are not on the list. If necessary, provide more than one
of each so you have enough for each child in your class or storytime
group. Give each child one picture and say that when you call a particular ingredient, the child with the picture should put it in the pot.
Give each child a turn to stir the pot. Or, you can make the center of
the circle the pot, and ask the children to be the ingredients. The children move to the center when their food is called while you pretend to
stir with a broom, large spoon, or your arm. Another idea is to place
enough pictures of each item around the room so that each child can
find pictures of all the ingredients. They can make baskets out of paper
lunch bags by attaching a construction-paper or yarn handle. They can
also make baskets out of construction paper. Using a pattern, they cut
out two pieces and then glue the ends together so they can slip paper
objects into them. Allow the children to walk around the room searching for one of each item and putting them in their baskets. Display pictures of all the items on the wall or a board so that they know which
ones they must find.

Bloom, Suzanne. 2001. *The Bus for Us*. Honesdayle, Penn.: Boyds
   Mills.

Summary:
Tess keeps asking Gus if different forms of transportation are her school
bus.

Activity:
Place pictures of different modes of transportation used in the story
around the room or use plastic toys if available, such as a taxi, tow truck,
fire engine, ice-cream truck, garbage truck, and a backhoe, finally ending with a school bus. Walk around the room with the children behind

you, asking, "Is this the bus for us, Gus?" You could also prop open books with these pictures in them, walk around the room with the book pointing out the pictures, or pretend you see the various types of transportation mentioned.

Blos, Joan W. 1984. *Martin's Hats*. New York: Morrow.

Summary:
Martin has a new adventure with every hat he tries on.

Activity:
Give each child a hat or picture of a hat that corresponds to one in the story, such as those worn by a chef, police officer, fire fighter, construction worker, farmer, and train engineer and let each child feel like Martin on an adventure. Let them act the part by pretending to cook, hose a fire, weld a building, and ride a tractor, or yelling "All aboard!" You could end by showing a variety of hats and asking who would wear these hats. To make it easier, you can just show pictures from books or magazines.

Bonning, Tony. 2001. *Fox Tale Soup*. Illus., Sally Hobson. New York: Simon & Schuster.

Summary:
This is a fox's version of *Stone Soup*.

Activity:
Have the children sit in a circle, and the center can be the pot of soup. Give each child a picture of a different vegetable, from the story or not, depending on what pictures you have. If you want ingredients from the story, you will need salt and pepper, a turnip, carrot, cabbage, and corn. You might also have someone contribute water. You can put in the stone and pretend to stir—with either a real or make-believe spoon. As the fox keeps deciding his soup is not quite right, have the children take turns coming up with vegetables and other things to add to it. The kids may not understand the fox's trick, so at the end of the story ask them what they think happened and explain it if they do not understand.

Bono, Mary. 2002. *Ugh! A Bug*. New York: Walker.

Summary:
Ugh! A Bug poses fanciful questions about what to do if different bugs were bothering you.

Activity:
Since the text is primarily questions, it is easy to involve the children by having them answer the questions. "If a FLY wouldn't split when you swatted at it, would you try to ignore it or throw a big fit?" Ask the children what they would do, or have them raise their hands for which action they prefer. "If an ANT were to ambush a crumb from your sandwich, would you ask him and all of his friends in for some?" Wait for the answer. To conclude, ask the children which bug is their favorite. You could also put pictures of each of the insects on a board and have the children take turns pulling off the one you are talking about. Otherwise, you could pull off a picture, bring it over to a child, and ask the child the question in the book that pertains to the bug you are holding. The creatures you need are a fly, spider, centipede, worm, ant, beetle, moth, inchworm, ladybug, flea, bumblebee, dragonfly, and mosquito.

Boujon, Claude. 1987. *Bon Appetit, Mr. Rabbit!* Illus., Claude Boujon. New York: Margaret K. McElderry.

Summary:
A rabbit that doesn't like carrots goes in search of other meal options.

Activity:
When Mr. Rabbit asks each animal what it eats, ask the kids what the animal eats before you read the reply. You could also set up puppets or pictures of the animals mentioned, including a frog, bird, fish, pig, whale, monkey, and fox. Then have the children follow you around the room asking each animal what it eats, or ask the children what they think the animals eat. Children can also play the parts of the animals while you or other children ask them what they eat. Either before or after reading the book, ask the children what they like or don't like to eat, or hold up pictures of food, insects, and other things, asking which they like or don't like to eat.

Bridges, Margaret Park. 2001. *Now What Can I Do?* **Illus., Melissa Sweet. New York: SeaStar.**

Summary:
A child is bored, and his mother convinces him to do chores by pretending they are adventures.

Activity:
This can be a clever idea book for parents. In a storytime or classroom, however, this can be used to spark the children's imagination. First, start off by asking the children what they think Little Raccoon should do so he will not be bored. When Mommy suggests something like "making your bed," ask the children if that is a fun thing to do. Then show the pictures and ask what Little Raccoon should do. When they see a boat, they will most likely suggest taking a boat ride. Tell them they can be explorers. Read the lines about making sails from the sheets that are folded neatly when the wind is calm. Look at the pictures of a cowhand who rounds up toys like cattle, an archaeologist who finds the oldest sock, a basketball player shooting socks into drawers, or a singer with a toothbrush. Pretend to fly on a book bringing it to other children to read and listen, go fishing for dinner as you set the table for a picnic, put on pajamas as a space suit, go to sleep, and rest the race car engine. This book can be read in tandem with one person reading the child's part and another reading the mother's. If you have the bedroom supplies, children can participate in the cleanup.

Brown, Marc Tolon. 1976. *Arthur's Nose.* **Boston: Little, Brown.**

Summary:
Arthur, dissatisfied with his nose, goes to a doctor to try on new animal noses, eventually deciding to keep his own.

Activity:
Use an Arthur doll or poster or even just a picture and keep placing new animal noses from the story on him and ask the children to decide which one they like best. You will need a nose for a chicken, fish, elephant, koala, hippo, armadillo, toucan, goat, rabbit, mouse, zebra, alligator, and rhino. Continue asking the children, "How about this nose?" "No!" they will yell.

Brown, Margaret Wise. 1947. *Goodnight Moon.* **Illus., Clement Hurd. New York: Harper & Row.**

Summary:
"Goodnight" is said to all the things in a room.

Activity:
After reading the descriptions of the things in the room, have the children repeat after you "Goodnight _____," inserting the name of each object. You could also just pause after "Goodnight" and have the children fill in the object. If you have the "Goodnight Moon" poster, it would be fun to point to the different pictures and say goodnight to them. You could also draw or find patterns for the objects in the story, place them around the room, and have the children say goodnight to them. Walk around in a line, pausing before each picture, saying "Goodnight" all together, or take turns. After finishing the story, do this with other objects in the room.

———. **1998.** *The Little Scarecrow Boy.* **Illus., David Diaz. New York: HarperCollins**

Summary:
A young scarecrow tries desperately to be scary.

Activity:
Let the children make scary faces to try to help the scarecrow scare the crows. You could begin by making six scary faces similar to the faces the scarecrow father tries to teach his son. Or you could have six children stand in front of the group, each making a different face. Pair with *The Perky Little Pumpkin* by Margaret Friskey, illustrated by Tom Dunnington (Chicago: Children's Press, 1990), in which the pumpkin tries to be scary, as well.

———. **2002.** *Sailor Boy Jig.* **Illus., Dan Andreasen. New York: Margaret K. McElderry.**

Summary:
A sailor does a dance.

Activity:
Dance steps are provided for you in this story. On some pages there are

blue-and-white drawings of the sailor doing the jig. "Jump Big. Jump little. Jump little." is written alongside the pictures. The next time it changes to "Dance Big. Dance little. Dance little." Then to "Step Big. Step little. Step little." and finally "Step loud. Step softly. Step softly." Model for the children how to jump, dance, and step big, little, soft, and loud.

———. 2001. *Two Little Trains*. Illus., Leo and Diane Dillon. New York: HarperCollins.

Summary:
A real train and a toy train both travel west at the same time.

Activity:
On a board, the floor, or the wall, put a picture of a real train and one of a toy train. Move the trains a step each time you read a new page of the story. You could also give each child a piece of paper with squares for game spaces and two small pictures of trains—one that looks real and one that looks like a toy—and have them move along with the story.

Brown, Ruth. 1996. *Toad*. New York: Dutton.

Summary:
A monster finally spits out a disgusting toad.

Activity:
Take a toad or frog toy and cover it with yarn or slime or clay or anything else you can find and start peeling away the layers as you read the description of the ". . . muddy . . . mucky . . . clammy, sticky, gooey toad, odorous, oozing, foul and filthy, and dripping with venomous fluid." When the monster spits out the toad in the end, throw it out into your audience.

Bruss, Deborah. 2001. *Book! Book! Book!* Illus., Tiphanie Beeke. New York: Arthur A. Levine.

Summary:
Animals enter the library looking for books, but the librarian does not understand them.

Activity:
Each time a new animal enters the room, point to the children so they can make the sound of that animal. Model the sound for them. Ask the children to repeat the sound if they don't catch on at first. If you have pictures or stuffed animals or puppets for the animals represented in this book, you could hold those up, too. Have the children make all the sounds in the end.

Bunting, Eve. 1994. *Flower Garden*. Illus., Kathryn Hewitt. New York: Harcourt Brace Jovanovich.

Summary:
A girl creates a flower garden for her mother's birthday.

Activity:
The first half of the book describes the places the flowers are located before becoming part of a garden, such as the shopping cart and laps on a bus. Instead of telling this to the children, point to the places and ask the children, "Where is the flower garden?" When the names of the flowers are given, first see if the children know the names of the flowers before giving the answers. You could also give each child a flower or picture of a flower to hold during the story. Save baby food jars or buy paper cups and seeds to let them make their own flower gardens in the end.

Burton, Marilee Robin. 1989. *Tail, Toes, Eyes, Ears, Nose*. New York: Harper & Row.

Summary:
One page lists the tail, toes, eyes, ears, and nose of an animal or person, while the next page reveals the creature to which they belong.

Activity:
Have the children guess which animal the tail, toes, eyes, ears, and nose belong to. You may want to cut out other samples for after the story to keep it going. You could also put the pictures on a flannel or magnetic board or just tape them to a poster or wall. Animals include a horse, pig, mouse, cat, dog, rabbit, elephant, bird, and also a boy.

Cabrera, Jane. 2001. *Old Mother Hubbard*. **New York: Holiday House.**

Summary:
Old Mother Hubbard goes shopping since she doesn't find a bone in the cupboard.

Activity:
Props can make this expanded version of "Old Mother Hubbard" interactive. When Old Mother Hubbard goes to several shops, have the items she selects on display and allow different children to take turns picking them out of the shop you create. You will need a coat, hat, wig, shoes, and, of course, a bone. Tape enough pictures of bones around the storytime room or classroom so that each child can find one to feed the dog puppet at the end of the story. This last activity would be enough by itself for this short book.

Calmenson, Stephanie. 1996. *Engine, Engine, Number Nine*. **Illus., Paul Meisel. New York: Hyperion.**

Summary:
Engine Number Nine makes stops on its journey to a fair.

Activity:
Blow a whistle, start choo-chooing, and call up kids as the train picks up different people and animals. The kids must pretend to be Bess and her pig; horses; Jake and his cow; roosters; ducks and geese; a band; and moms, dads, and babies. Depending on how many children you have in your group, you may use more or fewer of each animal, or leave some out. The book repeats the refrain, "Crowded Engine Number Nine, Rumbling, rumbling (or other phrases) Down the line. Wheels are turning. Whistle's blowing. Soon we'll find out where it's going." Each time you come to this part, ask the children to turn like a wheel, whistle, and guess where the engine is going.

———. 1984. *Ten Furry Monsters*. **Illus., Maxie Chambliss. New York: Parents Magazine.**

Summary:
Ten monsters disobey mother's orders and disappear one by one.

Activity:
Have ten children stand up, and each time a monster in the story disappears, have one child sit down until none are left standing. If you have more than ten kids, you can make two or more groups of ten or double up so everyone is involved. You can provide the children with numbers to put on their shirts like the numbers the monsters in the story wear on their shirts. If you have time, make the numbers different colors to match those of the monsters. Another option is to make a monster flannel board story using a monster pattern with a number and different color for each one.

Campbell, Rod. 1982. *Dear Zoo*. New York: Four Winds.

Summary:
Unwanted pets keep arriving from the zoo.

Activity:
Ask the children what animal they think is hiding behind each crate or package when the anonymous character keeps receiving unwanted pets from the zoo. It would be easy to make your own enlarged book using animal pictures from magazines or pattern books and hide them behind pieces of construction paper with flaps cut out so you can open the "crates or packages."

Carle, Eric. 1998. *Hello, Red Fox*. New York: Simon & Schuster.

Summary:
A frog has a birthday party and invites various friends who are not the colors they appear to be.

Activity:
Use the book as intended so the children can experience these optical illusions and visualize the animal or object in another color. After staring at the dot on one page, and looking at the next page, the children should see the same animal in a different color. Most will not see it unless they are older. Use only a few of the pictures, not the whole story. For older children you could also show other books or pictures of optical illusions to create a program.

————. 1986. *Papa, Please Get the Moon for Me*. **Natick, Mass.: Picture Book Studio.**

Summary:
A father goes to get the moon for his daughter.

Activity:
When a girl and her father are reaching for the moon, ask the children to reach their arms up too. When the father climbs the ladder, have the children stand and pretend to climb a ladder. You might want to ask the children why the moon keeps changing shape and size, and explain it to them if necessary.

————. 1984. *The Very Busy Spider*. **New York: Philomel.**

Summary:
A spider is too busy spinning her web to play with the other animals.

Activity:
Spin a web while telling the story. Use string to form one on the ground; tape string to a board; or draw a web on the chalkboard, dry-erase board, or paper. You could also ask children to take turns drawing the web. If you ask the children to draw a web on their own paper, you can take turns approaching each one, pretending to be a different animal disturbing the spider.

————. 1979. *The Very Hungry Caterpillar*. **New York: Philomel.**

Summary:
A caterpillar eats through everything in sight.

Activity:
Use a caterpillar puppet that turns into a butterfly for this book. Walk around the room with the toy, pretending to eat through the children. You could also cut pictures of the fruit and layer them on a board. Make it similar to the arrangement of the book, where you turn the page and there is another fruit under the last one. Remove the pieces as you tell the story.

————. 1995. *The Very Lonely Firefly*. New York: Philomel.

Summary:
A firefly searches for other fireflies in all the wrong places.

Activity:
Whenever the firefly flies towards a light that is not another firefly, ask the children what they think the light is. They will see a light bulb, candle, flashlight, lantern, dog, cat, cow's eyes, headlights, and fireworks. Finally, true to Eric Carle style, open up the last page to flashing fireflies. Perhaps you could instruct a volunteer or helper to turn off the lights when you give the cue.

————. 1990. *The Very Quiet Cricket*. New York: Philomel.

Summary:
Insects try to communicate with a cricket but he cannot make a sound.

Activity:
Every time a new insect is introduced, "the little cricket wanted to answer, so he rubbed his wings together. But nothing happened. Not a sound." Have the children rub their elbows together and try to make a sound, which will not happen with two elbows. In the end, when the book chirps, have the children imitate the sound.

Carpenter, Stephen. 1998. *The Three Billy Goats Gruff*. Illus., Stephen Carpenter. New York: HarperCollins.

Summary:
The traditional story of three goats that try to get past a troll to cross a bridge.

Activity:
Instead of only three billy goats, change the story to however many children you have in the room. Then have each one take turns crossing and have them beg you to not eat them and swear that the next goat to come along will be bigger. You may even want to line the children up in order of size if height is not an issue.

Catrow, David. 2002. *We the Kids: The Preamble to the Constitution of the United States.* **Illus., David Catrow. New York: Dial.**

Summary:
The preamble to the Constitution is illustrated.

Activity:
Do as you would for the "Pledge of Allegiance" and have the children hold their hands to their hearts and look at the flag. Hold the flag, use one in a stand or holder in the room, or ask a child to hold it. You could even let the children take turns holding it at each turn of the page. For older kids, you could go through each page and ask them what they think each statement means.

Chancellor, Deborah. 1999. *Copycat!: Animals.* **New York: Dorling Kindersley.**

Summary:
In this board book, children are dressed as different animals, and the text describes the sounds and actions they make.

Activity:
Children can pretend to be the same animals that the children in the story are dressed as. "Act like a CAT and lick your fur. Start to smile, begin to purr." Children can lick their hands and meow or purr like a cat. Children will also pretend to be owls with wide eyes hooting; a pig with a squished nose grunting and oinking, and crawling on the floor; a dog panting with his tongue out, perhaps barking, too; a rabbit twitching and munching; and a lion roaring and prancing. To conclude, walk around with a mirror to show the kids the animal faces they can make.

Chapman, Cheryl. 1993. *Pass the Fritters, Critters.* **Illus., Susan L. Roth. New York: Four Winds.**

Summary:
Animals pass food that rhymes with their own names.

Activity:
Have the children paired up or in a circle to pass things to one another throughout the story, including fritters, cantaloupe, muffin, éclair, cob-

bler, honey, carrot, chow, salami, cider, and snack. If possible, have the same objects, or pictures of the objects, that appear in the book. However, anything will do. Alternatively, have puppets of the animals with the objects in their mouths on a table, and when you say, "Pass the muffin, puffin," you could take the muffin that you drew or copied from the puffin's mouth or hands. Again, you could make up your own animal-food combinations and add them to the end of the story or use them instead of those in the story. The point is to get children to eventually say "please." You could first have the animals refuse to pass the food, and then ask the children why the animals won't share, until you get the suggestion that maybe you need to say "please" first. Or, simply pass around a paper plate and pretend a new food appears on it each time.

Christelow, Eileen. 2001. *The Great Pig Search*. New York: Clarion.

Summary:
Bert and Ethel's pigs escape from the back of their truck and they go on vacation to find them.

Activity:
Take the kids in your group on a pig search. Hide pig pictures, pig snouts, or pig toys; puppets; or stuffed animals around the room. When the kids start to point out the pigs to you, pretend you can't see them, just as Bert and Ethel keep missing the pigs they see on their search in the story. In the end, as Bert and Ethel see the pigs in the newspaper, finally show the kids that you see what they have been seeing—the pigs around the room.

Christiansen, Candace. 1997. *The Mitten Tree*. Illus., Elaine Greenstein. Golden, Colo.: Fulcrum Kids.

Summary:
A woman knits mittens for children in her neighborhood and hangs them on a tree by their bus stop.

Activity:
For this slow and quiet story, simply cut out mittens of different colors and hang them on a plant or on a tree that you have cut out of paper. When the children in the story pick their mittens off the tree, allow the children in your group to do the same.

Clark, Emma Chichester. 1990. *Catch That Hat!* Boston: Little, Brown.

Summary:
A young girl named Rose chases after her hat.

Activity:
Pass a hat around while the story is told. The children will feel like they are helping Rose find her hat as it lands on a roof, up a hill, in a lake, on a steeple, in a cave, and in a tree. Instead, it will be landing on the laps or in the hands of other children. If you want a wild time, you could also have the children chase around the room or an outdoor area for it, tossing it to a child each time it is almost caught, or throw it across a circle to one another.

Cleary, Brian P. 2000. *Hairy, Scary, Ordinary: What Is an Adjective?* Illus., Jenya Prosmitsky. Minneapolis, Minn.: Carolrhoda.

Summary:
A story is told mostly in adjectives.

Activity:
Older children can frantically raise their hands every time they hear an adjective. First make sure they understand the definition of an adjective. An activity for after the story could be to let the students choose an adjective they remember from the story and use it in a poem. Warn them ahead of time that they will need to remember some of the adjectives. You could make it more difficult by providing a list of adjectives after you have finished reading and have them check off the ones they remember from the story.

Compestine, Ying Chang. 2001. *The Story of Chopsticks*. Illus., Yongsheng Xuan. New York: Holiday House.

Summary:
A fictional story of how a boy who never gets to eat first because his food is too hot invents chopsticks.

Activity:
Give children chopsticks, craft sticks, or straws, and have them pretend

to use them as you tell the story. Since the story is rather wordy you may want to summarize it at times. You might even give the children some type of cereal to practice on and have them yell when they have lifted something with the sticks in any way. At the end of the book, there is an explanation of how to use chopsticks, which you might choose to read and demonstrate.

Conrad, Pam. 1998. *This Mess.* Illus., Elizabeth Sayles. New York: Hyperion.

Summary:
Brother and sister try to make their house look "better," but they actually make a mess instead.

Activity:
Without making the storytime area too messy, try doing some of the things in the book. Set a box of blown up blue balloons afloat, empty a box of blocks, stack up storytime mats and newspaper, place an upsidedown lampshade on the table, and put books of the same color in piles. Ask the children what they think is different. You might even try some of your own ways to make the area look like a mess to an adult, but heaven to a child. The children will enjoy being messy in the library or classroom.

Coxe, Molly. 1990. *Whose Footprints?* New York: Crowell.

Summary:
A mother and daughter try to figure out whose footprints are in the snow.

Activity:
Allow the children to guess whose footprints are in the snow. Give hints because the footprints all look pretty similar. You might even offer choices by putting out pictures or puppets of the animals, using a cat, rooster, mouse, pony, sheep, and dog. Ask the children to identify each animal. You could even draw or enlarge a picture of the footprints and add extra animals to the mix. Make it a game in which the children tape the footprint to the correct animal, and you tell them if they are right or if they have some wrong and need to change it around.

Crews, Nina. 1997. *Snowball*. New York: Greenwillow.

Summary:
A girl enjoys the winter snow and makes a snowball.

Activity:
Crinkle up scrap paper as snowballs and let children throw them at the end of the story when the girl throws her snowball. They can have a small scale "snowball" fight with each other. Maybe even try to build a snowperson out of the crinkled paper, providing objects for the eyes, ears, and nose and a hat and scarf. Unless glued, it won't stay up, but that's the fun of it. Just pretend it is getting too warm and the snow is melting. Alternatively, form a snowman that is lying down by making an outline of a snowman in wadded up paper balls. The last activity could involve holding a waste basket and having the children play the game of throwing the paper balls into the trash can, or better, a recycling bin.

Crisp, Marty. 2000. *Black and White*. Illus., Sherry Neidigh. Flagstaff, Ariz.: Rising Moon

Summary:
A boy loses his black-and-white dog among other black-and-white animals.

Activity:
Before you begin, give each child black dots cut out of construction paper with tape on the back or black dot stickers to put on themselves. Place white dots on a black stuffed dog, or vice versa, and put it somewhere in the room or give it to a child to hold. Walk around and pretend you have lost your dog, asking if the kids have seen him and pretending you do not. Then read the story, inquiring along the way about your dog until the end when you finally approach it. You could also put dots on other stuffed animals or puppets. Place these animals around the room, pretending to ask them about your dog as you read the story. The other animals in the story are all spotted or black and white, and the dog blends among them. Otherwise, simply ask the children if they have seen your dog as you walk around the room with a book and see if they spot him on the pages.

Cronin, Doreen. 2000. *Click, Clack, Moo: Cows That Type*. **Illus., Betsy Lewin. New York: Simon & Schuster.**

Summary:
Animals type their demands for a farmer before they will produce more milk and eggs.

Activity:
"Click, clack, moo" is repeated over and over in this story. Have the children pretend to type with their fingers and say "moo" each time they hear you read it in the story. You can also instruct them that you will point to them each time they are to say these words or have them repeat after you.

Cullen, Catherine Ann. 2001. *The Magical, Mystical, Marvelous Coat*. **Illus., David Christiana. Boston: Little, Brown.**

Summary:
A girl uses the magical buttons on her coat to help others until she finds they magically reappeared in her pocket.

Activity:
Find six large buttons or cut out six paper circles. Each should represent a different button from the story, although it does not have to look like the pictures in the text. One will say "cold," another "warm"; one plays a tune, another is a star; one is a stone, and the last is a doll with a coat. Bring in a coat of your own and tape the buttons or circles to it. Take off one at a time as you tell the story. When the tall man with the burnt head complains of pain, take off the cold button. You can give the buttons to children to hold. As a trick, put them in your pocket while the kids are not looking, or use duplicates and magically pull them out as the girl does at the end of the story.

Davis, Aubrey. 1998. *The Enormous Potato*. **Illus., Dušan Petrišić. Buffalo, N.Y.: Kids Can.**

Summary:
A farmer needs help to lift an enormous potato.

Activity:
Cut out a huge cardboard, paper, or poster board potato, or pretend to

have one. Ask the kids if they have ever seen such a huge potato before. Then say something like, "Well there was a farmer who wanted to win the state fair so badly with his enormous potato, but when he went to lift it into the truck, he could not get it off the ground. So he called for his wife to help. 'Wife! Wife!'" Have a child from the group grab on to you and try to lift the potato, which fails. Then call for the next person, such as the daughter, or have the last child call instead. Each child will grab on to the last person or on to the potato. This continues with different people and animals until the last child is the goldfish or another small creature, which has the miraculous strength to lift the huge vegetable. Start with cousins and aunts, lead into pets, and end with farm animals. You can change the ending to state that the potato was so heavy they dropped it and it broke, so they just ate it instead. The kids all gather around the potato and pretend to eat it. The story doesn't have to be followed word for word, and no memorization is required. It is just an adaptation of an obviously already adapted folk tale. Of course, these books can also be read instead of memorized, but it is easier to move about without the book in hand.

Davis, Katie. 1998. *Who Hops?* New York: Harcourt, Brace.

Summary:
Different animals perform different actions.

Activity:
The questions are already there for you: "Who hops?" "Who flies?" "Who slithers?" "Who swims?" "Who crawls?" Multiple answers are provided, but first see if the kids know them. Ask them what other creatures hop, fly, slither, swim, or crawl. There are also some tricks, such as "Elephants slither." If the kids don't catch it, flip the page and respond as the book does, "No they don't," or ask, "Do elephants really slither?"

Dealey, Erin. 2002. *Goldie Locks Has Chicken Pox*. Illus., Hanako Wakiyama. New York: Atheneum.

Summary:
The story describes what happens to Goldie Locks when she gets chicken pox.

Activity:
Get red dot stickers and put them all over yourself, a doll, a picture of a girl, or the children, as you tell the story. Find a coloring sheet of

Goldilocks, or any girl, and give the children crayons—red or any color—
to make her spots.

Denim, Sue. 1994. *The Dumb Bunnies*. Illus., Dav Pilkey. New York: Blue Sky.

Summary:
The dumb bunnies have a mixed up way of doing things.

Activity:
The Dumb Bunnies books provide a great opportunity for questions.
"Should the dumb bunnies have done that?" "Is that what you are supposed to do?" when they do things like put porridge in the microwave
because it is too hot, put their bikes on top of their car because they
could use the exercise, and bowl in the library. *The Dumb Bunnies* are
similar to *The Stupids* by Harry Allard and the *Amelia Bedelia* books by
Peggy Parish. Use questions for these books as well.

DePaola, Tomie. 1979. *Oliver Button Is a Sissy*. New York: Harcourt Brace Jovanovich.

Summary:
Oliver does not like to play sports; he would rather read and take walks
and dance.

Activity:
Use this book to ask questions and start a discussion on gender roles.
During the story, ask children if boys, girls, or both do the things that
Oliver does, such as jump rope, read books, play with paper dolls, and
dance. If they say boy or girl, ask, "Are you sure?" until you get the answer "both." Continue to ask questions throughout, such as, "Do boys,
girls, or both play sports?" "Do you think Oliver should win the talent
show?" "Will his class make fun of him?"

---

de Regniers, Beatrice Schenk. 1964. *May I Bring a Friend?* Illus., Beni Montresor. New York: Atheneum.

Summary:
A child keeps getting invitations to join the king and queen for meals
and asks to bring a friend each time. When it gets out of hand, they dine
at the zoo instead.

Activity:
Use the children as the different animals and bring them up to the front of the room or center of the circle each time new animals are invited to dinner. The children will pretend to be a giraffe, hippo, monkeys, an elephant, lions, and a seal. Count the children beforehand to make sure you have at least six. Leave out an animal if you have fewer children, or include some parents. If you have more than six children, you can use them as extra monkeys and lions.

―――. 1955. *What Can You Do with a Shoe?* Illus., Maurice Sendak. New York: Harper.

Summary:
The story asks what you can do with a shoe and other objects.

Activity:
When the book asks, "What can you do with a shoe?," ask the children the questions in the book, such as can you ". . . put it on your ear?" "On your head?" "Or butter it like bread?" Then ask what people really do with each object, wait for responses, and read the answers in the book. Do the same thing with the other things mentioned, a chair, hat, cup, broom, and bed. If possible, have the objects at hand to demonstrate the silly and proper uses or to point at when you ask the questions.

DeRolf, Shane. 1997. *The Crayon Box That Talked.* Illus., Michael Letzig. New York: Random House.

Summary:
Crayons don't get along until a girl buys them and uses all of them in a picture.

Activity:
Give each child a crayon in one of the colors mentioned in the book, including red, yellow, green, orange, blue, black, and white, and have each child stand up and then sit down every time you read the name of the colored crayon he or she is holding. You could also have the children stay standing or come to the front of the room after their color is called. You could also add other colors to the story or give out more of the same color crayon for variety or if you have more than seven children. For smaller groups, give each child more than one color. At the end you might ask them to use their colors to draw a picture or color a

picture of a crayon. Another option would be to end by having the children draw a little squiggle on a paper before returning the crayon to the crayon container.

Devons, Sonia. 1990. *Shut the Gate!* **Illus., Shoo Rayner. New York: Bedrick/Blackie.**

Summary:
A boy forgets to shut the gate and lets the different animals on the loose.

Activity:
This is already set up for you. Just ask the question, "Did he remember to shut the gate?" each time it appears in the book, with pictures of him passing the sheep, cows, bull, horse and donkey, and goats. Kids will wait until they get a chance to yell "No!" End by asking if they think John will remember to shut the gate next time. Ask the children if there is anything they ever forgot to do.

Diakite, Baba Wague. 1999. *The Hatseller and the Monkeys: A West African Folktale.* **Illus., Baba Wague Diakite. New York: Scholastic.**

Summary:
Monkeys steal a hatseller's hats and must be tricked into dropping them.

Activity:
Use this as an alternative to the older *Caps for Sale*, authored and illustrated by Esphyr Slobodkina (New York: W. R. Scott, 1940). The book suggests other versions at the end as well. Pile hats of any kind on your head and hand them to the children in the room when the monkeys steal them. They will catch on and do things similar to what the monkeys in the story do, such as pretending to throw things, waving the hats, and finally dropping them to the ground. Then collect the hats and pile them on your head again. You can make simple hats out of paper, either making them into a simple band or wizard's hat. Make more detailed hats if you choose to keep them a while. Kids can also make hats as a craft and use them for the story.

Dodd, Emma. 2001. *Dog's Colorful Day: A Messy Story about Colors and Counting*. New York: Dutton.

Summary:
A dog with one black spot soon has more colorful spots after a messy day.

Activity:
Copy an outline of a dog on white paper. Draw a black spot on it. As the story continues and Dog gets spots of colors on him from different food and fun, either draw the correct color spot on him or ask a child to come up and do so. Besides black, you will need red, blue, green, brown, yellow, pink, gray, orange, and purple. Make sure to count the spots along the way. You could also cut circles out of colored paper instead and tape them to the children in the room so that each has a color. Count the children as spots. You could also give the children coloring sheets and crayons and let them draw the spots themselves.

Dodds, Dayle Ann. 1992. *Do Bunnies Talk?* Illus., A. Dubanevich. New York: HarperCollins.

Summary:
The book gives the different sounds that animals and other things make—except for the innocent bunnies.

Activity:
Have the children repeat the sounds after you say them. For example, "Roosters cock-a-doodle. Chicks cheep-cheep. But quiet little bunnies don't make a peep." Every page has two or three different sounds. The quiet bunnies never say anything, so put your fingers to your lips to quiet the kids at this point in preparation for the next set of sounds.

Domanska, Janina. 1969. *The Turnip*. New York: Macmillan.

Summary:
Help is needed to pull a giant turnip from the ground.

Activity:
Just as with any story in which a large vegetable or fruit needs help to get off the ground, call children up to help. Either use the characters in

the story or make up your own animals and people so everyone in the room gets a turn. If using characters from the book, you will need a grandmother; grandfather; a child, Micky; dog; cat; geese; rooster and hen; pig; and magpie. Have all the children tumble to the ground in the end.

Donaldson, Julia. 2001. *Room on the Broom*. Illus., Axel Scheffler. New York: Dial.

Summary:
A witch gives animals a ride.

Activity:
Take a broom from the closet or a long stick or rope or even an imaginary broom and have the children climb on as you ask them to be the different animals in the story, including a cat, dog, bird, and frog. If you dare, you can extend the story by inviting even more children as animals onto the broom. Kids can also just hold onto the broom with one hand.

Emberley, Ed. 1992. *Go Away, Big Green Monster!* Boston: Little, Brown

Summary:
Using cut-out holes, each page turn reveals more and more and then less and less of the monster, as the book asks parts of him to "Go away."

Activity:
Start by asking if the children believe in monsters and if they are afraid of monsters. You might tell them you used to be afraid of monsters until you read this book and it showed you how to get rid of them. Go through the pages of the book describing the monster. Read the pages that go something like, "Go away, scraggly purple hair!" and ask the kids to repeat those phrases after you until you end with "Go away, big green monster! And don't come back!" The key is letting the children yell this out loud so they can think they helped get rid of the monster, even if only a monster in a book. You might also want to pause before you read "teeth" or "hair," etc., to see if the children can answer first. A craft could involve placing precut monster pieces on construction paper to be removed as the story is told. Turn this into a board story as well.

————. 1961. *The Wing on a Flea: A Book about Shapes*. Illus., Ed Emberley. Boston: Little, Brown.

Summary:
Different shapes can be seen on everyday things.

Activity:
Provide each child with an envelope of different cut-out construction paper shapes in different colors and see if each one can use the shapes to make some of the objects in the story. You could also make larger shapes and show examples on a board in the front of the room. Then see if the children can copy them or allow the children to come up and take turns making objects with the shapes on the board. After you read the story, see what other objects the children can make and ask them to share. The end of the book tells about Emberley's other books that show how to make pictures out of simple shapes.

Ericsson, Jennifer A. 2002. *She Did It!* Illus., Nadine Bernard Westcott. New York: Farrar Straus & Giroux.

Summary:
Four sisters blame each other for everything that goes wrong.

Activity:
Every time the mother asks which girl did something, they point and yell, "She did it!" When you read the story, point at a different child each time and yell, "He did it!" or, "She did it!" and have that child come up and do the same next time. You could also just instruct them all to point at someone at these moments in the story.

Evans, Lezlie. 1999. *Can You Count Ten Toes? Count to 10 in 10 Different Languages*. Illus., Denis Roche. New York: Houghton Mifflin.

Summary:
Count to ten in different languages.

Activity:
This book is more appropriate for classrooms as an introduction to different languages, and perhaps more appropriate when introduced a little at a time. Simply read the description of the scene and language. Pro-

nunciation of each number in a new language is given. Have the children repeat each number in a different language after you. Languages represented are Japanese, Russian, Korean, Zulu, French, Hindi, Tagalog, Hebrew, Spanish, and Chinese. You could also show the map at the back of the book or use a larger map to point out the countries where these languages are spoken.

Falwell, Cathryn. 1992. *Shape Space*. New York: Clarion.

Summary:
A gymnast dances on and around shapes.

Activity:
Cut out rectangles, triangles, semicircles, circles, and squares, each in a different color. Make sure there are more than enough shapes for each child in the group. Sprinkle them all around the room. As the story is told, let the kids find the shapes needed to act out the story. For example, when the story reads, "Hop on a rectangle," instruct the children to hop on one of the cut-out rectangles. Allow them to then "rock on a triangle," "swing a circle round," "try on a triangle," "take a shape take a step" and more. After reading the story, play a game of Twister with the shapes and colors on the floor.

Farley, Jacqui. 1998. *Giant Hiccups*. Illus., Pamela Venus. Milwaukee, Wisc.: Gareth Stevens.

Summary:
A giant has the hiccups and people in the town try to help get rid of them.

Activity:
Every time the giant hiccups and the word "hiccup" appears in the story, point to the children and ask them to make a hiccupping noise. You could also ask the children in your group to suggest ways to get rid of the giant's ailment as the children in the story do.

Feiffer, Jules. 1999. *Bark, George*. New York: HarperCollins.

Summary:
George the dog can't bark; he can only make other animal sounds until his visit to the doctor.

Activity:
Copy a picture of a large dog's head and put it on the front of a box or basket or on top of a blanket. Inside, hide pictures or puppets of a cat, duck, pig, and cow. When the doctor in the story reaches down George's throat to find these items, pull them out of your box, basket, or blanket one at a time. For more fun throw them out to the audience. You can simply have a dog puppet or stuffed animal on the side instead.

———. 2001. *I'm Not Bobby!* New York: Hyperion.

Summary:
Bobby does not want to answer when his name is called so he pretends to be other things.

Activity:
Have the children stand up and act out the different animals and objects in the story that Bobby becomes. They will roar like a lion, fly like an airplane, stomp like a dinosaur, make claw hands like a monster, stomp like a giant, gallop like a horse, drive like a racecar, and fly like an eagle and spaceship. You can follow by asking the children what else they can pretend to be and ask if it is a good idea to pretend to be something else when someone is looking for you and calling your name. Hope that the story won't give them any bad ideas to get them in trouble at home.

Fleming, Candace. 2001. *Muncha! Muncha! Muncha!* Illus., G. Brian Karas. New York: Atheneum.

Summary:
A man decides to build a garden, but no matter what he does bunnies keep getting into it.

Activity:
Let the kids repeat the sounds the bunnies make as they sneak into the garden each time the man tries to build another way to keep them out. First have them stand on tiptoe to "Tippy-Tippy, Tippy, Pat!" then say, "Muncha! Muncha! Muncha!" pretending to chew. Each time a new phrase is added along with these two.

Fleming, Denise. 1994. *Barnyard Banter*. New York: Holt

Summary:
Animals in a barn make different sounds.

Activity:
Have the children guess what sounds the animals make and then repeat
the sounds three times. Sounds you will be making are moo for cows,
cock-a-doodle-doo for roosters, cluck for hens, muck for pigs, mew for
kittens, coo for pigeons, squeak for mice, shriek for peacocks, heehaw
for donkeys, caw for crows, chirp for crickets, and burp for frogs. If you'd
like, replace sounds with more familiar ones, such as a grunt or oink for
the pig and a meow for the cats. Also use *Barnyard Song* by Rhonda
Gowler Greene illustrated by Robert Bender (New York: Atheneum
Books for Young Readers, 1997) in the same way.

———. 1992. *Lunch*. New York: Holt.

Summary:
A mouse eats a big lunch.

Activity:
Since only parts of the vegetables are shown at first, pause and point to
the pictures and let the children guess what the next food will be. You
will say, "sweet yellow . . . " and point to a picture of half an ear of corn,
wait for an answer, and turn the page to reveal the whole thing. Follow
by asking the children what other things the mouse should eat. You could
also cut out pictures of the fruits and vegetables and paperclip them in
the book to pull off and hand to a child or to a mouse puppet.

**Friskey, Margaret. 1990. *The Perky Little Pumpkin*. Illus., Tom
   Dunnington. Chicago: Children's Press.**

Summary:
A jack-o-lantern does not succeed in scaring the kids on Halloween, but
he does succeed in scaring himself.

Activity:
Each time the "Perky Little Pumpkin" tries to scare someone, ask the
children if he succeeded this time. For example, when the child dressed

as a pirate in the story runs by, ask the children if they think the pumpkin scared him. Then follow with the witch, ghost, and ballerina. In the end, when the pumpkin finally thinks he scares someone by looking in the mirror, see if they can guess who is really scared. You could also ask the children to be the pumpkin and make a really scary face. You are the judge as to whether you think the children could scare the trick-or-treaters.

Fuge, Charles. 2001. *Yip! Snap! Yap!* Berkeley, Calif.: Tricycle.

Summary:
Different dogs do different things and make different sounds.

Activity:
For every page, allow the children to repeat the words that describe the sounds the dogs make or the actions they perform. They will "Arf! Woof! Rruff!," "Chomp! Munch! Chew!" "Hrumph! Zzzzz! Shew . . . ," "Gruff! Grrr! Grrruff!" and more. Let children crawl around the floor like dogs while the story is read.

Gaga. 2000. *Pass the Celery, Ellery.* Illus., Jeffrey Fisher. New York: Stewart, Tabori & Chang.

Summary:
Phrases are repeated to show what each person passes using food that rhymes with each name.

Activity:
You can continue the story by making up rhymes about the children in the room, even if they don't make sense and it is not food you rhyme. In fact, the last page suggests this with the words, "Now it's your turn." For example, "Pass the chair-a Sarah," "Pass the muffin, Justin," or "Pass the cream, Reem." You can also copy pictures of the food represented in the book, choosing from abalone, chili, duck, date, eel, egg, fries, fish, food, sole, gum, ham, honey, ice, kidney, kale, linguini, leek, lasagne, meat, nutmeg, nectarine, olive, omelette, pasta, pan, pea, prune, quince, ratatouille, spaghetti, tea, tortilla, cake, veal, water, yam, and zabaglione. You don't have to use all of them, but sprinkle fake food you may have or pictures from pattern books around the room, and when you say a phrase in the story like "Pass the egg, Meg." Ask a child to be Meg and find the egg in the room. Have all the children stand when you say a

phrase such as, "Pass the meat, Pete," and have whoever finds the object first pass it to you.

Galdone, Paul. 1985. *Cat Goes Fiddle-I-Fee*. New York: Houghton Mifflin.

Summary:
Taken from an Old English rhyme, a boy tells about the different animals he feeds.

Activity:
Use a song version of this story to play along and sing along while the children look at the pictures. You can begin by teaching the children their line, "The cat goes fiddle-i-fee," and going over the other lines in the book they might want to repeat, such as the "Hen goes chimmy-chunk," "duck goes quack, quack," "goose goes swishy, swashy," "sheep goes baa, baa," "pig goes griffy gruffy," "cow goes moo moo," "horse goes neigh, neigh," and "dog goes bow-wow." You could also place pictures or puppets of the animals around the room so that you can point to them easily when it is time to sing their sound in the story.

———. 1983. *The Greedy Old Fat Man: An American Folk Tale.* New York: Clarion.

Summary:
A greedy old fat man eats everything and everyone in sight.

Activity:
If you don't think this story is too politically incorrect, then have some fun. Use a big blanket and pretend it is the fat man. Bring the children up one at a time to hide under the blanket as you pretend they are the people and animals the fat man eats in the story. You will need a little boy and girl, dog, cat, fox, rabbits, and a squirrel.

———. 1973. *The Little Red Hen.* New York: Seabury.

Summary:
The little red hen gets no help from her housemates, the dog, cat, and mouse, until they realize they won't eat unless they help.

Activity:
Children can repeat "Not I" at appropriate times when the hen asks the cat, dog, and mouse if they will help. You could even divide the children up in three groups, maybe even providing cat, dog, and mouse ears or masks for them to hold so it is easier for them to remember their parts or so they don't try to switch to their favorite animals during the middle of the story. Alternatively, have animal puppets or pictures on a table or on the floor and point to the one you are referring to when you want the children to repeat, "Not I."

———. 1982. *What's in Fox's Sack?: An Old English Tale*. **New York: Clarion.**

Summary:
In an Old English tale, Fox keeps tricking people into giving him a larger animal or person for his meal.

Activity:
Use this one for storytelling. Take a blanket, and each time Fox acquires someone new for his meal, have a child be that animal and hide under the blanket used as a sack. That child leaves when the next one is called and added to the sack. The animals (and the human) needed are a bumblebee, rooster, pig, a little boy, and dog. Children could also play the roles of the different women the fox tries to trick each time. Alternatively, use puppets as the animals and place them in a bag, pillowcase, or basket.

Gambrell, Jamey. 1996. *Telephone*. **Illus., Vladimir Radunsky. New York: North-South.**

Summary:
Different animals make telephone calls for different reasons.

Activity:
Pass a toy phone, a disconnected one from your desk, or your cell phone around the circle. The children can each take a turn as an animal makes the call. To make the story go faster, only read the print in the large font.

Gardner, Beau. 1986. *Have You Ever Seen . . . ?: An ABC Book.* **New York: Dodd, Mead.**

Summary:
On each page of this alphabet book there is a silly scenario that is unlikely to happen.

Activity:
Use some of the examples from the book. For a king in a kettle, put a plastic witch's cauldron on the table with a picture of a king or king doll in it, or make a turtle with a tie by putting a tie around the neck of a turtle puppet. Add some of your own creations from things you have lying around as well, such as taping a fake moustache on a monkey puppet for a monkey with a moustache. Then when you ask "Have you ever seen an egg with ears?" and kids say "No!" you can say, "Are you sure? Are you sure you haven't seen an egg with ears?" They look and yell, "Yes, there it is," when they realize their "mistake" and see that you have put a plastic or real egg with paper bunny ears on the table. When the story is over, start asking about the other things you have added (or hadn't included) and see if the kids can identify them by looking around the room.

Garland, Michael. 2001. *Mystery Mansion: A Look Again Book.* New York: Dutton.

Summary:
Hidden notes and objects give a boy clues.

Activity:
This is better for a one-on-one activity. Children can look at the pictures to find and count the animals and other objects according to clues. Perhaps for a group of older children, especially in a classroom, you could give a similar book to each child, such as Graeme Base's *The Eleventh Hour: A Curious Mystery* (New York: Abrams, 1989).

Garrett, Ann, and Gene-Michael Higney. 2000. *What's for Dinner?* Illus., Stephanie Peterson. New York: Dutton.

Summary:
Each double-page spread has a creature that eats another creature or thing. The mouths of the animals and human open up to show what they ate.

Activity:
Even though the rhymes tell what the animals or human ate, the kids will still think they are smart if you ask them. They can tell you what will be under the mouth when you lift the flap. "Surprises" include a mouse in a cat, clam in a walrus, fly in a frog, spider in a bat, fish in a shark, and a hot dog in a boy.

Geisert, Arthur. 2001. *Nursery Crimes*. Boston: Houghton Mifflin.

Summary:
A family of pigs has to find whoever stole their turkey topiaries.

Activity:
This is a strange but fun story with lots of opportunity for interaction. First explain to children what topiaries are by showing examples from books or maybe even a short clip from the movie *Edward Scissorhands*. Show the pigs looking in many places to find their missing topiaries, and ask the children if they think the topiaries are in each of those places. They look under a pumpkin, from a high ladder, in a car lot, in a junkyard, etc. When they go to the notorious topiary thief's home, ask the children if they think he stole them. Then ask if the children can tell the pig family's topiaries from Voler's (the thief) in the yard of turkey topiaries. Since the pigs cannot, they decide to make new ones and hide in pumpkins to catch the thief. At this point, give each child a piece of green or orange construction paper and a pair of safety scissors. With younger children, you may want to ask them to simply tear the paper into the shape of a turkey. You could also print a picture of a turkey on white paper and have some color them green and some orange, depending on the amount of time you have. Also provide pumpkin faces for the children to hold over their faces when the pigs hide, yet fall asleep, waiting for the thief. To save time and paper, you could ask only a few students to stand up front to do this. When the family goes back to the thief Voler's house, ask the children to hold up the turkeys they cut, colored, or tore. Point out, as in the story, that the orange ones were theirs because they made the last ones on special trees that will turn yellow and orange in the fall. Since the characters have French names, you might tell the story in a French accent.

Gelman, Rita Golden. 1992. *More Spaghetti, I Say!* Illus., Mort Gerberg. New York: Scholastic.

Summary:
Minnie the monkey doesn't want to play because she can't stop making and eating spaghetti.

Activity:
Wrap white yarn around yourself or a child while telling the story. When the story goes, "I am going to throw it all over the bed, in the air, on the

chair, on the floor, ON YOUR HEAD!" throw the "spaghetti" out to the children. You could also use shredded paper.

Gelsanliter, Wendy, and Frank Christian. 1998. *Dancin' in the Kitchen*. Illus., Marjorie Priceman. New York: Putnam & Grosset.

Summary:
A family prepares dinner together while they dance.

Activity:
As in the illustrations, have the children join hands and dance around in a circle until the story is done. Instead of continually dancing in a normal fashion, let them "kitchen-dance" by pretending to chop carrots, snap beans, add water, pile strawberries, add whipped cream, and end by sitting on the floor to pretend to eat. You could also hand out plastic bowls and spoons as grandma does in the beginning of the story.

George, Kristine O'Connell. 2001. *Book!* Illus., Maggie Smith. New York: Clarion.

Summary:
A boy describes what he can do with a book.

Activity:
Use *Book!* or another book to do the things the boy does in the story. It would be fun if you first wrap the book because the boy unwraps his gift, the book, in the story. Ask the children what they think is inside and then unwrap it or ask a child to do so. You could also pass it around the room and let everyone take turns slowly opening a little bit of the package until it is revealed. You can then pretend to be like the boy in the story and open and close the book, turn the pages, close it, read it to a toy cat, read it upside down, wear it like a hat, show it to a doll, read it, hug it, take it on a ride, put it on a shelf, hug it, and sleep with it. Have a child hold open the book and turn the pages as you pretend to do the same with a different book on the side. Ask the children to each select a book from the shelves or table and replicate the actions of the boy as you tell the story.

Gerstein, Mordicai. 1998. *Stop Those Pants!* San Diego, Calif.: Harcourt Brace.

Summary:
A boy has trouble getting dressed in the morning when his pants run away; the other clothes try to help him catch them. He finally bribes the pants by promising to put a yo-yo in his pocket.

Activity:
Put a pair of pants on a broom or stick or wave them around in the air and dance them around as you tell the story. You can even let the children try to catch them or have the children pass them around in a circle like a game of hot potato. You can add other items to the mix, like a shirt, socks, and a belt.

Gile, John. 1995. *Oh, How I Wished I Could Read!* Illus., Frank Fiorello. Rockford, Ill.: John Gile Communications.

Summary:
Bad things keep happening to a boy who can't read the signs around him.

Activity:
Perhaps a cruel trick to play on nonreaders or beginning readers, but you could hold up signs like the ones in the book (Wet Paint, Beware of Dogs, Wet Cement, Poison Ivy, No Crossing, Danger High Voltage) and then tell the children what the consequences would be if they couldn't read the signs. To make them know you are just tricking them, that it doesn't mean they can't read, you could hold up the sign quickly or take it away or the sign could be completely blank. You could also ask the kids what they think the sign says, even though they can't read it.

Ginsburg, Mirra. 1974. *Mushroom in the Rain.* Illus., Jose Aruego and Ariane Dewey. New York: Macmillan.

Summary:
Several creatures seek shelter from the rain under a mushroom that grows.

Activity:
Use a blanket as a mushroom or cut a large mushroom shape out of

poster board. As you tell the story, and as different creatures get under the mushroom for shelter, invite a different child to go under the blanket or behind the poster board. You will have an ant, butterfly, mouse, sparrow, and a rabbit, as well as a fox that they send away. Invent other animals to include more children.

Godwin, Laura. 2001. *What the Baby Hears*. Illus., Mary Morgan-Van Royen. New York: Hyperion.

Summary:
Pictures that show the loving things baby animals hear their parents doing.

Activity:
This is a simple book, so simply make the sounds such as "Guzzle, guzzle, guzzle," and "burp, burp, burp." First wait for children to guess what the sounds might be. They may instead make the actual animal sound first, so point out what the animals are doing in the pictures to get them to make the sounds written in the story.

Graham, Bob. 2001. *"Let's Get a Pup!" Said Kate*. Cambridge, Mass.: Candlewick.

Summary:
A family goes to a shelter to pick out a dog and ends up with two.

Activity:
Let the children have an opportunity to choose which pet they would like to bring home. Display stuffed animals or puppets around the room, and when the family in the story goes to choose their dog, let the children walk to a table or area set aside with different choices and, one at a time, let them pick an animal. They do not all have to be dogs, and pictures would work just as well. Then continue to tell the story, taking a vote on who would choose the puppy and who would choose the older dog.

Gray, Libba Moore. 1997. *Is There Room on the Feather Bed?* Illus., Nadine Bernard Westcott. New York: Orchard.

Summary:
As animals are floating in the rising water caused by rain, they join a wee fat man and his wee fat wife on their feather bed.

Activity:
Place a blanket on the floor and have the children lie on it one at a time as different animals are called out of the rising water to safety in the bed. Children can pretend to be a goose, duck, sheep, hen, pig, dog, cow, and cat. You could also have someone be the wee fat woman and the wee fat man. Children can also help repeat the phrase at the appropriate times, "Why, bless your hearts, such a noise, such a fuss. There's room on the feather bed for all of us." Longer dialogue towards the beginning can be abbreviated.

Greenberg, David T. 1999. *Whatever Happened to Humpty Dumpty? And Other Surprising Sequels to Mother Goose Rhymes*. Illus., S. D. Schindler. Boston: Little, Brown.

Summary:
New endings are given to Mother Goose rhymes.

Activity:
Use this with a Mother Goose or nursery rhyme lesson or storytime. Have the children repeat Mother Goose rhymes with you. Then read them the endings. Ask if that is how they think the story should have ended. Use this as a writing assignment for older children, assigning each child a rhyme for which to write a new ending.

Greenfield, Eloise. 1991. *I Make Music*. Illus., Jan Spivey Gilchrist. New York: Writers & Readers.

Summary:
A simple board book in which a child makes music in different ways.

Activity:
Let the kids "make good music" with you as they hit their thighs, bang on a fake drum, snap their thumbs, play a fake trombone or xylophone, and tap their toes along with the story. End by demonstrating or asking for other ways to make music with body parts.

Gross, Ruth Belov. 1988. *Hansel and Gretel*. Illus., Winslow Pinney Pels. New York: Scholastic.

Summary:
Two children get sent away from home and are caught by a witch whose house they tried to eat.

Activity:
Use any version of this tale and make your own gingerbread house. Use poster board or a cardboard box. Decorate it with pictures or patterns of candy and sweets. Let the children in your group pick off pieces as you tell that part of the story. You could even tape up actual cookies and let them eat. Gross's version is long, so tell it instead.

Grossman, Bill. 1996. *My Little Sister Ate One Hare*. Illus., Kevin Hawkes. New York: Crown.

Summary:
A little girl keeps eating gross objects in this cumulative tale until peas finally make her sick.

Activity:
This story is great for repetition. Instruct the children when it first comes up that you need them to say, "We thought she'd throw up then and there. But she didn't." Or simply say yourself, "We thought she'd throw up then and there, but what?" "But she didn't," they repeat. Try to tell the story really fast without looking at the words. In the end, you might want to ask the children what happened to make sure they got the point that after eating lizards, worms, polliwogs, mice, bats, shrews, ants, snakes, and a hare, that peas made her throw up.

Grover, Max. 1998. *So Many Kinds of Shoes!* San Diego, Calif.: Harcourt Brace.

Summary:
This board book shows different shoes and their uses.

Activity:
Ask the children what each shoe is used for, including sneakers, boots, and slippers. Since this is a simple board book and only three shoes are mentioned, you might want to bring in your own shoe collection and show different kinds of boots, athletic shoes, fancy high heels, or ski boots, etc., to continue the story. You could copy pictures or cut them from magazines instead. End with pictures of shoes around the room that children have to find. Have them tell you what the shoes would be used for or when they would wear them. You might also ask them what kinds of shoes they are wearing and where they would wear them. If they have no answer, suggest, "Would you wear them to the library/ school?"

Hall, Kirsten. 1995. *Duck, Duck, Goose!* Illus., Laura Rader. Chicago: Children's Press.

Summary:
Kids play the game "Duck, Duck, Goose!"

Activity:
Begin by showing the pictures of how the game is played and then let the kids play. Finish up with the ending of the story, where a boy takes off running faster. After the game is played you could have all the children get up and run around in a circle, pretending to fly.

Harder, Dan. 1997. *Colliding with Chris*. Illus., Kevin O'Malley. New York: Hyperion.

Summary:
A boy goes on an adventure with his new bike and doesn't realize his brakes are on the handlebars and not on the pedals.

Activity:
Like driving stories, have kids hold their hands like they are holding bicycle handles and take them on Chris's adventure by steering and grabbing and jumping when he does. The children will become familiar with the different things picked up along the way, such as a tuba, trout, bear, spider, roses, and a pig. You may have to point out the small spider in the pictures.

Harley, Bill. 1996. *Sitting Down to Eat*. Illus., Kitty Harvill. Little Rock, Ark.: August House.

Summary:
Animals keep knocking on a boy's door asking to join him for his meal until a caterpillar comes and the house just can't hold them all anymore.

Activity:
At the end of this cumulative tale, the author adds some suggestions of his own. He says it is best read with different voices for each animal. It actually started as a song, so if possible sing it. He called it a "zipper" song or story—the same words are used except a new animal is added each time, similar to Jan Brett's *The Mitten: A Ukrainian Folktale* (New York: Putnam, 1989). You don't even need to follow the exact story or

even have it in hand. Use the recurring phrases in the story, "I was sitting down to eat, just about to begin, when someone knocked on the
door and said, 'Can I come in?' When I opened up the door what did I
see? It was a great big _____ looking at me! I said, 'Oh no! What can I
do?' 'If you've got enough for one, you've got enough for two.'" Keep
substituting then replacing all the animals' names you add when you say
or sing, "I've got enough for _____." You could have the children act as
the animals: either they can remember who they are and make the appropriate animal sounds or movements, or you can provide masks for
them to wear or puppets for them to hold. Otherwise, just display the
puppets or pictures at the front of the room and point to them so the
children can shout out the animals at the appropriate times. It is most
fun when you have the children join you at a table or on a blanket and
you ask them to be the different animals. Add more of some animals or
add different animals at the end to make sure everyone is involved.

Harris, Lee. 1999. *Never Let Your Cat Make Lunch for You.* Illus., Debbie Tilley. Berkeley, Calif.: Tricycle.

Summary:
A girl describes how her cat makes her breakfast and lunch.

Activity:
Use a toy sandwich or hamburger or use two fresh pieces of bread and
hide disgusting things inside, preferably a fake fish, even if out of paper, to represent the anchovy. Keep this in a lunch bag that you keep
touching or shaking to keep the kids interested and pull out the sandwich as the girl does in the story.

Harrison, David Lee 1994. *When Cows Come Home.* Illus., Chris L. Demarest. Honesdale, Penn.: Boyds Mills.

Summary:
The story tells what cows really do when they come home and the farmer
is not looking, such as square dancing, fiddling, and bike riding.

Activity:
Let the children be the cows. Maybe even provide them with a few black
spots to tape onto themselves so they can feel like real cows. At the beginning, tell them to act like real cows, mooing, swishing their tails, and
chewing their cuds, as in the story. When the farmer looks away, and as

you pretend to look away, have them go a little wild. Tell them to join in the secret cow world and do the things you say and act out for them. For "cows play tag," tap a child and say, "You're it," and instruct him or her to run around and tag someone else. You can cut this game short or continue it as long as the children enjoy it. Then have the children pretend to play a fiddle, then square dance, and then pretend to ride bikes. Next, as the cows jump into a pond, have the children jump and pretend to swim. Laugh with the donkeys and roll on the floor instead of doing a summersault. When the cows in the story escape, pretend to open the gate and let your "cows" run around the room or in place until the farmer comes into view again.

Harter, Debbie. 2000. *The Animal Boogie.* **Illus., Stella Blackstone. New York: Barefoot.**

Summary:
Animals dance and move the way they do to the animal boogie.

Activity:
Here the activity is right there for you. For each animal there is a rhyme that involves the animal movement along with the words "boogie, woogie, oogie." If you read the page with the leopard, you will say, "She goes leap, leap, boogie, woogie, oogie!" So involve the children by wiggling and shaking their bodies to the "boogie, woogie, oogie" and moving for each of the animals, including a bear who shakes, a monkey who swings, an elephant who stomps, a bird who flaps, and a snake who slithers.

———. 1997. *Walking through the Jungle.* **New York: Orchard.**

Summary:
A girl meets different animals while traveling the world.

Activity:
Set stuffed animals—or puppets—representing the animals from the book in a circle around the room and walk to each animal with the kids behind you. Have them repeat the statements as well, "Walking through the jungle, Walking through the jungle, what do you see? What do you see? I see a ___." Wait for them to name the next animal, such as a wolf, and continue, " . . . chasing after me." Then run to the next animal. In the end, when you read that you have been around the world and back, point to all the animals and have the children shout out the names of

what they have seen. When you do this, you can walk around with the book or a copy of the story.

Haynes, Max. 1997. *In the Driver's Seat.* **New York: Bantam Doubleday Dell.**

Summary:
A wild driving experience continues through city and country.

Activity:
Give all the children paper plates cut into the shape or drawn in the pattern of steering wheels and read the story, asking the kids to follow along with the words. Read "Turn!" and the kids turn. "Honk!" and they honk.

Heap, Sue. 2002. *What Shall We Play?* **Cambridge, Mass.: Candlewick.**

Summary:
Friends decide what to play and pretend to be different things.

Activity:
Instead of using the names in the story, replace them with the names of children in your class or storytime. "Matt was a big tree. Martha was a shaky tree. Lily May was a quiet tree." When you say their names ask them to act out what you say. Matt, or whomever else you choose, can lift his arms high, Martha can shake, and Lily May can remain silent or hold her finger to her lips. Continue this with all the games the children play in the story.

Heide, Florence Parry. 2000. *Some Things Are Scary.* **Illus., Jules Feiffer. Cambridge, Mass.: Candlewick.**

Summary:
A story that describes things in life that might be scary.

Activity:
Turn the statements in the story into questions. For example, instead of saying "Getting hugged by someone you don't like is scary," Ask the children if they find that scary. "Yes!" they will shout. Is "seeing something

on your plate you know you're not going to like" scary? Is "being on a swing when someone is pushing you too high" scary? Is "discovering that your hamster cage is empty" scary? Then follow with some of your own statements about things that may or may not be scary, or have older children ask the class some of their own ideas of what might or might not be scary. Ideas might be, "Is going to the library scary?" "Is the first day of school scary?" "Is such and such movie scary?" It is okay to ask questions that will get a "No" answer. It is actually recommended to end that way to ease their minds and assure them that not everything is so scary.

Hendra, Sue. 2001. *Moley Gets Dressed for All Weather*. Illus., Sue Hendra. New York: Penguin.

Summary:
A board book with magnetic clothing shows what Moley wears in each season.

Activity:
The activity is right here for you. Ask children to come up one at a time and pick a different piece of clothing from the pile that Moley would wear in each season. Question them if they try to put shorts or a bathing suit on Moley in the winter. There will be extra pieces. If you don't have the book, play the game with pictures of clothes for all seasons and a picture of any animal or person to put them on.

Henkes, Kevin. 1996. *Lilly's Purple Plastic Purse*. New York: Greenwillow.

Summary:
Lilly's purple plastic purse is confiscated after she won't stop playing with the objects inside it.

Activity:
Purchase a purple purse or make a purple purse out of paper. Inside include objects similar to those in Lilly's purse, including quarters and sunglasses. Show off your purse to the children and put it aside, pretending the purse was taken away from you as you tell the story.

Hershenhorn, Esther. 1998. *There Goes Lowell's Party*. Illus., Jacqueline Rogers. New York: Holiday House.

Summary:
Lowell is afraid his birthday party will be cancelled because the animals' behavior and the environment are showing signs of a possible storm.

Activity:
The author has already set up an activity for you, only you wouldn't know it because it was left out of the final edition. On the last page, Hershenhorn provides a list called "How to Know if It's Likely to Rain: Some Weather Proverbs." Examples include, "floorboards creak," and "cows scratch their ears or tail-thump their ribs or run across the meadow, tails atop their backs." These proverbs are actually hidden in the pictures, according to Hershenhorn. You could walk around the room and ask the children to help you find these things in the pictures. Ask if they see anything different in the pictures. Older children could take time during silent reading to locate as many as they can using a list of the proverbs. In the story you will find things such as the word "creak" written or scratched in the porch steps and a cow's tail on her back. When the author visits libraries or schools, before she reads the story she often will have the children come up and dress as different characters in the book, with hats, overalls, and accessories. If you choose, have the children come up as you read the story and have them spin in the wind as they arrive ready for the party.

Hillenbrand, Will. 1999. *Down by the Station*. San Diego, Calif.: Harcourt Brace.

Summary:
A train picks up and passes by different people and animals along the way.

Activity:
Invite children to the front of the room or middle of the circle and pretend to be part of the train that picks up different animals and people. They can also repeat the sound effects such as, "Puff, Puff, Toot, Toot . . ." You will need children to be the engine driver, elephants, flamingos, pandas, tigers, seals, and kangaroos. If you have more children, call up several of each animal, as in the story. If fewer, call only one of each animal, exclude some, or be the engine driver yourself. Each animal has

its own sound repeated. Make sure each child or group of children know what sounds their animals make, such as "Flip, flop" for the seals, and instruct them that when you point to them, they make this sound. Reciting the sounds as a group might work better. The story continues to add on new animals and repeat each sound, ending with the most recent.

Hilton, Nette. 1990. *The Long Red Scarf*. Illus., Margaret Power. Minneapolis, Minn.: Carolrhoda.

Summary:
Grandpa can't get anyone to knit him a scarf, so he does it himself.

Activity:
While the story is being told, slowly pull out a long red ribbon or piece of yarn and pass it to the children, who continue to slowly pass it to one another until the scarf is made. This is a long story, so you will probably want to summarize the events, asking all the people who refuse Grandpa, such as Aunt Maude, Cousin Isabel, and maybe even adding some more characters of your own.

Hindley, Judy. 2002. *Do Like a Duck Does!* Illus., Ivan Bates. Cambridge, Mass.: Candlewick.

Summary:
A duck family proves a fox is not a duck.

Activity:
As the five ducklings follow their mother, have the children stand up and join you in the moves. "Flop! Flop! Flop! Flop! Flop!" "Quack!" says Mama Duck. "That's the way to be! Do like a duck does! Do like me!" Save two children to be the fox and pig, who come later. Sounds and motions also change a little throughout. Add more movements to a follow the leader game afterwards, pretending to do as other animals do. For a simpler activity, just have the children act like ducks.

————. 1999. *Eyes, Nose, Fingers and Toes: A First Book About You*. Illus., Brita Granström. Cambridge, Mass.: Candlewick.

Summary:
Children tell you what you can do with different parts of your body.

Activity:
Have children point to the body part mentioned in the story and hold their fingers there until another body part is mentioned. Children will be pointing to eyes that wink, a nose that blows, a mouth that yawns, lips that whistle, necks that tickle, a back to stretch, arms to reach, hands to clap, fingers and toes to count, legs to leap, feet to stomp, knees to bend, and bottoms to bump. Besides these, there are many other actions for each body part that the children can demonstrate and act out after they identify each part.

Hinds, P. Mignon. 1995. *What I Want to Be*. Illus., Cornelius Van Wright. New York: Golden.

Summary:
A girl gets ideas from things in her grandmother's trunk for what she might want to be when she is older.

Activity:
You don't even have to read the full text. Just start each time with the first half of what is written on each page, such as, "Next I found this cool red fire truck and ... helmet ...." Then ask, "What do you think she might want to be?" Children will answer, "A firefighter." Take out words that might give away the professions.

Hoban, Tana. 1978. *Is It Red? Is It Yellow? Is It Blue?: An Adventure in Color*. New York: Greenwillow.

Summary:
Photographs show different colors.

Activity:
At the front of the book is a chart with circles of colors next to the name of colors that will be in the book. Duplicate this chart on paper or on a board in the room. Next, show each picture and ask, "What colors are in this picture?" The circles of the colors are below each picture to make it easy. For slightly older groups, or when you have time or want to thoroughly cover the concepts of color, ask, "What in this picture is yellow?" Continue with different colors.

————. 1997. *Look Book.* **New York: Greenwillow.**

Summary:
Parts of pictures are seen through a small hole.

Activity:
Hoban's books are intended for interaction. Go around the room allowing children to guess what is behind the holes. This can be used as a
filler for programs with older children, as well, or when there are a few
minutes left in class. You can also make your own version using a piece
of black construction paper with a circle cut out and holding it over pictures. Be silly and hold the paper over your face and the faces of other
children in the room and ask them to identify who is behind the hole.
They will feel intelligent if you hold it over objects in the room that they
are already familiar with.

**Hoberman, Mary Ann. 1999. *And to Think That We Thought That
We'd Never Be Friends.* Illus., Kevin Hawkes. New York: Crown.**

Summary:
A brother and sister make up after having numerous arguments that
spread to others as well.

Activity:
This is better for older children, as the text is rather long. Instruct the
children to repeat the title of the book, "And to think that we thought
that we'd never be friends" every time you point to them after the sib-
lings make up. For younger crowds you can skip over some of the situations.

————. 1997. *One of Each.* **Illus., Marjorie Priceman. Boston:
Little, Brown.**

Summary:
A dog is happy just having one of everything until he meets a cat and
decides he would like to share the things in his life.

Activity:
Find patterns or pictures of the objects in the story that Oliver has one
of, such as a pear, an apple, a plate, and a chair. Make two copies of

each, and tape one set around the room. Tape the other set to the front of the room, arranged as if the items were in a house. At the point in the story when Oliver decides he needs two of everything to share with a friend, ask the children to look around the room to see if they can find the matching objects as you mention those in the story. Children can remain seated or look around the room one at a time or all together. If you don't have pictures of the objects in the story, substitute those you do have.

————. 2001. *You Read to Me, I'll Read to You: Very Short Stories to Read Together.* **Illus., Michael Emberley. Boston: Little, Brown.**

Summary:
These stories are poems that can be read in tandem.

Activity:
The obvious activity is to read this book together with children. For storytimes it would be best to choose selections and have another staff member or volunteer read them with you. Some lines are read together, while other lines should be read by different readers.

Holden, Robert. 1997. *The Pied Piper of Hamelin.* **Illus., Drahos Zak. Boston: Houghton Mifflin.**

Summary:
The Pied Piper leads the children of Hamelin away after the townspeople refuse to pay him for ridding the town of rats.

Activity:
You be the Piper. Just get a flute, recorder, or even a whistle and toot a little bit as the children follow behind you, first pretending to be the rats and then the children in the story. End with a game of follow the leader.

Holsonback, Anita, and Deb Adamson. 1997. *Monkey See, Monkey Do: An Animal Exercise Book for You!* **Illus., Leo Timmers. Brookfield, Conn.: Millbrook.**

Summary:
Animal movements are demonstrated for children to follow.

Activity:
Let the children act out the different animal movements in the book. A picture and animal name precede a short rhyme. For example, "Be a caterpillar—hug a tree—give each leaf a nibble. And when you want to move along, wiggle and wave your middle!" Model the movements for the children.

Holub, Joan. 1999. *I Have a Weird Brother Who Digested a Fly*. Illus., Patrick Girouard. Morton Grove, Ill.: Albert Whitman.

Summary:
Unlike the traditional story, this book shows what happens to the fly as it moves through the body.

Activity:
Use the picture in the back of the book or find an enlarged picture of the body or even use your own body to point to or attach pictures to and show where the fly is heading next in the human anatomy. This is not difficult because the book shares little side notes and pictures along the way. Starting in the mouth, the fly travels to the throat, stomach, and intestines until it is flushed. You could even end by pressing the button on the book *Flush the Potty* by Liza Baker, illustrated by Ken Wilson-Max (New York: Scholastic, 2000), to make the flushing sound or have the children imitate the sound of the toilet. It can also be useful as a fun science activity for older students.

Hort, Lenny. 2000. *The Seals on the Bus*. Illus., G. Brian Karas. New York: Holt.

Summary:
Just like "the people on the bus," different animals do different things on the bus.

Activity:
Perhaps an obvious one. Sing the song to the tune of the traditional song, "The Wheels on the Bus," and have the kids say the sound or act out the motion in the book. For example, "The tiger on the bus goes roar, roar, roar," "The snakes on the bus go hiss, hiss, hiss," and "The geese on the bus go honk, honk, honk."

Howard, Arthur. 2001. *Hoodwinked*. San Diego, Calif.: Harcourt.

Summary:
Mitzi tries to find a creepy pet until an adorable kitten comes her way.

Activity:
Set up a pet store with stuffed animals, puppets, or pictures. Let the children help decide which is the creepiest or let them each choose their own. Save the adorable kitten for the end. You might want to set aside a bat for Mitzi's first choice of a pet.

Hru, Dakari. 1996. *The Magic Moonberry Jump Ropes*. Illus., E. B. Lewis. New York: Dial.

Summary:
Two girls make a wish on their new magic jump ropes.

Activity:
Twirl a rope while telling this story or ask two of the children to twirl it. At some point, let each child take a turn and make a wish out loud. To conclude, you might want to play a game of jump rope with the children—even if it doesn't work out perfectly.

Hubbell, Patricia. 2000. *Bouncing Time*. Illus., Melissa Sweet. New York: HarperCollins.

Summary:
A baby bounces all day long.

Activity:
Save this for when you want to wear out the children, perhaps before a quiet story. Allow the children to bounce up and down while sitting or standing throughout the whole story, just like the baby in the book. It begins, "Will you bounce like a grasshopper, cricket, or frog?" and continues to explain how other animals bounce. Try to bounce a little differently for each animal in the way that each animal might move. Move your arms like monkeys, for example, when you bounce as they come into the story, jump hard on two feet for the elephants, squat like a frog, roll around the ground like a tiger, jump like a giraffe, pounce like a lion, and slither like a python. Continue to bounce in between the animal activities.

Huliska-Beith, Laura. 2000. *The Book of Bad Ideas.* **Boston: Little, Brown.**

Summary:
This book suggests some bad ideas that could happen in everyday life.

Activity:
Ask the children if they think the suggestions mentioned in the book are bad ideas, such as, "volunteering to test the rope swing your brother just put up (again)." or "rollerblading with your dog even though he was kicked out of obedience school." You might also want to add some bad ideas of your own or ask the kids if they have any. This is better for older children, since some of the ideas like "parking your truck in the oven" and "making fun of someone else when you have toilet paper stuck to your shoe" might create ideas. Let's not encourage making fun of someone even with toilet paper stuck to our shoes. Ask for the children to offer some of their own rules.

Hutchins, Pat. 1986. *The Doorbell Rang.* **New York: Greenwillow.**

Summary:
The children have to keep giving up their cookies as more guests arrive, but finally Grandma brings more.

Activity:
Cut out cookie-shaped circles out of brown construction paper and draw chocolate chips on them or copy a pattern in a cookie-like color. Start off by giving all the cookies to two children in the room. Then as more guests arrive in the story, start dividing the cookies up among other children in the room. When Grandma comes, a real treat would be to pull out a box of real cookies!

———. 1994. *Little Pink Pig.* **New York: Greenwillow.**

Summary:
Little Pink Pig keeps lagging behind and his mother keeps looking for him, but Little Pink Pig doesn't hear her calling.

Activity:
Ask the children if they see Little Pink Pig in the pictures and walk around the room having them point out his location. End by having

enough little pink pig pictures scattered around the room so that the children can pretend to be mother pigs searching for their little pink pigs. This would also work well for a flannel board story, hiding a little pink pig behind the other animals, like the horse, cow, sheep, and hens. There is also a point in the story where you can have the children make animal sounds.

Inkpen, Mick. 1992. *Kipper's Toybox*. San Diego, Calif.: Harcourt Brace Jovanovich.

Summary:
Kipper the dog looks in his toybox and keeps counting one too many noses until he realizes that mice have somehow gotten inside.

Activity:
Use a cardboard box just like Kipper's and put different toys inside. They don't necessarily have to be the animals mentioned in the story. You can change the names. In the end, show the side of the box with a hole in it that you uncover and then pull out the sock with a mouse toy inside it. Have the children help you count the toys and noses as you pull them out of the box and read this part in the story.

Jackson, Shirley. 2001. *9 Magic Wishes*. Illus., Miles Hyman. New York: Farrar Straus & Giroux.

Summary:
A girl makes nine magic wishes.

Activity:
Simply ask a different child or several children what they would wish for as the girl in the story makes each wish. You could also ask them if they think her wishes were good wishes or why they would or would not wish for things she wished for. You could also have a paper bag of star confetti to let the children pick one each time they make a wish or walk around with a magic wand and tap a child's head when it is that child's turn to wish.

James, Betsy. 1997. *Flashlight.* **Illus., Stacey Schuett. New York: Knopf.**

Summary:
A girl uses a flashlight to feel safe at night.

Activity:
Tell the story in the dark, shining the flashlight on the book. Ask a child to help hold the flashlight or to shine a different one on the book. You could also pass it around as the pages turn to give everyone a chance. You may also place other objects mentioned in the story around the room, for example, a music box, and then shine the flashlight on that object at the appropriate point in the story.

Johnson, Angela. 1990. *Do Like Kyla.* **Illus., James E. Ransome. New York: Orchard.**

Summary:
Kyla does everything that her sister does.

Activity:
After Kyla does what her sister does and says, "I do like Kyla," point to your group and say, "Now you do like Kyla." Let them act out the scenes as best as they can, such as pretending to put a sweater on, twisting their hair, pouring honey over cereal, putting on a coat, and more.

———. 1993. *The Girl Who Wore Snakes.* **Illus., James E. Ransome. New York: Orchard.**

Summary:
After a zookeeper brings a snake to school, a girl buys some of her own and wears them everywhere.

Activity:
Wear a snake puppet or plastic snake around your neck, pretending to be the zookeeper who visits the school. Pretend to be Ali, and add some more snakes when she buys them at the store and then wears them everywhere. You could also ask a child to represent Ali and put the snakes around herself. Make sure in the beginning you walk around the whole room showing the snake to all the children just as the visitor from the zoo in the story does.

Johnson, Crockett. 1955. *Harold and The Purple Crayon*. New York: Harper & Row.

Summary:
Using a purple crayon, Harold draws what he needs and sees during his walk.

Activity:
Use a dry-erase board, overhead projector, or large piece of white paper. Take a purple marker or crayon and draw everything, or just about everything, Harold draws. You could also give each child paper and a crayon of any color to draw along with the story.

Johnson, Lindsay Lee. 1998. *Hurricane Henrietta*. Illus., Wally Neibart. New York: Dial.

Summary:
Henrietta has really long hair that is always getting in the way and causing problems until she gets it cut off.

Activity:
Use a wig or create one out of yarn or paper to place on your head as you tell the story. Cut it off at the end of the story. You could also have a picture of a girl with really long hair and cut it off in the end. Give the children a piece of paper with the outline of a head and facial features and ask them to draw Henrietta's really long hair as you tell the story. Give them safety scissors to cut it off and give her a new hairstyle at the end or ask them to just tear the paper with their fingers.

Jonas, Ann. 1995. *Splash*. New York: Greenwillow.

Summary:
Different animals keep jumping and falling into a pond.

Activity:
Instruct the children to say "Splash" whenever you point to them. You can also ask the question at the end of each page, "How many are in my pond?" and wait for the children to respond with how many animals have fallen into the pond. Another possibility is to take a large piece of blue construction paper and cut around the edges in a wavy pattern to make it look like a pond. Then you will need to cut out pictures of a turtle,

two catfish (or any black fish), three frogs, and four goldfish. By yourself or with the help of the children, put the other animals into the pond when the animals in the story jump in. Leave the fish in at all times. Then ask for the children's help in counting how many there are in the pond each time. Be careful to watch for which animals get out on the next page. When the story is over, you can continue with other combinations of animals. Let the children make some, too. This would be a good story to precede the song "Five Little Speckled Frogs" or the finger play "Five Little Froggies."

Jones, Bill T., and Susan Kuklin. 1998. *Dance*. Photos, Susan Kuklin. New York: Hyperion.

Summary:
Basic dance moves are demonstrated.

Activity:
Have the children mimic the dance moves in the book. They will stretch their bodies, make lines and curves, and jump and lie on the ground. Children can copy the pictures in the book, make their own moves, or follow yours.

Jorgensen, Gail. 1997. *Gotcha!* Illus., Kerry Argent. New York: Scholastic.

Summary:
A bear has a birthday party that is interrupted by a fly.

Activity:
Have the kids yell, "Gotcha!" when you point to them whenever the exclamation comes up in the story. You could also put a little fake bug, or picture of one, on a stick and wave it over the children's heads and let them try to catch the fly so they can yell, "Gotcha!" You could also just pretend that you are trying to catch a fly as you read the story and say, "Gotcha!" and "Missed!" throughout. Move around the room as you pretend to catch that fly.

Kalan, Robert. 1981. *Jump Frog, Jump!* Illus., Byron Barton. New York: Greenwillow.

Summary:
This is a cumulative tale in which a frog tries to get away from danger.

Activity:
When the book reads, "How did the frog get away?" wait for the children to respond "Jump frog, jump!" as instructed. You could also make a board story out of this by making each picture of an animal larger than the last to cover the creature it eats in the story. Starting with the smallest, you will need a fly, fish, snake, turtle, and a child. The frog can stay on the side.

Kalman, Maira. 2001. *What Pete Ate from A-Z: Where We Explore the English Alphabet (In Its Entirety) In Which a Certain Dog Devours a Myriad of Items Which He Should Not.* **New York: Putnam.**

Summary:
A girl goes through the alphabet to describe the objects her dog eats but should not.

Activity:
Use this book in several ways. Although the objects in the pictures are rather small, you could walk around the room, or use the book with smaller groups, and have the children pick out all the objects that begin with a certain letter to show what Pete ate. You could let go of the book and fill the room with objects starting with all the letters of the alphabet, or just use the objects in an already busy room and ask children to spy different objects starting with different letters. One final option would be to copy pictures of objects starting with the different letters of the alphabet. Use a pattern book or clipart to locate pictures easily. Then when you get to each letter ask the children to walk around the room finding objects that start with a letter and bring them to the dog. You will have a puppet of a dog whose mouth opens for the children to place the food in his mouth. Optionally, you could create a cardboard dog or paste a picture of a dog with a slit for his mouth on two pieces of poster board taped together so that the pictures of the object fall to the center when children feed the dog what they have found.

Karas, G. Brian, illus. 1994. *I Know an Old Lady.* **New York: Scholastic.**

Summary:
An old lady swallows a fly and many other things after. Perhaps she'll die.

Activity:

There are so many ways to tell this story. Use a flannel board, make a picture of a lady and a skirt to hang over her, placing items under the skirt. Use a piece of cardboard with another behind it and cut a slit for a mouth on a drawn woman figure. Give kids copied pictures of the types of animals in the story and let them feed them to the old lady one at a time. Put an apron on yourself and be the old lady, stuffing things into a secret compartment beneath you. Use actual stuffed animals to put under a long skirt you have propped up over a hanging doll head. Use a blanket to hide animals under. Purchase one of the already made dolls with pieces to go along with this story. There are also many versions of this story. Try Simms Taback's *There Was an Old Lady Who Swallowed a Fly* (New York: Viking, 1997), which, because of the cutouts could be used on its own. You can also play a version of the song. In the Karas version, you will be using the following animals: fly, spider, bird, cat, dog, and goat. You could make substitutions if you have a limited puppet collection. Some might find it preferable to end with "She got sick, of course!" rather than "She died, of course," which is how the story ends.

––––––––. 1998. *The Windy Day*. New York: Simon & Schuster.

Summary:

A boy experiences a powerful wind.

Activity:

As you tell the story, have the children stand up and spin around and wave their arms as you move in a circle or around the room. Fall down when the wind goes away.

Karlin, Barbara. 2001. *James Marshall's Cinderella*. Illus., James Marshall. New York: Dial.

Summary:

This is the typical Cinderella story in which a fairy godmother turns the ragged girl into a princess for one night. Cinderella must try on a glass slipper she lost to prove she is the prince's true love.

Activity:

As you can do for any Cinderella story, although this is a short version, have objects such as a plastic pumpkin and a mouse puppet. Then use a magic wand to turn them into a carriage and horses by using a picture or a carriage drawn on poster board and using a horse puppet or picture. Also have a crown or fancy shawl to drape over the child who turns into Cinderella. Then when it is time for the prince to try the slipper, try it on every child, pretending it doesn't fit until you reach the child you dressed up. Alternatively, make this book into a flannel board story, covering the pumpkin and mice with pictures of a coach and horses. Have fancy shoes for the children to try on to see which child is Cinderella. If the shoe is yours, the children can probably all fit their feet into it for an even game.

Katz, Alan. 2001. *Take Me Out of the Bathtub and Other Silly Dilly Songs*. Illus., David Catrow. New York: Margaret K. McElderry.

Summary:
Silly songs are the result when the lyrics of well-known songs are changed.

Activity:
Pick some of the songs in this book to use with the children. Instead of "London Bridge" you will sing, "Brother Mitch keeps falling down." Each song provides its own interactive fun. For this one, instead of forming a bridge, ask kids to stand and flop down. Use this for a fun music or writing exercise, and ask kids to write their own lyrics to one of the songs in the book or another one they choose. Even the youngest can at least come up with one line.

Katz, Bobbi. 1998. *Lots of Lice*. Illus., Steve Björkman. New York: Scholastic.

Summary:
Lice describe where they like to go and what they like to do.

Activity:
Tell the kids that whenever they hear you say the words "Lice," "Nits," "Louse," or "Cooties," to scratch their heads. This is a good example of how you can use any book with a repeated or similar word or phrase to have children perform an action.

Keats, Ezra Jack. 1966. *Jennie's Hat*. New York: Harper & Row.

Summary:
Jennie doesn't like the plain new hat her aunt sent her until some birds help her along.

Activity:
When Jennie tries on household items as a hat, such as a basket, lampshade, flowerpot, TV antenna, and pan, provide the children with objects to try on, or put these objects on your head. Then have a plain hat and ask the children to be birds and look around the room to see if they can find anything that will make this plain hat prettier. You will have placed plastic flowers, leaves, ribbon, and pictures around the room for them to find. Children can decorate their own birthday hats or hats made from construction paper as a craft.

Kelley, Marty. 2000. *The Rules*. Madison, Wisc.: Zino.

Summary:
Different rules that kids should follow are described with humorous illustrations.

Activity:
Ask the children to raise their hands if they follow the rules in the book. For example, "Wipe your feet." Children should raise their hands if they always wipe their feet. It will get tricky with phrases like, "Don't eat dog food for a snack." Kids may not raise their hands, but they should if they "don't eat dog food." Basically, they should have their hands raised the whole time, but it will make them think. To make it clearer, start each phrase with, "Raise your hand if you ____." You might also want to change the rules to "If" statements. "If you don't eat dog food, raise your hand," for example. You could end with stating rules not mentioned in the story or asking kids for their own rules, especially older children.

Kellogg, Steven. 1998. *A-Hunting We Will Go!* New York: Morrow.

Summary:
Describes what children see while hunting and doing other things to the tune of the song "A-Hunting We Will Go."

Activity:
Hold up the book as the children form a line behind you or a circle around you. Walk in the line or circle as you sing the book to the tune of the song or play the song in the background. The book also changes the lyrics to "A-reading we will go!" so you may have to sing louder than the music if the words are different. Use this with other songbooks as a writing exercise for children to write their own lyrics to popular songs.

————. 2000. *The Missing Mitten Mystery.* New York: Dial.

Summary:
A girl searches everywhere to find her missing mitten.

Activity:
Find a mitten pattern or draw one yourself and make enough copies for everyone in your class. When Annie searches for her mittens in the story, have the children look around the room to find one, too. If you make each pair a different color, give each child his or her own color. Then, as the story progresses, keep inviting a new child to go find his or her matching mitten, which you will have taped around the room.

Kerins, Tony. 1996. *Little Clancy's New Drum.* Cambridge, Mass.: Candlewick.

Summary:
Clancy bangs his drum and other objects while his friends are trying to nap.

Activity:
Wake up the whole library and give each child rhythm sticks, plastic spoons, or other objects and allow them to bang on toy drums, bowls, boxes, or other objects while the story is read. "Ting! Ting! Ting! Tap! Tap! Tap! Klok! Klok! Klok!" Other sounds such as "Bang! Bang!" are repeated throughout this quick story. Perhaps the craft of the day might be to make a drum out of a box or other container, or even a small one out of toilet paper tubes or cups, and then use it with this story for a finale or maybe even a parade around the library. If you know ahead of time, ask the children to bring in an object that could be used as a drum.

Kessler, Leonard. 1980. *Mixed-Up Mother Goose.* **Illus., Diane Dawson. Champaign, Ill.: Garrard.**

Summary:
Mother Goose is really mixed up. She keeps telling a story that goes with the wrong character or calls people by the wrong names.

Activity:
Just ask the children if Mother Goose is right every time she says something wrong and ask them to tell you how the real nursery rhyme goes. The Mother Goose rhymes included are Little Bo Peep, Jack and Jill, Jack Horner, Jack-Be-Quick, Little Miss Muffet, Simple Simon, Little Boy Blue, Jack Sprat, and Old King Cole.

———. **1994.** *That's Not Santa.* **New York: Scholastic.**

Summary:
Santa cannot find his suit, so he tries on other uniforms, such as a baseball outfit and fireman's hat, but the children keep repeating, "That's not Santa."

Activity:
First begin by pretending to be Santa and looking around the room, as if you had lost something, finally admitting you cannot find your Santa suit and it is Christmas Eve. Have different hats to go along with the story, including those of a baseball player, cowboy, pirate, court jester, and fire fighter, and tell the story by putting on the different hats and pretending to be Santa trying to make a substitute. Ask the children to yell out "That's not Santa," if they don't think it is Santa. You might want to have a little bag of small novelty gifts to pass out at the end.

Ketteman, Helen. 1992. *Not Yet, Yvette.* **Illus., Irene Trivasa. Morton Grove, Ill.: Albert Whitman.**

Summary:
An anxious girl helps her father get ready for her mother's birthday party.

Activity:
Yvette is impatient and keeps asking questions of her father. Every time the story reads, "Not yet, Yvette," point to the children as their cue to

say this phrase. Take time before the story to instruct them on their role
in the story.

King, Karen. 1993. *I Don't Eat Toothpaste Anymore!* Illus., Lynne Willey. Singapore: Tamarind.

Summary:
A girl describes things she does now or that she used to do when she
was a baby.

Activity:
There is not much activity here, but you can still ask questions of the
children in your group or class. When the book reads, "I don't throw
my dinner on the floor . . . ," follow by asking the children if they throw
their dinner on the floor. Continue by asking similar questions that re-
late to all the things the girl does or no longer does in the story.

Kirk, David. 1994. *Miss Spider's Tea Party*. New York: Scholastic.

Summary:
Miss Spider throws a tea party, but no one wants to come because each
bug is afraid that Miss Spider will eat it.

Activity:
Hold a tea party for the children by giving them cups and plates. Give
out nametags to tape to the children with a different bug on each. When
a new bug is mentioned in the story, invite it to the tea table. The children can walk away from the table when the bugs do the same in the
book. They can then all come to the table in the end to celebrate the
end of storytime with juice and cookies and their own tea party. The insects you need are beetles, fireflies, bumblebees, rubber bugs, and ants.
Have several nametags prepared for each bug so you can give them to
more than one child if necessary. Make sure to change the number from
11 guests to however many come to storytime for the final guest count.
Save this for a last story.

Kleven, Elisa. 1996. *Hooray, a Piñata!* New York: Dutton.

Summary:
A girl gets a piñata for her birthday party, but decides to keep it as a pet
instead.

Activity:
Use a dog puppet or stuffed animal, and as the story progresses continue to ask the children if they think the girl in the story should put candy in the piñata or keep it as a pet. Ask if she should take the piñata to all the places she brings it, such as the store and the merry-go-round. Continue to ask the questions until you get to the part in the story where the family brings in a new piñata and, if possible, have a piñata for the children to use, even if it is as simple as a paper bag they toss around until it breaks, spilling out candy, cheap toys, or confetti.

Kline, Suzy. 1988. *Ooops!* Illus., Dora Leder. Niles, Ill.: Albert Whitman.

Summary:
A girl keeps causing minor accidents and sees that others do, too.

Activity:
Children can repeat the word "Ooops!" every time you point to them throughout the story—when the girl drops her soap and towel in the bathtub, spills her juice, trips on a cat, drops her coat, and when she points out other people or animals in the house who do an "Ooops." They may even catch on by themselves. To make it easier, you could have them say "Ooops" at the end of each situation. Then, ask what they do that would be an ooops or what other things they can think of that might be an ooops.

Kneen, Maggie. 1996. *When You're Not Looking . . . A Storytime Counting Book*. New York: Simon & Schuster.

Summary:
A counting book in which each double-page spread is a new scene with a phrase beneath it, along with the number of objects that can be located in the picture.

Activity:
Besides asking the children to help find the correct number of objects in the pictures, you can also ask them to help tell the stories using the phrases below the pictures, as with Chris Van Allsburg's *The Mysteries of Harris Burdick* (Boston: Houghton Mifflin, 1984). Both are great for a creative writing assignment for older children. For example, one phrase reads, "The only sounds were the crackling of the fire and the muffled

thump from the window seat." Ask, "What could be in the window seat? Why?" Other "stories" include toy planes loose in a child's room and bunnies planning an escape.

***

Koller, Jackie French. 1999. *One Monkey Too Many*. Illus., Lynn Munsinger. San Diego, Calif.: Harcourt Brace.

Summary:
Each time the monkeys go to a new place, another monkey joins them.

Activity:
Call up the children one by one to join the monkeys. Ask them to act and sound like monkeys. If you choose, at the end, when the story reads, "One monkey too many got into this book," you can call all the children up to start coloring on paper or poster board as the monkeys are seen doing on the second to last page.

***

Kotzwinkle, William, and Glenn Murray. 2001. *Walter, the Farting Dog*. Illus., Audrey Colman. Berkeley, Calif.: Frog.

Summary:
Walter the dog has chronic flatulence, and the family tries to cure him until he saves the day.

Activity:
If you dare to ever use this book, get a whoopee cushion and squeeze it every time any variation of the word "fart" is used. Probably best for a silly storytime for older kids. Children can add sound effects too.

***

Krull, Kathleen. 2001. *Supermarket*. Illus., Melanie Hope Greenberg. New York: Holiday House.

Summary:
This story shows how a supermarket works.

Activity:
Start collecting food and beverage containers or ask other staff members to donate some, and bring in real or plastic fruit, or even pictures of all these items to display around the room. Give each child a paper bag or plastic bag that you have collected or purchased from the store. Walk around the room as you read the book and let the children do some

shopping, selecting what they want, perhaps limiting them to only a few items, depending on how much you have collected. When you are done, and at the point in the book when the shoppers line up to check out, look at each item, press the keys of your large calculator, and come up with a fake amount asking children for the fake money you have given them. This may work well in a grade school class when children learn about money. Alternatively, you could have signs posted on the different foods with the price and a little envelope beneath each picture. The envelope can be full of little slips of paper that have the names of the food on them. The children can collect the papers of the food they select and place them in a paper lunch bag; they then bring the bag up to the checkout counter. Adapt this to a program for selling real candy, food, used books, or other items.

Kunhardt, Edith. 1989. *Which One Would You Choose?* New York: Greenwillow.

Summary:
A day in the life of a brother and sister is augmented with other choices of things to do.

Activity:
The book is already set up for involvement. After each statement of what Will and Maggie do, there are four choices with a question, such as, "What do you like for breakfast?" which has pictures of toast, a banana, an egg, and a bowl of cereal. Either all the children respond at the same time with their favorite, or they answer one at a time as you take the book around the room. If there is time, you could even have pictures of these objects on the board where children could come up and point so you do not have to move around the room for them to see such small images.

Larios, Julie Hofstrand. 2001. *Have You Ever Done That?* Illus., Anne Hunter. Asheville, N.C.: Front Street.

Summary:
The book asks if you have done these many activities in nature.

Activity:
Ask the questions to the children in this quiet book and wait for their responses. "Flown with wings. Have you ever done that?" "Nursed a baby bird. Have you ever done that?"

Lass, Bonnie, and Philemon Sturges. 2000. *Who Took the Cookies from the Cookie Jar?* Illus., Ashley Wolff. Boston: Little, Brown.

Summary:
Someone took the cookies from the cookie jar, and skunk asks around to find the culprit.

Activity:
There are several things you can do. If you are musically talented, the music for the song is provided at the beginning of the story. You could always have everyone sing as you go through the pages of the story. Even if you read rather than sing the book, point to a child each time an animal is introduced. Say something like, "Mouse took the cookies from the cookie jar!" Ask the child to reply, "Who me? Couldn't be." Finish the rhyme for them. Along with the song at the beginning, the traditional game is suggested where everyone stands in a circle and gets an animal name, or uses numbers, colors, or even their own names. They chant, "Who took the cookies from the cookie jar?" If the skunk starts (the starter would most likely be the librarian or teacher), he or she will call on the next person and say something like "Raven took the cookies from the cookie jar!" Then it goes back and forth again "Who me?" "Yes, you," "Couldn't be," "Then who?" Make up animal names—unless the children use their own names—until everyone has a turn. If you are short on time, or if you have a younger group who may not catch on, just use a few children to portray the animals in the story and call on them. If food is allowed and money is available for purchase or if you are willing to spend a couple dollars, provide a cookie jar of cookies for children to take at the end of the story. Change the rules, and let them each take a cookie as their turn is over—almost as if they really did take the cookies.

Lavis, Steve. 1998. *Jump!* New York: Dutton.

Summary:
A child wants to do the same things as animals, but sometimes his teddy bear doesn't want to participate.

Activity:
Have the children perform the same actions as the animals in the story. Jump like a tiger and frog, swing like a monkey, roar like a lion, slither like a snake, fly like a toucan, stamp like an elephant, munch like a gi-

raffe, jump like a frog, snap like a crocodile, march like a tiger, dance like a monkey, march like an elephant, and more. Hold a teddy bear in your arms during the story so you can make it shiver when the bear is afraid of the snake and to help demonstrate the actions the children should perform. You could ask the children to bring in teddy bears or provide them each with a puppet instead.

Lawrence, John. 2002. *This Little Chick*. Cambridge, Mass.: Candlewick.

Summary:
A chick visits other animals and learns the sounds they make.

Activity:
The same phrase is repeated several times while changing the animal each time. "This little chick from over the way went to play with the pigs one day. And what do you think they heard him say?" Repeat the last sentence if children don't respond with the animal sound. You will do this for the ducks, cow, frogs, and lambs. In the end, when the chick goes home, have the children repeat all the sounds. You may have to show the book again and point to the pictures.

Legge, David. 1994. *Bamboozled*. New York: Scholastic.

Summary:
A girl visits her grandfather and can't figure out what is wrong in this mixed-up house until she decides it is because her grandfather is wearing two different colored socks.

Activity:
Walk around with the book and let the children each pick out something that is wrong or mixed up in the story, such as slanted pictures, a watering-can pitcher, a card-playing dog, fish in a cabinet, and so much more. For older children, pass the book around or assign each one a different page and see how many objects they can find. You might also change some things around in the room and ask the children what is different.

LeSieg, Theo. 1965. *I Wish That I Had Duck Feet*. Illus., B. Tobey. New York: Random House.

Summary:
The troubles and the joys that would arise if a boy had duck feet or other animal parts are explored.

Activity:
As the teacher, librarian, or storyteller, you can don duck feet, antlers, a whale spout (squirt toy or funnel), tail (rope), and an elephant trunk. Add each piece to your attire as the boy adds them in the story. You can also ask the children during the story if the additions are good ideas and ask the problems or benefits of each new body part.

Lester, Mike. 2000. *A Is for Salad*. New York: Putnam & Grosset.

Summary:
An atypical ABC book in which the letter does not match the word it is referring to.

Activity:
Although this can be a confusing book for young children, older kids can have fun with it. Ask questions like, "F is for soup. Is F for soup? Are you sure F is for soup?" Hopefully they will notice the frog sitting in the soup. "Could F be for frog?" Continue this way throughout the book. Other examples include "C is for hot dog," with a cat eating a hot dog; "G is for soccer," with a soccer ball hitting the goat's head; and "S is for tennis," with a snake and a tennis racket. Try adding some of your own examples from objects and puppets around the library for extra fun.

Linn, Margo. 2001. *Scratches and Scrapes*. Illus., Doreen Gay-Kassel. New York: Scholastic.

Summary:
Alex keeps hurting himself in different ways.

Activity:
Waste a box of bandages for this book and keep putting them on yourself, a child, different children, or a doll or stuffed animal as you tell the story. You could also provide children with a calendar and bandages

you copy on paper and have them glue one to the date on which Alex hurts himself each time.

Lionni, Leo. 1959. *Little Blue and Little Yellow: A Story for Pippo and Ann and Other Children*. New York: McDowell, Obolensky.

Summary:
Little Blue and Little Yellow are friends that turn green when they are together.

Activity:
Tear construction paper dots to tell the story on a board, or give the children in your group their own dots to act out the story. You do not have to use all the colors in the book for the parents and friends. You will need at least a yellow dot and a blue dot and then a slightly larger green dot to put over the two when they change colors.

Livingston, Myra Cohn. 1989. *Up in the Air*. Illus., Leonard Everett Fisher. New York: Holiday House.

Summary:
A poem and the illustrations describe what can be seen from a plane high above.

Activity:
Children can sit still or stand up with arms stretched out to simulate airplanes. As you turn the pages, the children can pretend they are flying and seeing the scenes in the book from above. In the end, ask the children where they would like to fly to keep the story going.

Lodge, Bernard. 2001. *How Scary! Who Scares Who from One to Ten?* Boston: Houghton Mifflin.

Summary:
New scary creatures keep entering the picture to scare away the last scary creatures, and each time there are more than before.

Activity:
Point to the pictures in the story, and instead of saying something like, "It's four wicked witches," ask, "It's four, what?" And make sure they understand what is happening by asking, "And who are they scaring?" They

should reply, "Sharks." Alternatively, if you want to stress numbers, ask, "How many wicked witches are scaring the sharks?" In the end when all the creatures are displayed together, count them.

London, Jonathan. 1992. *Froggy Gets Dressed*. Illus., Frank Remkiewicz. New York: Viking.

Summary:
Froggy wakes up early from hibernation and wants to play in the snow but he keeps forgetting to put something on, even his underwear.

Activity:
This is great for a flannel board story. Find a picture of a frog, or use a frog puppet or stuffed animal. Cut out pictures of all the different clothing used in the story and add and remove them from the picture or toy as requested in the story. You will need socks, boots, a hat, scarf, mittens, pants, a shirt, coat, and underwear. If time allows, have the children put on and remove Froggy's clothing. You could also provide each child with a photocopied picture or coloring sheet of a frog along with clothing to fit the story and have the children play along, like a puzzle or bingo. Such clothing patterns, for a child or bear, can be found in storytime books like *Felt Board Fingerplays* by Liz Wilmes and Dick Wilmes, illustrated by Janet McDonnell (Elgin, Ill.: Building Blocks, 1997).

———. 2002. *Froggy Plays in the Band*. Illus., Frank Remkiewicz. New York: Viking.

Summary:
Froggy forms a band with his friends to enter a contest.

Activity:
As the story mentions different friends with instruments, start passing out different instruments to the kids in your group. Then, when they form a line to start marching, get the kids up in a line as well. Instruct the children not to stop for anything, just like the teacher in the story. Keep yelling "Frrooggyy!" as in the story, and try to distract them. Keep playing this game after the story by yelling, "Frrooggyy!" as they are marching and try to make them stop. You could also turn it into a game of "Hot Music," like "Hot Potato," and pass around an instrument and tell the children to stop when you yell, "Frrooggyy!"

Long, Melinda. 2001. *Hiccup Snickup*. Illus., Thor Wickstrom. New York: Simon & Schuster.

Summary:
A girl tries to get rid of her hiccups using strange suggestions from her family.

Activity:
As the story goes on, ask children what they think you should do to get rid of your "hiccups" as you pretend to hiccup during the story. Also have them do the dance with you that continues throughout the story. It goes "Hiccup snickup, rear right straight up. Three drops in the tea cup, will cure the hiccups." Children can also practice their own fake hiccups. You could go around the room and ask the children how each one would cure your hiccups. Be surprised when they yell "Boo!" and then continue to hiccup and have a glass of water and paper bag on hand in case they suggest these remedies. If not, you can suggest these methods to them.

————. 2000. *When Papa Snores*. Illus., Holly Meade. New York: Simon & Schuster.

Summary:
A girl tries to decide who snores louder, Papa or Nana.

Activity:
First divide the room in half. One group will be Papa and one group will be Nana. This is not necessary, but it makes it more fun, like a competition. Ask one half to make snoring noises whenever you say "Nana," and the other to snore when you say "Papa." They can also repeat the sounds of other objects in the house that are affected by the snoring, such as "When Nana snores, the blinds on the window clink-clank together." The blinds have the words "Clinka-linka" on them and across the page of text are the words "Carrroosh. . . . Carrroosh." Many other funny sounds follow like "Snoooga" and "Gidda-Giodda-Gidda-Idda." Towards the end, signals to yawn are in parentheses. Expect a noisy time. You may have to skip over some of the text as it can get long.

Lotz, Karen E. 1993. *Can't Sit Still*. Illus., Colleen Browning. New York: Dutton.

Summary:
A girl describes what she sees in the city during each season.

Activity:
Instead of reading the name of each season first, show the pictures and read the words. Then ask the children which season they think it is. Go back and point to pictures or repeat words if necessary.

MacDonald, Alan. 2002. *Scaredy Mouse*. Illus., Tim Warnes. Wilton, Conn.: Tiger Tales.

Summary:
Two mice set out on an adventure through the house, and one repeatedly thinks he sees the cat.

Activity:
Every time the mouse gets scared and says, "It's the cat! It's the cat!" point to the children and have them repeat this phrase. Then turn the page and point to the picture of what the mouse actually saw, like a scarf or pillow, and ask the kids, "Is it really a cat?" Or ask, "What is it?" Continue to read the rest of the story. At the end, when the cat gets tied up in string, you could also wrap yourself, a toy cat, or a child in string or yarn.

MacDonald, Amy. 1996. *Cousin Ruth's Tooth*. Illus., Marjorie Priceman. Boston: Houghton Mifflin.

Summary:
Cousin Ruth lost her tooth and the whole family is called to help find it.

Activity:
Hide one or more teeth cut out of white paper around the room. Tell the story while you pretend to look around the room for the tooth or teeth. One at a time, as new family members are called to help in the story, bring up children to help look for the tooth. Read "Norma Jean and Aunt Bodine, go check the attic for the tooth," and bring up two more kids to help in the search.

MacDonald, Elizabeth. 1991. *John's Picture.* **Illus., David McTaggart. New York: Viking.**

Summary:
A boy draws a picture and the characters in the picture draw what they need.

Activity:
Give each child a piece of paper and crayons. Ask them to draw the same things as are being drawn in the story: house, man, wife, children, backyard, dog and cat, car, and food. Even if the children are younger and cannot draw anything remotely resembling the people and objects in the story, they will think they are. You could also draw the pictures yourself on a flip chart, dry-erase board, or overhead. Ask the children to take turns drawing a different part of the story, adding to what has already been drawn. This could be a useful book if you invite a local artist to the library to draw as you tell a story.

————. 1990. *Mike's Kite.* **Illus., Robert Kendall. New York: Orchard.**

Summary:
Mike's kite blows him around town while others try to ground him.

Activity:
There are two options for this story. Since the pictures are rather basic, you might want to turn this one into a board story. The characters don't have to look like those in the book; just draw or find pictures of different people to copy. You will need two gentlemen with dogs, three nannies, four people on horseback, five fishermen, six farm workers, seven bakers, eight sailors, nine shoppers, and ten firemen. Of course, to simplify you might just have one of each, and if you use a flannel board the children will never know how many of each character are actually in the story. Add one at a time as they try to catch the kite. In the end, when the wind stops blowing, knock them all off the board to show how the wind knocked them down and have children pick them up one at a time, returning them to the board as the characters pick themselves up in the story. You could also use the children in the class as the characters. Provide a kite and string or make a kite shape out of paper and attach yarn, and one at a time, let a child join you by holding the string as the story progresses. All fall down at the end when the wind stops blowing. You

can also have the children help you repeat the phrase, "The wind is strong, and the kite is too, but it's sure to come down if we help you." Let the children make kites of their own as a craft.

MacDonald, Margaret Read. 1998. *Pickin' Peas*. Illus., Pat Cummings. New York: HarperCollins.

Summary:
A girl tries to capture the rabbit that keeps eating her peas.

Activity:
The endnote, "About this Tale," gives ideas on how to use this book.

> When telling this story, it is fun to repeat the "pickin' peas" refrain twice and let the listeners join in. I make a picking motion and slap one hand into the other palm on the word "pail." When Mr. Rabbit sings, I slap my legs on "land on my knees...." This story is also fun to act out, dividing your listeners into "young gardeners" and "pesky rabbits." The phrases that will be repeated are "Pickin' peas. Put 'em in my pail" and "Pickin' peas. Land on my knees!"

You could also cut small circles out of green paper and place them around the room to help children pretend they are picking peas, too.

MacDonald, Margaret Read, and Supaporn Vathanaprida. 1998. *The Girl Who Wore Too Much: A Folktale from Thailand*. Illus., Yvonne Lebrun Davis. Little Rock, Ark.: August House.

Summary:
In a folktale from Thailand, Aree loves all her clothes and cannot decide what to wear to a dance. In her vanity, she decides to put on as many of the clothes as she has.

Activity:
MacDonald suggests, in an afterthought called "About the Story," that you can play with the audience. Tell the story without the book and ask questions such as, "Should I wear the red? Yes! I will!" or "Who has another ring I can wear?" Ask the children what color you should wear next, and make up many things such as "Polka dots? Stripes?" Besides dresses, ask what hats, scarves, and jewelry you should put on next, continuing for as long as you have time and can keep the children's inter-

est. You can have fun with audiences of all ages using this story. Also use the similar story, *Hannah and the Seven Dresses*, by Marthe Jocelyn (New York: Dutton, 1999). Use this story when you need to fill time as you can continue the story for as long as needed by adding more and more articles of clothing and jewelry.

MacDonald, Suse. 1995. *Nanta's Lion: A Search-and-Find Adventure*. New York: Morrow.

Summary:
A child looks for a lion that others are hunting.

Activity:
Each time the half-cut pages are turned, ask if the children see the lion anywhere. It will slowly be revealed at the top of each page. In the end, when the book asks if the reader saw the lion and the reader says, "Yes," pretend like you don't see it and let the children point it out to you.

Mack, Stanley. 1974. *10 Bears in My Bed: A Goodnight Countdown*. New York: Random House.

Summary:
The traditional story in which bears roll off the bed because of lack of room until only a child is left.

Activity:
Use this story or any other version. Have the children all lie on the ground and one at a time roll off to the side or sit up as the story unfolds. You might have to make it more than "ten in the bed" to include everyone and, instead, have two or three roll off at a time. You could also invite ten kids in the group to lie on the floor in the front of the room and act as your ten bears. Of course, this could also be a flannel board with ten bear pictures, or you can even change the story to ten of anything in a bed. For a simpler option, find a copy of the song and play it as you turn the pages of the book, allowing the children to sing along. Ask the children at the end what the one remaining child says. Do they know the book's version with the answer "Good night," or another where the child says "I'm lonely," or have they heard something else? Make sure the children sing along or at least repeat "Roll over! Roll over!" Use other versions instead, such as *Ten in a Bed* by Mary Rees (Boston: Joy Street, 1988).

MacKinnon, Debbie. 1996. *Billy's Boots*. Photos, Anthea Sieveking. New York: Dial.

Summary:
A simple board book in which Billy can't find his boots and the reader must lift the flap to see if they can be found in other objects.

Activity:
As with most lift-the-flap books, children can participate by taking turns lifting the flap to see if the boots are inside. When the boots are not in the closet, for example, children can then name the objects that are in the closet. Before Billy finds his boots in the end, and before you turn to the last page, you can set a pair of boots under some jackets just like where Billy is found with his boots at the end of the story. You can also ask the children along the way if they think Billy's boots are in the storytime or classroom closet, in a desk or file cabinet drawer, under a table, in a box, or other places in the room. Allow a different child each time to peek in those places to check, or allow them to yell "No!" if you just point at different places in the room. You could also hide other objects in these places so children can name what is there instead of the boots.

———. 1998. *Eye Spy Colors*. Photos, Anthea Sieveking. Watertown, Mass.: Charlesbridge.

Summary:
Bright photographs show objects of different colors.

Activity:
Like all I-spy-type books, ask the children what objects on the pages are the color you mention. Then ask them what objects in the room are also that color and what other objects of each color they can remember. Hold up the book for small groups to see, and walk around the room for larger groups. Use this book as a time filler or in between longer books.

Maestro, Betsy, and Giulio Maestro. 1984. *Around the Clock with Harriet: A Book About Telling Time*. New York: Crown.

Summary:
The time is given as Harriet performs different activities throughout the day.

Activity:
Make a clock or use a real clock so children can move the hands to show the different times throughout the story. Since the time only increases by one hour, children will easily catch on to the concept. You could also do things the opposite way. Read the description of what Harriet does and ask the children to move the hands on the clock to the time they think Harriet would do something, for example, eat breakfast or go to the library. To involve the children all at one time, you could make clocks for them or make a clock as a craft, providing the children with 12 numbers, two hands, a fastener, and a cardboard/cardstock paper-clock background. You could also purchase a set of individual clocks at a teacher supply store or borrow a set from a teacher in your school. Have the children participate throughout the whole story.

————. 1981. *Traffic: A Book of Opposites*. New York: Crown.

Summary:
Opposite phrases show different aspects of traffic.

Activity:
Let the children do all the work. Show each double-page spread to the group, asking questions such as, "Which picture shows a car going over the bridge? Under the bridge?" "Which car is taking a left turn? A right turn?" Or instead, point to the pictures and say, "Is this car going over or under the bridge?" If you have little cars or pictures of cars you could also demonstrate the concept on a board, table, or floor. You could even have the children pretend to be the different modes of transportation simulating the opposites in the story. They can stretch their bodies for a long train, or scrunch them together for a short one. Opposites used include over and under, left and right, stop and go, slow and fast, big and little, empty and full, closed and open, narrow and wide, dark and light, long and short, far and near, high and low, front and back, and day and night.

Mahurin, Tim. 1995. *Jeremy Kooloo*. New York: Dutton.

Summary:
The letters of the alphabet are used to tell the story of a cat.

Activity:
This book can best be used as a writing exercise for older children. Have

the students write out the alphabet vertically and create a story using the letters of the alphabet. Use this book as an example. For younger children, put up an alphabet chart and have children point out the letters of the alphabet as the story goes along or do it yourself. You could also give each child one or two letters of the alphabet to hold up at the right time in the story. It will work best if the children are seated in order of the letters in the alphabet.

Mahy, Margaret. 1997. *Boom, Baby, Boom, Boom!* Illus., Patricia MacCarthy. New York: Viking.

Summary:
A baby gives all her food to the animals that come in the door while the mother is busy banging on the drums.

Activity:
Provide something for the children to bang with, such as rhythm sticks or spoons. You could also give them something to bang on, like boxes, but that is not necessary. You could even give each child a different instrument if you have a variety of them. Play up the sound of "BOOM-BIDDY-BOOM-BIDDY-BOOM-BOOM-BOOM!" and have the children beat out the rhythm. When each new animal comes into the picture, the last three "booms" are replaced by the sounds the animals make. You will probably have to repeat the phrase each time so the children have a chance to repeat the new animal sound with you. You will be repeating the words "mew" for the cat, "bow-wow" for the dog, "cock-a-doodle-doo" for the rooster, "baa" for the sheep, and "moo" for the cow. Finish with "Yum-Yum-Yum." Keep continuing with other animal sounds if you choose, and ask the children what animals might come in the room next. You could even put down the whole book and just tell the story, asking kids what animal they think will want food. Instruments are not necessary. If you want to shorten the story, ignore the text and just introduce the new animals and sounds.

———. 1999. *Simply Delicious!* Illus., Jonathan Allen. New York: Orchard.

Summary:
A father tries to avoid obstacles to bring his son an untouched ice cream cone.

Activity:
Hold an ice cream cone with cotton inside for the ice cream and tell the story without the book. Pretend to balance the cone and wobble around, acting out the motions in the story to avoid losing the cone. Balance the cone on your nose, as the father does in the story. For more fun, give each child a cone or a cup that they can stuff with cotton and have them try to balance it in various places as the story is read. Pointed cones are more fun to balance.

Maitland, Barbara. 2000. *Moo in the Morning*. Illus., Andrew Kulman. New York: Farrar Straus & Giroux.

Summary:
Mom brings her child from the city to the farm to get away from the noise.

Activity:
Sounds make the interaction for this book. Read the story slowly, allowing children to repeat the noisy sounds of the city and the farm. Some sounds will be given for you, like "Vroom" and "Quack." Others may require that you ask the question yourself. For example, after reading the phrase, "There are people slamming doors," ask, "How does it sound when a door slams?" End by asking children what sounds they think are noisy and if they would prefer to live in a city, on a farm, or just where they are.

Malone, Peter. 1996. *Star Shapes*. San Francisco, Calif.: Chronicle.

Summary:
The many constellations in the sky are described.

Activity:
Each double-page spread has a picture of the real animal on one side and a picture of the constellation on the other. First explain the concept of constellations, or "star shapes," to the children. Then show them the pictures in the book and ask if they can identify which animals the stars represent. This will be easy because the animal shape surrounds the picture of the constellation, and the actual animal is pictured on the opposite page, but let the children feel intelligent for a while. If possible, make other star shapes on the ceiling or wall, or show other constellation pictures to the children.

**Maloney, Peter, and Felicia Zekauskas. 2001. *His Mother's Nose.*
New York: Dial.**

Summary:
A boy disguises himself so he won't have the features of the others in
his family, but then the features disappear from the family members.

Activity:
You could play the game where the children point to the correct body
part every time it is mentioned in the story. You could also make or copy
a picture of a body to place on a board. Start adding the pieces of the
face as the story is told. Children could add them as well. Take off the
features as they disappear from family members in the story. Add them
back in the end. Alternatively, provide the children with a picture of their
own on which to draw body parts.

**Mammano, Julie. 1996. *Rhinos Who Surf.* San Francisco:
Chronicle.**

Summary:
Whimsical rhinos surf.

Activity:
Depending on what region you live in, children may or may not be familiar with surfing. They may need a brief explanation. You can begin
by asking if they know what surfing is. Have the children stand up in a
surfboarding stance, with legs spread and bent and arms out. As you read
the words, have the children move with you as they pretend to surf. Wax
the boards and paddle. The author uses surfboarding terms that will be
new to them, so show them how to "go vertical" and "pull killer aerials."
Let the children also have a "full-in gnarly wipe-out" and fall to the
ground. Most important, just keep them pretending to sway and dodge
waves as you read the story. If you are ambitious, you could cut large
construction paper or cardboard in the shape of surfboards on which
the children can stand. This could also be the art project, and the children could decorate their surfboards. Skip words you are unfamiliar or
uncomfortable with.

Marceau, Marcel, and Bruce Goldstone. 2001. *Bip in a Book.* **Photos, Steven Rothfeld. New York: Smith, Tabori & Chang.**

Summary:
Pictures of a mime in action tell the story.

Activity:
Show each picture of the mime and ask the children what they think he is doing, acting out, or trying to be. Many answers may be correct. Ask the children to act out the same movements as Marcel Marceau in the book. Afterwards, play mime, imitating the pictures in the book or ones that you create on your own; have the children follow your lead. You could also ask the children to each take a turn miming something after you explain what miming is. Create some of your own moves, like washing the floor and windows, checking out books, or hailing a cab.

Martin, Bill Jr. 1967. *Brown Bear, Brown Bear, What Do You See?* **Illus., Eric Carle. New York: Holt, Rinehart and Winston.**

Summary:
Different animals tell what animals they see.

Activity:
Before turning each page say, "I see a what looking at me?" The children will answer with the next animal as you turn the page. In the end, when all the animals are on the last two pages, point to each one for them to repeat together. If you have puppets or pictures of all the animals, you could display them in a circle and walk around the room with the children while asking them what they see next. For this you would need a bear, bird, frog, sheep, goldfish, duck, horse, cat, and dog.

———. 1991. *Polar Bear, Polar Bear, What Do You Hear?* **Illus., Eric Carle. New York: Holt.**

Summary:
The book asks each animal what they hear. The answer is another animal and the sound it makes.

Activity:
Use this popular book in the way in which it is set up. There are two possibilities. First, simply ask the questions, "Polar Bear, Polar Bear, what

do you hear?" and answer for the children, "I hear a lion roaring in my ear." Then ask the children to roar like a lion. A second possibility would be to say, "I hear a what roaring in my ear?" Then show the picture on the next page and allow the children to make the sound. Animals (or humans) included are polar bear, lion, hippopotamus, flamingo, zebra, boa constrictor, elephant, leopard, peacock, walrus, zookeeper, and children.

Martin, Bill Jr., and Michael Sampson. 2001. *Rock It, Sock It, Number Line.* **Illus., Heather Cahoon. New York: Holt.**

Summary:
Numbers and vegetables dance together to make a soup.

Activity:
While reading the story, have the children stand up and dance along with the rhymes. In the end, have the children sit down one at a time in a circle to pretend they are forming a vegetable or number soup. You could also assign each child a number or vegetable. As the story progresses, the children take turns standing up and dancing as their numbers or vegetables are called, and then sitting in a circle until the soup is complete.

———. 1997. *Swish!* **Illus., Michael Chesworth. New York: Holt.**

Summary:
The Cardinals and Bluejays play a basketball game against each other.

Activity:
Have a wild time with this one. Divide the children into two teams, the Cardinals and the Bluejays. Give the Bluejays blue and the Cardinals red nametags or construction paper bands for their heads or something similar. Then throw a small ball out and let them all pretend to play and act out the story. For a more quiet time, they could sit in a circle or across the room from each other and roll or toss a ball or balloon back and forth to one another.

Marzollo, Jean. 1978. *Close Your Eyes.* **Illus., Susan Jeffers. New York: Dial.**

Summary:
A father tries to put his child to bed.

Activity:

When the book reads "Close your eyes," ask the children in storytime to close their eyes. Continue reading to the next page, where you then say, "Open your eyes," which is not an instruction in the book. Allow them to look at the pictures until the next time you instruct them to close their eyes. You might also want to use words like "imagine" and "pretend," so while they close their eyes they can picture what is happening in the story. This could also be used at the end of a bedtime storytime while children have their heads on a pillow or mat. Instead of showing the pictures, just read and let them imagine with their eyes closed.

—————. 1992. *I Spy: A Book of Picture Riddles*. Photographs by Walter Wick, design by Carol Devine Carson. New York: Scholastic.

Summary:

Find pictures hidden within pictures along with rhyming text.

Activity:

All the "I Spy" books are meant for interaction. They are best to use with small groups or one on one, but there are ways to make it work with a larger group. You could just hold up the book and ask what pictures the kids see. They will probably see things you do not. For an in-between or after game, put pictures up around the room from magazines or use all the bulletin board decorations you have. Hang them with tape or simply lean them against the wall or on tables and chairs. Then say, "I spy a Christmas tree," and have the children locate the tree picture in the room. This would be a good way to introduce the "I spy" concept to children if working with the book is not possible.

Mason, Ann Maree. 1991. *The Weird Things in Nanna's House*. Illus., Cathy Wilcox. New York: Orchard.

Summary:

Nanna just smiles every time her granddaughter questions the "odd" objects in the house.

Activity:

Grandma may just smile when a girl complains that there is a doll over the toilet paper, a giant's spoon and fork on the wall, and a dog by the fireplace that does not bark or move, but you can use this as a way to ask the children questions. Ask them what the doll is doing over the toilet paper, why there are huge spoons on the wall, and why the dog won't bark. In case you haven't figured it out, the doll is a cover to hide the unsightly toilet paper, the spoon and fork are just wall decorations, and the dog is a sculpture. More follow, such as a grandfather clock, plastic fruit, gnomes in the yard, and fairy cakes.

Maynard, Bill. 1999. *Quiet, Wyatt!* Illus., Frank Remkiewicz. New York: Putnam.

Summary:
Wyatt is always told to be quiet until others see the importance his words could have.

Activity:
Instruct the children to yell, "Quiet, Wyatt," whenever you point to them. Then, when Wyatt sees things he should tell people about, ask the children, "Was Wyatt quiet?" They should say, "Yes." In the end, discuss in what situations you should or should not be quiet.

Mayo, Margaret. 2002. *Dig Dig Digging*. Illus., Alex Ayliffe. New York: Holt.

Summary:
Rhymes tell what the jobs that different work vehicles do.

Activity:
For these large pictures, ask the children the name of each work vehicle. Next ask them the job of each vehicle. Then read the rhyme that follows. There will be diggers, fire engines, tractors, garbage trucks, cranes, transporters, dump trucks, rescue helicopters, road rollers, bulldozers, and trucks. An alternate game would be to first ask the children to name some vehicles or types of transportation used for work. Then find the pages that you have marked in the book that show those vehicles. Another way to do this would be to give each child the name of one of the vehicles in the book. Ask each child to bring it to you as you find the matching description in the book.

Mayper, Monica. 1991. *Oh Snow*. Illus., June Otani. New York: HarperCollins.

Summary:
A child goes outside to enjoy the snow.

Activity:
Crinkle paper to make fake snowballs and throw them about the room as you tell story. You could also cut out snowflakes instead. During the story, the children could make snow angels and roll on the ground as if they were rolling down a hill at the appropriate parts in the story.

McBratney, Sam. 1996. *The Dark at the Top of the Stairs*. Illus., Ivan Bates. Cambridge, Mass.: Candlewick.

Summary:
Mice want to go to the top of the stairs for an adventure.

Activity:
Use questions to add suspense to the story. "Should they go on their journey?" "What do you think is really at the top of the stairs?" "Do you really think there is a monster at the top of the stairs?" and "What do you think the monster is like?" After the mice peek through the door and see the cat that goes "Meow," ask the children, "What is it? What is it? Are you sure?" Have the children stand up with you and pretend to slowly walk up the stairs and peek through the door. The children can bounce when the book reads "bumpety-bump," feign ice-skating moves when it reads "Slippity-slide," and plop down to the ground when it reads "tumble-thump" and the mice fall down the stairs back to safety.

McClintock, Barbara. 2001. *Molly and the Magic Wishbone*. New York: Farrar Straus & Giroux.

Summary:
Molly gets a magic wishbone with one wish and she waits for the right moment to use it.

Activity:
This is a good storytelling book. Read the story and describe all the things Molly almost wishes for and what her brothers and sisters want her to wish for, such as toys, a horse, a big house, a lifetime supply of cakes

and candies, a broken bowl to be fixed, and other things. Then ask the children for their wishes. Finally, you will end with Molly's wishing to find her sister.

McCully, Emily Arnold. 1992. *Mirette on the High Wire*. New York: Putnam.

Summary:
Mirette learns to walk tightrope from a famous performer.

Activity:
Put out some ropes, yarn, string, or tape around the room. Allow the children to walk on your "tightrope" as you tell the story or after you tell the story. You could also have children take turns walking the tightrope, or choose one child to be Mirette.

———. 2000. *Monk Camps Out*. New York: Arthur A. Levine.

Summary:
Monk wants to camp outside but ends up sleeping inside while his parents sleep outside.

Activity:
Do what you can do for any camping book and what children love to do at home—make a tent in the library. Push some chairs together and drape a large blanket over it so the children can still see out the sides. Bring a flashlight inside and continue to tell the story. Use a real tent if one is available. In the end, you can be the parents and decide to sleep outside the tent. Instruct the children to run out of the tent back to their seats just as the parents and Monk switch sleeping places in the story. Make the most of being inside the tent and sing campfire songs and pretend to roast marshmallows.

———. 1999. *Mouse Practice*. New York: Arthur A. Levine.

Summary:
A mouse is the worst player on the team until he begins to practice.

Activity:
When Monk begins target practice, give the children beanbags or crumpled-up balls of paper to throw at a target you make and hang on

the wall. During the rest of the story children can act out the actions of the game, like swinging a bat and raising their arms in the air to catch a ball. If you really want to act out the story with the group, you can allow some of the children to be members of the band and give them instruments to cheer after big plays are made in the game.

McDonald, Megan. 1992. *Whoo-oo Is It?* Illus., S. D. Schindler. New York: Orchard.

Summary:
An owl tries to figure out what sound she is hearing.

Activity:
There are many sounds in this book. At least one on every page. Have children repeat sounds like "tat-a-tat-a-tat," "sssssssssssssssssssssss," and "Clk-clk-clk." Instead of telling them which animal makes the sound, you might ask first which animal makes these sounds. Towards the end of the book where all the sounds are mentioned on one page, you could assign each child a different sound and hear what the room sounds like when they all make different sounds from the book at the same time.

McDonnell, Flora. 1999. *Splash!* Cambridge, Mass.: Candlewick.

Summary:
Animals are so hot they all splash into the water to cool off.

Activity:
Cut a pond shape out of a large blue piece of construction paper, use a blanket of any color, or just form a circle. Choose different children to be the elephants, tigers, and rhinos. Have the children wipe the fake sweat off their foreheads and fan their faces with their hands when you read the first part of the book, where the animals are hot. Then have them jump into the center or into the pretend pool of water when you read aloud the names of the animals they represent. When you read, "Splosh! Goes rhinoceros," all the children pretending to be rhinos can jump into the pool. Decide whether you want them to jump back out as soon as their turn is over or join one another until all the children are together, as in the story. You can even have them wave their arms and fake trunks as they pretend to splash each other with water, carefully and at a good distance, of course.

McElmurry, Jill. 2000. *Mad about Plaid.* **New York: Morrow.**

Summary:
A girl finds a plaid purse, which puts a curse on her and turns her and
everything around her plaid.

Activity:
Tell this story with or without the book. Purchase cheap plaid material,
copy a plaid pattern from the Internet, or make a plaid pattern on paper with construction paper, markers, or crayons. Cut out squares to pass
to the children at the point in the story where everything turns plaid. If
possible, drape yourself in plaid material. Do the same with blue paper
or material when the girl turns the purse inside out and everything turns
blue. Another possibility is to use the page in the book titled "How to
Cure a Plaid Curse." Instruct children to do the following: "Sit still, be
quiet, eat a special low-plaid diet, no kissing or hugging, don't use the
phone, don't belch, don't burp, don't moan and grown, don't laugh or
cry, don't lose your head." Otherwise the curse will last longer than a
week. If you want to expand this story, when the children break those
rules and laugh or move around, keep giving them more squares of paper or material. Of course, the children will love this and continue it
until you are out of paper. Write the rules on a board or a large piece of
paper for older kids.

McFarland, Lyn Rossiter. 2001. *Widget.* **Illus., Jim McFarland.**
    New York: Farrar Straus & Giroux.

Summary:
A dog named Widget wants so badly to be warm and have food and a
home that he pretends to be a cat.

Activity:
This is fun to act out if you have all the children in the room pretend to
be cats while you pretend to be the dog. Otherwise, hold up a dog puppet and pretend to have it act out the actions of the cats. If possible,
use a volunteer or several volunteers to act out the scene. The dog pretending to be a cat will puff up with its tail sticking straight up, hiss,
spit, and purr, play with a toy mouse, go in a litter box (could be a cardboard box), and eat from a cat bowl. Put out paper plates or bowls or
even plastic bowls from which cats can eat. In the end, when the dog
needs to bark for help and reveal his true identity, then ask all your cats

to bark as well. You may also want to provide cat masks or simply give the children cat faces copied on paper to hold during the story. More simply, divide the room up: half can be the cats and the other half the dogs. They can then act out the motions and sounds in the story. Alternatively, choose the dog or the cat and have everyone do the same things.

McGrath, Barbara Barbieri. 1998. *The Cheerios Counting Book.* Illus., Rob Bolster and Frank Mazzola, Jr. New York: Scholastic.

Summary:
Cheerios cereal is used to demonstrate counting up to the number 100.

Activity:
There are many possibilities for using this book. Buy a box of Cheerios or a generic equivalent and give each child a cupful. When you show and say a number or hold up a page in the book, ask the children to count out that many Cheerios from their cups. Continue counting to the number 10, or maybe 20. Any number after that would be excessive for preschool children and require the purchase of multiple boxes of cereal. Another option would be to provide each child with a paper numbered from 1 to 10 and have them glue the correct number of Cheerios next to each number. Otherwise, have one large board of numbers and allow children to take turns gluing Cheerios to it to show the increasing numbers. If you want to spend more money, do the same for *The M & M's Counting Book* (Watertown, Mass.: Charlesbridge, 1994) by the same author. This book provides more options for interaction by later suggesting mixing and matching colored candies to reach a number and making different shapes. You could also do the same thing with shapes for the *Cheerios Counting Book*. This is best for classes learning addition and subtraction.

McMillan, Bruce. 1988. *Dry or Wet?* New York: Lothrop, Lee, & Shepard.

Summary:
One page shows a child who is dry while the next page shows another child in the same setting who is wet.

Activity:
An opposites book that is simple to use. Simply ask the children, "Which

child is wet and which one is dry?" Let the children take turns answering, and ask the group if they all agree. Fold the book over so you only see one child at a time or point to only one picture at a time and ask, "Is this child wet or dry?" You can make it fun by asking, "Are you sure? I think she is dry," when she is actually wet. You could also ask the children in your group what the children in the photographs are doing. Then follow up by asking if they are wet or dry. "Is a swimmer wet? A fish dry?" After the story, on the page titled "About This Book," there are suggestions for other wet and dry words to use along with the story. Ask older children if they can think of any other words to describe wet and dry. Put the suggested words, such as downpour, spurt, waterless, and thirsty, on the board for readers and allow them to choose the correct words for each of the pictures. As a writing assignment, let the children use one of the words in a story or poem.

―――. 1988. *Growing Colors.* New York: Lothrop, Lee, & Shepard.

Summary:
Each page shows a different color along with a fruit or vegetable to match.

Activity:
McMillan's colorful photography is a great way to show color in the real world. Show each page to the group, first asking what color they see and then asking what fruit or vegetable is on the page. Never fear, if you don't know your fruits and vegetables, a list by color is provided in the back of the book. You might also ask children to name the other colors on the page, which are mostly brown and green. You could turn this into a bingo game as well by providing the children with a bingo card and dots or circles of color for each of the colors in the book. Perhaps this could be an activity for volunteers to prepare in advance. Then give the children a crayon or bingo markers to mark off the colors as they are displayed in the book. You can make each card different or some or all of them the same.

―――. 1989. *Time To . . .* New York: Lothrop, Lee, & Shepard.

Summary:
The clock on each page shows a different time and describes what activities occur for a child at this time of day.

Activity:
You can do the same as you do for all books about time: give each child his or her own cardboard clock with hands either made or purchased, and allow him or her to move the hands to the correct time as you tell the story. Alternatively, display the time on a large clock or have children take turns changing the time on a single clock. You could even pass a clock around the room. After you have set the clock for the time on each page, ask the children what activity they think the boy in the story does at this time, using the pictures provided. Most will be pretty obvious, such as paint a picture or eat lunch.

McPhail, David. 1998. *The Day the Sheep Showed Up.* **New York: Scholastic.**

Summary:
No one on the farm can identify what the sheep is.

Activity:
Every time the animals try to guess what animal the sheep is, you can ask the children what they think it is. "Well, it has four legs, and so do I. Maybe it's a pig." Then you can ask, "Do you think it is a pig?" They will all continue yelling, "No," and "It's a sheep." Another idea might be to have pictures of all the animals mentioned in the story, such as a duck, goose, pig, cow, rooster, and sheep, on a board. After each suggestion the animals make as to what creature the sheep might be, you can eliminate the picture of what it is not. You or the children can remove the photos. You could also provide a coloring sheet with pictures of all the animals from a pattern book and let the children cross off the pictures on their sheet with a crayon until all are eliminated except for the sheep. You might not want to use the book when you start so that you can keep the pictures of the sheep a secret. End with a game of tag as they do in the story.

———. 1972. *The Glerp.* **Lexington, Mass.: Ginn.**

Summary:
A Glerp will eat anything until after eating too many animals he gets sick.

Activity:
"A Glerp eats anything." Throughout the book he eats one animal after another. You can either use stuffed animals to represent the different

animals in the story and slowly cover them with a blanket one by one, or use the kids as animals, calling them up one at a time. When it comes to the part where the animals dance around inside the Glerp, the children, without even being asked, will dance around making the big blanket move about. Then, when the Glerp gets sick and begins to regurgitate, the children or animals all exit the blanket one at a time as their animal names are called. Again, they never have to be asked. You have their full attention.

Meade, Holly. 1998. *John Willy and Freddy McGee*. New York: Marshall Cavendish.

Summary:
Two guinea pigs escape from their cage and have an adventure.

Activity:
One option is to copy pictures of guinea pigs in two different colors and hide them around the room so the children can pretend they are chasing John Willy and Freddy McGee. Another option is to put a small guinea pig puppet or stuffed animal on a string, and maybe even attach the string to a pole, and wave it over the children's heads as you tell the story so they get the feel of the frantic movements of John and Freddy. When the animals find the pool table and when the cat jumps on top scattering the balls, you could throw a toy cat into the crowd of children. Then throw a bunch of bean bags, crumbled papers, or sponge balls at the children so they can experience what it was like when the pool balls went scattering and John and Willy got trapped in the commotion.

Meyer, Eleanor Walsh. 1998. *The Keeper of Ugly Sounds*. Illus., Vlad Guzner. Delray, Fla.: Winslow.

Summary:
A boy makes disagreeable sounds all his life until he becomes the keeper of ugly sounds and realizes the noise he has made.

Activity:
After every page ask a different child, or all the children, to imitate the sounds in the book or make the sound they think the boy is making. On pages where the forest shows all the sounds, children can make their individual sound or any sound all together. If you want to make things

even more fun, blow up balloons before storytime and draw squiggles on them or the names of sounds for older children. Provide each child with a plastic or paper bag; at the point in the story where the boy gathers up all the sounds and ties them in bags to throw in the water, let the balloons loose and give each child a bag to catch one. Then allow them to pretend they are throwing the bags into the water, which may be just returning them to the bag or container you used to hold the balloons or designating another area for the water where the sounds are drowned.

Milgrom, Harry. 1970. *ABC Science Experiments*. Illus., Donald Crews. New York: Crowell-Collier.

Summary:
Each letter of the alphabet is used to demonstrate a science-related concept with a very simple science experiment.

Activity:
There are activities on every page, along with "a message to parents and teachers" in the front of the book. For example, the letter A is for the word air. The experiment is to blow air through a straw onto your hand. Questions to ask include, "Can you feel the air? Can you hear it? Can you see it?" Teachers can expand on the children's answers, and brief explanations are included in the back of the book. For an early science class, this book could be used as a combination lesson on the alphabet and science, using a different concept each day or each week in conjunction with other lessons. For a storytime, library program, or classroom lesson, this could take up the whole 45 minutes, allowing each child to try the experiments. Most can be easily prepared with objects found in the school or library. To complete every experiment in the book, you would need a straw, ball, cup, pennies, water, bowl, waxed paper, hardboiled egg, fork and string, glove and ice cube, hoop, long balloon, key and magnet, paper clips, nail polish, cooking oil, pencil, quarter, rock and magnifying glass, spinning top, sink (or vortex made out of two 2-liter bottles taped together at the opening and filled with water), food coloring, xylophone (or other instrument), yo-yo, and a zipper.

Miller, Margaret. 1998. *What's on My Head?* New York: Simon & Schuster.

Summary:
A board book in which photographs of babies show different objects, including hats, on their heads.

Activity:
Simply show the pictures and ask what is on each baby's head. Answers will be a puppy dog, fire hat, fancy hat, froggy, pretty bow, and rubber ducky. Then walk around with a box, bag, or basket and put different hats, toys, stuffed animals, or puppets on the children's heads and ask them one at a time what is on their heads as they then return the objects to the container. Alternatively, they could each pick an object from a table and have the teacher or librarian guess what is on their head, or call in another librarian or teacher or student waiting in the hall to make the guesses.

———. 1988. *Whose Hat?* New York: Greenwillow.

Summary:
Pictures of hats represent a chef, fire fighter, pirate, construction worker, nurse, police officer, cowhand, magician, and witch, followed by a page with a person in that profession wearing the hat and a picture of children wearing the hat.

Activity:
On the pages that read, "Whose hat?" wait for children to respond. Then flip the page revealing whether or not they were right. They will likely get stuck on the nurse's hat and you may need to change their answers of "cowboy" and "fireman" to the politically correct "cowhand" and "fire fighter." Perhaps you'll want to discuss if you could have a woman fire fighter or if the children have ever seen anyone in these professions.

Millman, Isaac. 1998. *Moses Goes to a Concert*. New York: Farrar, Straus, & Giroux.

Summary:
Moses and his fellow deaf classmates go to a concert.

Activity:
Since the students in the story are deaf, you can use this as an opportunity to introduce sign language and deafness to even the youngest of children. This might especially be a nice addition if there are deaf students or students with deaf parents in your storytime or class. Even the youngest of children will be able to make simple signs during the story. Try words such as "my," "wave," and "beautiful." The signs are included in the book. If this is too difficult for the age group you have, or even for

you, stick with the sign for "wave" and "applaud," and show how deaf children cheer by waving their arms instead of clapping. Have them do this after each page. During the part of the story when the children try the instruments, let the children in your group pick up one or several instruments to try as if they had just attended the concert. If this is too much of a distraction, wait until the story is over. The signed alphabet is included in the back as well as other signs.

Miranda, Anne. 1996. *Pignic*. Illus., Rosekrans Hoffman. Honesdale, Penn.: Boyds Mills.

Summary:
Each pig brings an item that starts with the same letter as his/her name to the annual pignic.

Activity:
As you can do with other picnic books, provide the food or substitute other foods to give to the children and have them put the items on a table at the appropriate point in the story. When you say, "Fern fried fifty fish," whoever is holding the toy fish or picture of a fish would bring it to the table. When you read a letter of the alphabet, substitute names of children in your class or storytime and have them come up and bring the foods in the book or alternate foods. Children will be waiting for the initials of their names to be called. Make sure to go over their initials before you start the book. If following the book, you will need the following foods or pictures: apple pie, beans, carrot cake, dates, eel and eggplant, fish, gazpacho, hominy, ice cream, jam, kumquat mousse, lemon tarts, mush and meatballs, nectarines, onion sauce, pickled peas, quince, rice, spaghetti, tea, ugly fruit, vermicelli, watermelon, extra jelly, yams, and zucchini bread. You could use a lemon instead of lemon tarts, for example, or a carrot instead of carrot cake.

———. 1997. *To Market, To Market*. Illus., Janet Stevens. San Diego, Calif.: Harcourt Brace.

Summary:
Using the popular nursery rhyme starting "To Market, To Market," a woman shops for many animals that keep getting away.

Activity:
Turn the room into a store. Around the room place stuffed animals or

puppets or pictures to represent the following animals: pig, hen, goose, trout, lamb, cow, duck, goat, and duck. Use a basket (or bag) as a shopping cart and have the children follow you, helping to spot the animal you are looking for and place it in the basket. The story has a twist. As soon as one animal enters the bag or cart, the last one to enter escapes. So make sure you toss the other out of the basket or bag and throw it across the room or to the floor or out of the way. Then, when the woman gives up and decides to make vegetable soup, walk around the room shopping for the vegetables mentioned in the book and then have the children help you place them in a pot or bowl to make the soup. You will need the following pictures or real or plastic foods: potatoes, celery, beets, tomatoes, pea pods, peppers, garlic, spice, cabbage, brown rice, okra, onions, and carrots. You can replace any of the foods with others if you prefer.

Moler, Robert E. 1999. *If I Were a Halloween Monster*. Boston: Little, Brown.

Summary:
Each double-page spread is a different monster with holes for your own eyes and a backwards message only to be read in a mirror.

Activity:
Younger children may be afraid of the "scary" monster pictures. Even though the text is simple, it has many uses for all ages. Tell the story as it is with phrases like, "If I were a Halloween monster, I might be a witch casting spells." Have children take turns holding the book over their faces and peering out through the holes in the monsters' eyes. Then read the backwards mirror phrase to the group, or provide a mirror for older children to hold so they can read the message to the group. Another option for older students is to use this book as a prop in storytelling. One possibility would be to tell a story using each creature, giving the book to a different child when you mention a monster. Make it fast and silly by having eight children stand up front to be the pumpkin, witch, werewolf, ghost, boogie man, vampire, creature resembling Frankenstein, skeleton, and a mummy, and they must pass the book to the correct person each time a monster is mentioned in the story you read or make up as you go along. You could also pass the book around the room, instructing the children to turn to the next mask each time. Let the children tell the progressing story using the creature they have when it is their turn. For older children you can pass out note cards with other scary words like

"haunted house," "attic," "midnight," and "graveyard" to add more twists to the story.

Mora, Pat. 1996. *Uno, Dos, Tres: One, Two, Three*. Illus., Barbara Lavallee. New York: Clarion.

Summary:
Like "The Twelve Days of Christmas," two girls shop for their mother's birthday up to the number ten in both Spanish and English.

Activity:
Use this book to introduce the Spanish numbers one through ten. Show the pictures to the class or group and have them count with you in English. Then go over them in Spanish. Do the opposite if you have Spanish-speaking children. You could also add other objects in the room, such as three/*tres* books, six/*seis* instruments, or whatever you have around the library or classroom. Ask the children if there is anything else in the room you can count to further practice the numbers. You can even count the children. Begin the book by introducing all the numbers and repeat them all at the end.

Mosel, Arlene. 1968. *Tikki Tikki Tembo*. Illus., Blair Lent. New York: Holt, Rinehart and Winston.

Summary:
A boy almost drowns because of his long name in this Chinese tale.

Activity:
Everyone has fun saying the name "Tikki Tikki Tembo-No Sa Rembo-Chari Bari Ruchi-Pip Peri Pembo." Have the children repeat this after you every time it is mentioned in the story. You could also repeat it for them many times at the beginning of the story until they can say it without hearing you first, so all you will have to do is point to them when it is time to say it in the story.

Moss, Lloyd. 2001. *Our Marching Band*. Illus., Diana Cain Bluthenthal. New York: Putnam.

Summary:
Children all play an instrument alone until they decide to start a marching band.

Activity:
Have each child pick up an instrument. Ask them to play badly, which won't be hard. When the band in the story finally gets together, have the children march in a straight line or in a circle around the library or room. Ten children's names are mentioned, but you can make up names to add more kids, take some names out, or use the real names of your children.

———. 1995. *Zin! Zin! Zin! A Violin.* **Illus., Marjorie Priceman. New York: Simon & Schuster.**

Summary:
Different instruments keep joining the orchestra increasing its size.

Activity:
You don't need a trumpet, French horn, or other professional instruments to involve kids in this story. Read each page, introducing a new instrument, such as "FLUTE that sends our soul a-shiver: FLUTE, that slender, sliver sliver. A place among the set it picks to make a young SEXTET—that's SIX." Ask, "Who wants to be number six?" and pick a child, handing or allowing him or her to pick out a different instrument from your collection or those borrowed from the music teacher. If you do not have instruments, anything will do. Give markers to bang on boxes or beanbag toys to shake or puzzle pieces with knobs to bang together. Skip pages in between if you do not have enough children in the room to complete your orchestra. Make sure they are not playing throughout the story. When each new member joins the orchestra, ask the group to all play together. Instruct them to stop when you begin the next page. You can even wave your hands as a conductor to let them know when to begin and end.

Moss, Miriam. 1997. *Jigsaw.* Illus., Tony Smith. Brookfield, Conn.: Millbrook.

Summary:
Clues in the text and puzzle pieces lead to a final picture.

Activity:
The simple way to read this book would be to read the clues on each page and show the puzzle pieces to the children, asking them what the picture is. You will have to move closer or have the children come to

you one at a time. For example, when the page reads "By a thorny rose a long sharp nose—sniffed," and the puzzle piece shows an animal nose, children can guess the animal. Older children might be able to offer suggestions as to why the animal might be sniffing flowers. In the end, ask who the children think the characters in the book are as they see a wolf in a red cape in one picture and the girl in the red cape in another. When they guess Little Red Riding Hood and the Big Bad Wolf, you might have older children make a guess as to why the wolf would be giving the girl a flower.

Most, Bernard. 1996. *Cock-a-doodle-moo!* San Diego, Calif.: Harcourt Brace.

Summary:
A rooster isn't loud enough to wake the farm animals and the farmer, so he gets some help from the other animals.

Activity:
At first when the rooster tries to wake everyone with a quiet "Cock-a-doodle-moo," let the children repeat it quietly after or with you. You could also ask the children to pretend they are asleep and pretend not to hear you when you whisper the rooster's call. Then have children repeat after you the cow's different silly attempts at saying the word until he gets to "cock-a-doodle-moo." If you assign children to be different animals, they can snore when the rooster tries to wake them and wake with a laugh when the cow tries to wake them.

———. 1978. *If the Dinosaurs Came Back.* New York: Harcourt Brace Jovanovich.

Summary:
If they still existed, dinosaurs could use their height and strength to help humans in many ways.

Activity:
Use questions with this book. When you read a phrase like, "If the dinosaurs came back, they could help fire fighters put out fires," ask the children how the dinosaurs would be able to put out a fire. Do this for each of the different scenarios. Then ask if they would like the dinosaurs to be able to do this or if it would cause problems. In the end, ask the children if they would want the dinosaurs to come back. Ask for other

suggestions of things dinosaurs could do or what the children would like dinosaurs to do for them. The last page shows simple drawings of many different dinosaurs and their names. You might provide larger pictures of dinosaurs and ask if the children can identify them or introduce the children to the variety of these prehistoric creatures.

————. 1999. *Z-Z-Zoink!* San Diego, Calif.: Harcourt Brace.

Summary:
A pig wakes up the whole barnyard with her snoring.

Activity:
This is a sound book, so children can repeat the animal sounds and snoring. You might want to divide the group: half can be the ones who snore and half can be the other animals. Provide pig noses so they remember their parts. Perhaps give others a picture or puppet of animals in the story so they don't feel left out.

Mould, Wendy. 2001. *Ants in My Pants.* New York: Clarion.

Summary:
Imaginary animals keep a boy from getting his clothes on so he can go out with his mother.

Activity:
Use props for this story, perhaps not for all the animals in the book, but try to provide as many as you can. For example, when the boy claims he has ants in his pants, shake a pair of pants and allow little black dots to drop out of the pocket. Put socks on a fox puppet, a sweater on a goose, a coat on a goat, a scarf on a giraffe, a newt in a boot, a bat in a hat, and a kitten in a mitten. You might want to invent your own if you do not have the exact props to fit the story, or use pictures instead.

Munsch, Robert. 2000. *Aaron's Hair.* Illus., Alan and Lea Daniel. New York: Scholastic.

Summary:
Aaron hates his hair until it runs away and he wants it back.

Activity:
This is a great Munsch tale for storytelling. Put the book down, and use

a wig, mop head, or bunched up yarn for Aaron's hair. First keep it on your head, and when it jumps off Aaron's head in the story and jumps onto others, choose children in your audience who put the wig on as it jumps from person to person. You could also do this while reading the story—move around the room or throw the wig around, asking children to throw it to someone else. Add onto the story until everyone has had a turn.

———. 1997. *Alligator Baby*. Illus., Michael Martchenko. New York: Scholastic.

Summary:
Kristen's mom accidentally has her new baby at a zoo and keeps bringing home animal babies instead.

Activity:
Find a stuffed animal, picture, puppet, or plastic toy for each of the animals in the story, including an alligator, a seal, and a gorilla, or animals similar to these, and wrap them each in a blanket or cloth. Substitute if necessary. If you use a big blanket, you can layer it in a large basket or laundry bushel and cover each animal under a different layer. Tell the story without the book and pretend to be showing the kids your new baby. Make a fake scream and throw the animal into your audience when you open the blanket and reveal the animal baby instead. You could even change the story to use animals that you do have puppets for or just to keep the story going. Have a baby doll wrapped up or at the bottom of the basket for when the girl finally brings home their real baby.

———. 1979. *The Dark*. Illus., Sami Suomalainen. Toronto, Canada: Annick.

Summary:
A girl finds "the Dark" in her cookie jar, which eats shadows and gets bigger.

Activity:
Memorize this story, carry a blanket around the room and when the Dark eats different shadows cover a different child with the blanket each time. You could also walk around the outside of the children's seating area and pretend to see the objects mentioned in the story, such as a car and telephone pole, and cover them with the blanket or sheet instead. This is

perhaps better used with older children who are less likely to be scared. Provides a good Halloween story.

———. 2001. *Makeup Mess.* **Illus., Michael Martchenko. New York: Scholastic.**

Summary:
A girl buys makeup and scares people with her new look until she discovers she is more beautiful without it.

Activity:
Bring in your makeup collection and tell the story with or without the book. When the part comes where Julie puts makeup on herself, start applying makeup to yourself in all the wrong places, too dark and too much. Have wipes or paper towels available to wash it off and do it again as Julie tries for the second time. Be sure to act out the parts of the characters who scream and fall back when they see her. If you have a willing older volunteer or a doll, you could also put makeup on him, her, or it as well. Children can also draw makeup on a picture.

———. 2000. *Mmm, Cookies!* **Illus., Michael Martchenko. New York: Scholastic.**

Summary:
A boy tricks people with fake cookies made from clay.

Activity:
Tell this story without the book and even without props. Use facial expressions to show how the parents are disgusted when they eat the fake cookie. Get wild with creating the cookie, using the sounds in the book, such as "Whap," "Swish," "Chick," "Glick," and "Plunk," over and over again. You can even let the children repeat the sounds. End by letting the children make clay cookies or design one using paper.

———. 1979. *Mud Puddle.* **Illus., Sami Suomalainen. Toronto, Canada: Annick.**

Summary:
No matter what a girl does to get and keep clean, a mud puddle keeps finding her until she finds a way to make it go away for good.

Activity:
Robert Munsch writes some of the best books to act out for storytime. With that in mind, know that you can make any of Munsch's books interactive by simply acting out the story and maybe even letting the kids take part. For *Mud Puddle* there are a couple of other options. As suggested for his book *The Dark*, use a big blanket to throw over a child or the whole group of children each time the mud puddle attacks. Before the story begins, introduce the blanket as the mud puddle. If you want to be messy you can also cut out pieces of black or brown construction paper or use confetti and have cups filled ahead of time to throw over the kids each time the mud puddle returns. You can also have the children act out the motions each time Jule Ann's mother cleans the mud puddle off of her in the story. The repetitive lines read, "She washed out her ears. She washed out her eyes. She even washed out her mouth." Her nose and belly button are added later. So rub your ears and eyes, make spitting sounds with your mouth, rub your nose or make a fake sneeze, and rub your belly as examples of how the children can help act out the cleaning process. Have a sponge or a bar of soap to throw at the blanket at the end of the story when Jule Ann does so to finally make the mud puddle go away.

———. 1982. *Murmel, Murmel, Murmel*. Illus., Michael Martchenko. Willowdale, Ontario: Firefly.

Summary:
A girl finds a baby and tries to find someone who will take it.

Activity:
When the girl finds the baby, have a basket or bucket with a blanket in it and pretend it is a sandbox. Look inside, pretending to hear the sound "Murmel, murmel, murmel," which you might want to play on a tape recorder, and pull out a baby doll. This story might work for storytelling as the girl asks people if they want a baby and listens to their excuses. After a couple of examples, you might want to ask the children in your group if they would like the baby, instructing them to say no, and ask them why not. Even if they say yes, you could change the story and decide that they would not be good parents and that they look too young to be parents.

————. 1996. *Stephanie's Ponytail*. Illus., Michael Martchenko. Toronto, Canada: Annick.

Summary:
Stephanie tries a new hairstyle at school but everyone copies her, even when she says she will shave her head.

Activity:
Stephanie keeps asking for a different style ponytail, including one on the top of her head like a tree and one dangling in front of her face. Everyone at school keeps copying her new looks. If your hair is long enough you can pull it into the different types of ponytails Stephanie asks for, but you could use a wig, yarn, rope tied together, or even a doll. You could also hold the hair of a child or have her hold her own hair. Children also repeat the phrase, "Ugly ugly very ugly," which is the initial reaction of the children at Stephanie's school when they see her new hairdos. They may also repeat the line, "Well, it's my ponytail and I like it." They can also hold their own hair, even the boys, as you show them the different ponytails that Stephanie wears.

Muntean, Michaela. 1981. *The Very Bumpy Bus Ride*. Illus., B. Wiseman. New York: Parents Magazine.

Summary:
A bus takes people and more on a bumpy ride to the fair.

Activity:
Have the children bounce up and down as the story is read or paraphrased. Then have the children pretend to push the bus up the hill and sit back down as it rolls down the other side.

Naylor, Phyllis Reynolds. 1997. *Ducks Disappearing*. Illus., Tony Maddox. New York: Atheneum.

Summary:
A boy watches a family of ducks fall in a storm drain and tries to help them.

Activity:
This is one where you need either a bunch of rubber ducks, perhaps used in a carnival or fun fair game, or you need to copy pictures of 11

small ducks and 1 large one. Slowly, as you progress through the story, ask a child to take one duck at a time off the board and place it in a basket or box or other object as all the ducks disappear in the storm drain. Towards the end of the story, when they are being rescued, ask the children to then take one out of the storm drain and put it back on the board or table to safety. Because the story is longer at some points, you may want to paraphrase the beginning.

Newcome, Zita. 1999. *Toddlerobics: Animal Fun.* Cambridge, Mass.: Candlewick.

Summary:
Children use animal movements as exercise in their class.

Activity:
Newcome's books are set up for action from the children. They will "waddle like a penguin," flip their fins, swim, "scuttle like a crab," stretch fingers like starfish, float like a jellyfish, move elbows like a duck, "squat like a frog," roar like a lion, snap like a crocodile, hop like a kangaroo, swing arms like a monkey, "stomp like an elephant," put hands together like a snake, gallop like a horse, flutter their wings, and "wriggle like a worm." Every word in the book adds up to an action that can be performed by the children. Let the children do their favorite actions at the end or show other children what their favorite actions were.

Nikola-Lisa, W. 1991. *1, 2, 3 Thanksgiving!* Illus., Robin Kramer. Morton Grove, Ill.: Albert Whitman.

Summary:
A counting book that shows what and how much is needed for a Thanksgiving dinner.

Activity:
Provide pictures of the objects in the story for the children to count, such as one turkey, two pumpkin pies, three cups of cranberries, and four tomatoes. Alternatively, ask the children to count how many objects are in the book for each number. The end page provides a chart of the pictures to make gathering pictures easier.

———. 1997. *Shake Dem Halloween Bones*. Illus., Mike Reed. Boston: Houghton Mifflin.

Summary:
Different fairy tale characters join the pumpkin man in a Halloween dance.

Activity:
This is a fun story to get the children up and moving. After every new character is introduced and asked to dance, get the children dancing to the phrase "shake, shake, shake dem bones now. Shake, shake, shake dem bones now. Shake, shake, shake dem bones at the hip-hop Halloween ball." Alternatively, you can bring one child up at a time to dance with you, pretending each is a different character in the book. Just bring them up as they are, or provide some type of prop to differentiate them from the others. The characters will be Li'l Red, Jack, Tom Thumb, Snow White, Goldilocks, Mister Pig, Rapunzel, Rumpelstiltskin, Cinderella, and Big Puss. Since the pictures in the story represent the characters as average children, you don't have to give them props that match their fairy tale, but perhaps different hats or bows to show the difference. Maybe a cut-out pig nose for Mister Pig, a baseball cap for Tom Thumb, and a wig or rope for Rapunzel. Another option for this story, so that you can use it at times other than Halloween and for a fairy tale unit or theme, would be to cut out the dancing part and read the phrases describing each character, such as "Snow White is here in a fancy dress, with seven little men, no more, no less. Come on, Li'l Snowy, won't you dance with me at the hip-hop Halloween Ball?" Only cut out the word "Halloween" and replace it with another word to suit your needs, such as "Birthday Ball" or "Winter Ball" and leave out the name of the fairy tale character. Instead allow the children to guess who the character is by the clues in the phrase you read (seven little men = Snow White) and by the pictures, which sometimes provide clues.

———. 1997. *Tangletalk*. Illus., Jessica Clerk. New York: Dutton.

Summary:
Strange mixed-up things happen.

Activity:
Ask the children if the silly things in the story make sense. This is bet-

ter for older children who will better understand. For example, "In a pot, my socks were simmering. Lunch was pinned to the line." Ask, "Do you simmer socks in a pot?" and "Do you pin lunch to the clothesline?" At the end you can make up some of your own if there is still interest.

Noakes, Polly. 1990. *Sally Sky Diver.* Nashville, Tenn.: Ideals Children's Books.

Summary:
A girl is picked up by the wind with her umbrella for an adventure.

Activity:
The activity is obvious from just looking at the cover of a girl with her umbrella in the night sky. Open up an umbrella and let it carry you about the room as you tell the story. Children can raise one arm pretending they have an umbrella as well and follow you. You could provide an umbrella for each child from the lost and found, but it might prove to be dangerous. It could also be an activity used on a rainy day with older children who have brought their umbrellas to the classroom. Children can all thump back down in their seats on their bottoms when Sally returns.

Noble, Trinka Hakes. 1980. *The Day Jimmy's Boa Ate the Wash.* Illus., Steven Kellogg. New York: Dial.

Summary:
A pet boa constrictor causes havoc on a school field trip.

Activity:
Turn this one into a flannel board story. You will need a cow, a haystack, and a tractor or farmer on a tractor to run over the haystack and knock it off the board, making room for the next scene. Next you will need pigs on a bus, corn, and of course a boa constrictor. For the next scenario you will need a chicken and an egg. You could also leave all the objects on the board to show what mass confusion was occurring on the class trip. Although the book never does explain, but rather shows that the boa eats the wash, you could provide the children with small articles of clothing and let them dress a boa constrictor or snake puppet, stuffed animal, or even a rubber snake or tube.

Noll, Sally. 1987. *Jiggle Wiggle Prance.* **New York: Greenwillow.**

Summary:
Different words describe the actions of animals.

Activity:
Have the children stand up and get ready to move. They will act out every word as you hold up the pictures in the book so that they can see what the animals are doing. They will "walk rock drop push pull flop hop spin dance jiggle wiggle prance" and much more. When the book ends, ask them to perform their favorite action from the story or create some new ones of their own.

Novak, Matt. 1990. *Mr. Floop's Lunch.* **New York: Orchard.**

Summary:
Mr. Floop gives his lunch away to all the animals that join him on the park bench.

Activity:
You can act out this one as a storyteller to make it more exciting to the children. As you tell the story, pull out a different animal from a basket or from underneath a blanket and offer it food. It doesn't have to be presented in the order of the book, nor do you have to use the same animals as in the story. You can even ask children to bring up a different animal and pretend to be that animal, or simply have the children pretend to be any animal they like. Maybe you can even give them nametags with their animal names. Then, as each comes up, hand that animal some of the food from a paper bag or lunchbox until the food is all gone.

———. 1998. *The Pillow War.* **New York: Orchard.**

Summary:
A brother and sister fight over who gets to sleep with the dog and try to resolve it with a pillow fight.

Activity:
The title is the first clue to the activity you can use. Ask the children to bring pillows, provide them, or use a handful of stuffing or cotton balls and have a pillow fight in the room. You could even crinkle up balls of

paper to make pretend pillows. As a craft, make pillows by cutting a cloud, quilt, or pillow pattern out of paper or felt or other material and allow the children to glue the edges together after stuffing the inside with cotton balls or some kind of stuffing. Then they can use these as their pillows. Let them begin throwing as the pillow fight in the story begins and end when it ends. If you prefer, take breaks in between some of the pages to make sure they are hearing part of the story, although it is more fun to keep going, or only throw a few pillows out at certain times in the story. End with forming a circle of children and allowing them to toss a few pillows back and forth to each other.

Numeroff, Laura Joffe. 1995. *Chimps Don't Wear Glasses*. Illus., Joe Mathieu. New York: Simon & Schuster.

Summary:
Different animals are in unlikely situations.

Activity:
In any book with silly pictures like this, you can ask the children if the situations would actually occur. For this book, first read a phrase like, "Tigers don't ice-skate." Then ask, "Do they?" Your answers should be "no" every time. As suggested for all books like this, you may just have some props lying around that would match the pictures in the book. For the phrase "Zebras don't cook," for example, you might want to have a zebra puppet or picture of a zebra and place or tape it in a pot. Then ask the children, "Are you sure zebras don't cook? Look around. Can you see a zebra cooking?" You can also add other objects on your own using your puppet collection or pictures of animals. Then you can follow up at the end of the book with some animals and activities of your own. Other simple examples to create from the book could be a chimp with glasses, a kangaroo reading a book, a piglet saving money in jars, a seal flying a kite, a chipmunk king, and a turtle that dines.

————. 1985. *If You Give a Mouse a Cookie*. Illus., Felicia Bond. New York: Harper & Row.

Summary:
The classic story tells what happens when you give a mouse a cookie.

Activity:
If you don't have the mouse puppet that comes with the props that go

with the story, then you can easily cut out pictures to match the objects the mouse asks for or uses in the story, attach tape to them, and place them on the hand of a mouse puppet, doll, or picture, unless you can find the real props around the room. Everything is a general household or workplace item that will be easy to locate. If you have a volunteer or use a child, put mouse ears on him or her and hand the props to a live person. Children can also come up to you and put the pictures or pieces on the mouse. The objects and pictures you need include a cookie, glass of milk (or a cup or milk carton), straw, napkin, mirror, scissors, broom, mop, blanket and pillow, storybook, paper and crayons, pen, wall or board as refrigerator, and tape. Of course, you can also use Numeroff's books *If You Give a Moose a Muffin* (New York: HarperCollins, 1991) and *If You Give a Pig a Pancake* (New York: Laura Geringer, 1998). Both are illustrated by Felicia Bond.

———. 2002. *Laura Numeroff's 10–Step Guide to Living with Your Monster*. **Illus., Nate Evans. New York: Laura Geringer.**

Summary:
The title explains this guide to taking care of your monster.

Activity:
Read each rule and ask children to raise their hands if they think it is a good rule. Some rules will have several parts to them. For example, step two reads, "On the way home, be sure to get your monster a checkup. Hold his hand and make sure he gets a lollipop. Do not give him green lollipops. Give those to your dad." At the end ask the children if they have any rules of their own. This could lead to a writing assignment for older kids in which you ask them to write more monster rules or to write rules for their pet, someone in their family, or for something else.

———. 1998. *What Mommies Do Best/What Daddies Do Best*. **Illus., Lynn Munsinger. New York: Simon & Schuster.**

Summary:
Mommies and daddies do the same things although they may or may not be typical for both genders.

Activity:
Use this book for much discussion. Ask specific questions for each picture. For example, for the phrase "Daddies can teach you how to ride a

bicycle," ask the group if their daddies taught them to ride a bike. Then flip the book over and ask if their moms helped them to ride a bike or if it was someone else entirely. Be careful using this book with children who may not have a mother or father. It is better to use when paired with books using other family members so everyone is included. Consult the theme index for ideas.

————. 1996. *Why a Disguise?* Illus., David McPhail. New York: Simon & Schuster.

Summary:
The story tells when you should or should not wear a disguise.

Activity:
Don a pair of glasses, big nose and beard, or any kind of hat, wig or mask that will work as a disguise while reading the story and describing the different situations. Let the children take turns wearing the disguise. Involve them with questions as well by saying something like, "Is it a good idea to wear the disguise when playing hide and seek?" "How about when kissing your grandmother?" These are situations in the book, but you could also make up your own.

Nygaard, Elizabeth. 1998. *Snake Alley Band.* Illus., Betsy Lewin. New York: Doubleday.

Summary:
Snake joins other animals to create a new sound for his band.

Activity:
Let the children be the band. First teach them to sing as the snakes do, "shhh shhh shhh." "BOOM BOOM BOOM." "Shhh-BOOM Shhh BOOM Shhh-Boom." Then later assign children to be other animals and add the sounds of the cricket, "Chew-up chew up"; fish, "POP-POP-DOO-WOP"; frog, "Cha-BOP cha-BOP cha-BOP"; bird, "Tweet-tweedle-dee-deet"; and turtle, "TA-BOOM TA-TOOM TOOM." If children are unable to remember their own parts then teach everyone the sounds and have them repeat the sounds together when they occur in the story.

O'Brien, John. 1999. *Poof!* **Honesdale, Penn.: Boyds Mills.**

Summary:
A wizard couple keeps magically changing things to avoid work.

Activity:
Use a magic wand or make one out of a straight object covered in aluminum foil. You can simply keep tapping the wand and repeating "Poof!" as the wizards change things in the story. To make it more fun, though, hide the different animals in the story in a box or on the side and keep pulling them out as the wizards change one into another. You will need a doll, cat, dog, and duck. Three ducks would be best for the end when the wizards change themselves into ducks. Make magic wands in storytime and let the children be magical, too.

Ochiltree, Dianne. 2002. *Pillow Pup.* **Illus., Mireille d'Allancé. New York: Margaret K. McElderry.**

Summary:
A girl fights for a pillow with her dog.

Activity:
If it is a bedtime storytime, ask the children to bring pillows and act out the pulling and tugging of the pillows with a partner. You can also do this if you happen to have enough pillows or mats or carpet squares around the room. Alternatively, use one pillow and have the children toss it around. They could also sit in a circle and take turns tugging one pillow with another child.

Ohanesian, Diane. 1991. *Can You Find Sadie?* **Illus., Susan Miller. New York: Golden Book.**

Summary:
A girl and her mother search the house to find their puppy.

Activity:
The book is already set up for an activity. On each page, after reading the text, simply read the final question to the children, "Can you find Sadie?" and move about the room until you get the answer. Give each child a turn at a different page or let each child have a turn at the same page, depending on the size of your group. To end, hide pictures of dogs

around the room and ask the children if they can find Sadie in the room. Otherwise, just hide one stuffed dog toy or puppet and have them all search for the same one. You might want them to close their eyes, turn around, and hide the same toy over and over again until they all have had a turn.

O'Keefe, Susan Heyboer. 1989. *One Hungry Monster: A Counting Book in Rhyme.* **Illus., Lynn Munsinger. Boston: Little, Brown.**

Summary:
Monsters keep asking for food until they add up to ten.

Activity:
The first option is to make or copy ten monster pictures and have children take turns placing them on a board as the numbers increase and more and more monsters keep entering the picture. A second option would be to allow the children to be monsters, perhaps even providing them with masks and have them one at a time go to the table as you read the story so that they can get ready for the food you will bring in the second half of the book. In the story, after the monsters are seated, the boy begins to bring the food. It is easier to pretend to have food and ask the kids to pretend they are eating. However, if you are ambitious you could copy pictures of the items and place them on the table. You could also give each child a piece of paper and crayons to draw the pictures for the objects you mention. They would draw two loaves of bread and five pears, for example.

O'Malley, Kevin. 1997. *Velcome.* **New York: Walker.**

Summary:
A seemingly scary man tells scary stories that turn out not to be very scary.

Activity:
This is definitely a book for storytelling and definitely for older children. Have a few props on the side, such as wrapping paper, a plate of vegetables, and a bucket. Pull the appropriate prop out after you tell each "scary" story and reveal that the "Viper" was really a window washer with a bucket, that the rapping noise was really wrapping paper, and the scariest thing of all is actually a plate full of vegetables. Use for scary stories.

Oppenheim, Joanne. 1989. *Left & Right*. Illus., Rosanne Litzinger. San Diego, Calif.: Harcourt Brace Jovanovich.

Summary:
Two cobbler brothers are used to making either a right or left shoe and realize they need to work together.

Activity:
One activity could be to have the children either hold up their right or left arm or foot, or point to the right or the left each time the words "right" or "left" are recited. Another fun game would be to have the children take off their shoes and hold up the right or left or mix them up. At the end, play the game where everyone puts their shoes in the center and see who can be the first to put on his or her shoes. Of course, you may find yourself tying lots of shoes.

Ostrow, Vivian. 1996. *My Brother Is from Outer Space (The Book of Proof)*. Illus., Eric Brace. Morton Grove, Ill.: Albert Whitman.

Summary:
A boy believes his brother is from outer space because he is so different from him.

Activity:
For older children who are writers, give them notebooks or paper, like the format of the book. Let them make their own notes as you read the story and ask them to write down all the clues they hear as to how the brother could be an alien. Then, when the book is over, ask them to check off all the points that they find logical. Then ask the class to determine whether or not they think the brother is truly from outer space.

Palatini, Margie. 2001. *The Web Files*. Illus., Richard Egielski. New York: Hyperion.

Summary:
The ducktectives try to solve the crime of the missing pilfered peck of perfect purple almost-pickled peppers.

Activity:
This could be acted out, if you have enough volunteers to play the char-

acters as you read the story. An easier activity, however, would be to have a large clock up at the front of the room, and as the story progresses and time passes, move the hands of the clock to the times in the story. Children can take turns at this as well.

Paraskevas, Betty. 1996. *Cecil Bunions and the Midnight Train*. Illus., Michael Paraskevas. San Diego, Calif.: Harcourt Brace.

Summary:
A boy and a private eye take a strange train ride in their dreams.

Activity:
This is actually a rather spooky story as the train keeps seeming to chant the message, "Never Coming, Never Coming, Never Coming Back." When these lines are repeated, ask the children to say the words with you or point to the children when it is time for the phrase. Make sure they say it in almost a whisper. You could even have them parade around the room like a train as you read the story and chant the phrase. Say the phrase more often as it is not repeated on every page.

Parish, Peggy. 1963. *Amelia Bedelia*. Illus., Fritz Siebel. New York: Harper & Row.

Summary:
Amelia Bedelia takes her job as a housekeeper literally.

Activity:
Cut down the length of the book by paraphrasing and only reading the actual instructions left by the owner of the house where Amelia Bedelia is working. Then read or tell the children how Amelia Bedelia follows through with these chores, and ask them if they think that is what the owners meant. For example, when the instructions read, "Change the towels in the green bathroom," tell the children that Amelia Bedelia decided to cut them to make them look different. Ask the children if they think that is what she was supposed to do and ask them what she was really supposed to do.

Parker, Vic. 1997. *Bearobics: A Hip-Hop Counting Story.* **Illus., Emily Bolam. New York: Viking.**

Summary:
A bear teaches other animals to do Bearobics, which they all perform in their own way.

Activity:
This is one of those books where the activity is already set up for you. You could start by getting a rhythm going. Perhaps repeat some of the sounds from the first page over and over until the rhythm is set. "Deep in the forest there's a thumping bumping sound, a drumming and a humming, a stomping on the ground." Repeat the words "With a thumping and a bumping and a drumming and a humming and a stomping on the ground." Allow the children to thump their chests, bump by jumping up and down, drum their thighs, hum, and stomp their feet on the ground. Then read the story as new animals join the bear. Now use the new phrase and show the new actions such as "Seven swinging penguins can't get quite enough. With a slide to the side they shake and strut their stuff." Let the children perform these actions. In between each page you might want to go back to repeating, "With a thumping and a bumping and a drumming and a humming and a stomping on the ground."

Parnall, Peter. 1988. *Feet!* **New York: Macmillan.**

Summary:
Describes the feet of different creatures.

Activity:
There are two options for using this book interactively. The first is to have the children act out the types of feet. Take giant steps for "big feet," run for "fast feet," stretch your toes for "long-toed scaly feet," wiggle your toes for "hairy feet," walk cool and strut for "tough feet," lift your feet up one at a time for "wet feet," stomp hard for "hard feet," tiptoe and move in slow motion for "slow feet," put your legs together for "thin feet," shake your feet for "dry feet," shake for "cool feet," walk like a duck for "webbed feet," and wipe your feet for "clean feet." Another option is to ask the children what animal belongs to each pair of feet, as the rest of the body is not shown. These answers are in the back of the book in order of appearance. Combine the two activities by first asking the children to act it out and then to guess the animal, or vice versa, or read the book twice.

Parr, Todd. 1999. *Things That Make You Feel Good/Things That Make You Feel Bad.* **Boston: Little, Brown.**

Summary:
Each double-page spread has something good and something bad.

Activity:
Say the names of the objects or people and then ask the children if they are good or bad. For example, "Are bubble baths good or bad?" Children will most likely say "good," unless they dislike the water. Then ask, "Are smelly feet good or bad?" and hope they reply bad. Follow with some of your own or ask the children for their suggestions of things that are good or bad.

Partridge, Elizabeth. 2000. *Pig's Eggs.* **Illus., Martha Weston. New York: Golden.**

Summary:
When Hen steps out from sitting on her eggs, the artist Pig decides to paint them each a different color. When they hatch, each chick is the color of the egg.

Activity:
Buy plastic Easter eggs and cut out or copy a picture of a chick to match the egg color and place it inside. You could also make construction paper eggs, cutting them in half in a zig zag pattern and reattaching them with a fastener, gluing a chick the same color partway on the bottom half of the egg, so its head appears when the egg is separated by the fastener. Before you get to the part in the story when the eggs hatch, let each child open an egg and discover the surprise. More simply, make egg shapes out of colored paper with a chick drawn on the other side or placed underneath. The kids can turn over the eggs.

Paterson, Bettina. 1991. *My First Wild Animals.* **New York: HarperCollins.**

Summary:
Collage pictures of animals are shown.

Activity:
This entire book is pictures of animals and their names. Simply show

the pictures to the children and ask them to shout out the names of the animals. Or take turns and let one child at a time name an animal, maybe giving a small prize as they guess correctly. Follow by allowing children to make their own animal picture using cut or torn construction paper and, maybe, provide a pattern to put the paper on for younger children.

Patrick, Denise Lewis. 1996. *See What I Can Do!* Illus., Thomas Hudson. New York: Golden.

Summary:
This simple board book describes things a girl can do.

Activity:
Simply ask the children if they do these things instead of reading "I can . . ." For example, change, "I can drink from a cup . . ." to "Can you drink from a cup?" Follow with other questions that you make up on your own and let the children take turns saying things they can do and asking the class if others can too.

Patterson, Elizabeth Burman. 1997. *Whose Eyes Are These?* Nashville, Tenn.: Thomas Nelson.

Summary:
Pictures and words give hints to the animals they describe.

Activity:
Children will probably be able to identify most of the animals from the pictures even though the whole body is not shown. After reading a description for each animal, ask the question as the book does, "Whose eyes are these?" The answer is upside down below the pictures in case you do not recognize them.

Paye, Won-Ldy, and Margaret H. Lippert. 2002. *Head, Body, Legs: A Story from Liberia.* Illus., Julie Paschkis. New York: Holt.

Summary:
Separate body parts join together to form a whole body in this creation story.

Activity:
Cut out patterns of arms, a head, a body, and legs. Put each piece onto a flannel board whenever it enters the story. Ask the children to help put the body parts where they belong. You could also give each child a set of all the pieces and have them put together their own bodies as the story is told. They could also draw the different body parts or point to them on their own bodies.

Peek, Merle. 1987. *The Balancing Act: A Counting Song*. New York: Clarion.

Summary:
From the lyrics of a song, elephants balance on string, adding one more until they have ten.

Activity:
Place a piece of string or yarn on the ground and have the children come up one by one, as if they were the elephants, to balance on it. You could even extend the story or shorten it for however many children are in your class or storytime. Alternatively, cut out ten elephants and use this as a flannel board story. Find a copy of the song "One Elephant."

Pelletier, David. 1996. *The Graphic Alphabet*. New York: Orchard.

Summary:
The alphabet is shown using simple drawings to represent words starting with the corresponding letters.

Activity:
Simply point to the pictures and say which letter is represented. Then ask the children what word they think the letter is trying to show. An "H" floating represents "hover" and an "I" sinking represents an "iceberg," for example. Many will be too difficult for your younger crowd, but the guessing will be what makes it fun. You could also play the game where you offer suggestions, "Could this be a kangaroo? A knot?"

Peters, Lisa Westberg. 2000. *Cold Little Duck, Duck, Duck*. Illus., Sam Williams. New York: Greenwillow.

Summary:
A duck waits for the pond to unfreeze.

Activity:
Have the children act out the motions and activities of the duck in the story. For "brisk brisk brisk" hold your arms across your chest and shiver, for "creak creak creak" tiptoe on the fake ice, for "stuck stuck stuck" you try to lift your feet from the ground, for "shake shake shake" shiver in the cold, for "quick quick quick" run fast in place, for "drink drink drink" pretend to sip, for "snack snack snack" pretend to eat, and for "flock flock flock" pretend to fly. Blink for the words "blink blink blink," look around for "look look look," dip down for "dunk dunk dunk" and "shrink shrink shrink." Slide for "slick slick slick," fall for "crack crack crrr...ack," and kick your legs for "kick." Other things in the story are quack and wiggle.

Peterson, Jeanne Whitehouse. 1981. *While the Moon Shines Bright (A Bedtime Chant)*. Illus., Margot Apple. New York: Harper & Row.

Summary:
A granddaddy tells a boy what to do before bed.

Activity:
After each direction from the grandfather comes the phrase, "I can do this. I can do this." Let children know this phrase before the story is read and instruct them to repeat it when you point to them. You could also ask the children if they do these things before bed, and ask them what else they do before going to bed.

Pfanner, Louise. 1990. *Louise Builds a Boat*. New York: Orchard.

Summary:
Louise imagines building a boat.

Activity:
Use a chalkboard or any type of surface to draw on. Draw a boat and have the children help finish the drawing by adding the other parts of the boat as you show them the pictures in the story. Start with the wooden deck and let the kids fill in the mast, crow's nest, flags, gangplank, figurehead, cabin, galley, anchor, lanterns, dinghy, and canvas sails.

————. 1987. *Louise Builds a House*. New York: Orchard.

Summary:
Louise imagines building a house.

Activity:
Put up a dry-erase board, poster board, or paper and draw the house as Louise imagines it being built. You don't even have to hold up the book. You will start with a rectangle and gradually add windows, a tower, clock, moat, drawbridge, arch, gardens, and more. Give the children a piece of paper to draw the house as you read the story or let them draw as you draw.

Pfister, Marcus. 1997. *Milo and the Magical Stones*. Translated by Marianne Martens. New York: North-South.

Summary:
Two different endings, happy or sad, tell what happens when Milo finds a magical shiny stone.

Activity:
Tell the story and ask the group of children if they want to hear the happy story or the sad story. When you are finished, ask if they still want to hear the other story. The length and two endings make this more appropriate for grade school children. After reading the endings, you could hide paper stones around the room and have the children help look for them. After both endings have been read ask the children which ending they preferred and why. This could also be a classroom writing exercise in which they develop their own endings instead.

————. 1992. *The Rainbow Fish*. Translated by J. Allison James. New York: North-South.

Summary:
A beautiful fish soon shares his scales with other fish.

Activity:
Make a fish with different colored seals or with shiny scales. When the part in the story comes where the Rainbow Fish gives away his scales, take turns giving the children in your class or storytime scales. If pos-

sible, use sticky notes or easily removable tape to put the scales inside the book.

Piers, Helen. 1999. *Who's in My Bed?* Illus., Dave Saunders. New York: Marshall Cavendish.

Summary:
A donkey searches a farmyard to find animals sleeping in other animals' beds.

Activity:
In this story, pages fold over to reveal who is sleeping in each bed. The donkey keeps asking, "Who's that in there?" Ask each child this question, and see if the children can guess before revealing what is behind each door. You might want to peek and give clues.

Pilkey, Dav. 1994. *Dog Breath: The Horrible Trouble with Hally Tosis*. New York: Scholastic.

Summary:
A family tries to cure their dog's bad breath until he saves the day.

Activity:
Have the children hold their noses every time you say words like "bad breath," "breath," "stunk," "Hally Tosis," "smelly," or anything relating to the dog's bad breath. Model what to do for the children, and instruct them to hold their noses when you do.

———. *The Hallo-Wiener.* 1995. New York: Scholastic.

Summary:
Dogs make fun of Oscar the Daschund when he is dressed as a hot dog for Halloween until he saves them.

Activity:
First of all, have children repeat the phrase "Wiener Dog" with you whenever it is read in the story. Ask questions about the story: "Does Oscar like his costume? Do you like Oscar's costume? Do you like the costumes the other dogs are wearing? Do you think Oscar will save his friends? Should he? Who do you think is inside the monster costume?" and others. Perhaps give out candy at the end to share, just as the dogs do.

Pinczes, Elinor J. 1995. *A Remainder of One*. Illus., Bonnie MacKain. Boston: Houghton Mifflin.

Summary:
A queen wants her army of bugs to divide evenly, but there is always one remaining.

Activity:
You would need exactly 25 children to act this story out. If you have that number, divide the children as they are divided in the story, marching in rows of twos, threes, and fours—until rows of five finally make them even. This could also be used in a math class. If you have older children, cut out twenty-five bugs for each to make the lines themselves. Younger children may be able to do this with help, especially if you have already cut out the correct amount of insects. This would also work as a flannel board story.

Pinkney, Brian. 1994. *Max Found Two Sticks*. New York: Simon & Schuster.

Summary:
Max makes music with the two sticks he finds.

Activity:
Pull out your rhythm sticks or anything similar, like straws, plastic spoons, or craft sticks. Let the children beat out the rhythms as Max does when he beats to the sound of a band, church bells, a train, and more, playing sounds like "THUMP-DI-DI-THUMP!" and "Di-di-di-di. Dum-dum." Follow with more rhythm stick games or songs. When Max finds his own sticks, let the children find their own sticks, which you have placed around the room.

Pinkwater, Daniel. 1972. *Bear's Picture*. New York: Holt, Rinehart and Winston.

Summary:
Bear paints a picture.

Activity:
As bear paints different colors, do the same with markers or crayons on

a board or poster for the children in the group to see. Alternatively, give the students each a piece of white paper and crayons to create their own pictures, or have them take turns coming to the front of the room to draw what bear draws.

———. 1998. *Rainy Morning*. Illus., Jill Pinkwater. New York: Atheneum.

Summary:
A man and woman keep letting animals and people come in out of the rain and into their home.

Activity:
Each time an animal or person is let into the home of Mr. and Mrs. Submarine, invite a different child to come to the front of the room. You could also form a circle and let them enter the center, or section off an area with chairs, or even use a tent.

Pizer, Abigail. 1990. *It's a Perfect Day*. New York: Lippincott.

Summary:
Animals wake up and say what they will do on a perfect day and make their animal sounds.

Activity:
When each animal makes a sound, ask the children to repeat it. "It's a perfect day to crow, thought the rooster. Cock-a-doodle-doo!" Then have the children repeat "Cock-a-doodle-doo." The story continues with a bee buzzing, cat purring, cow mooing, duck quacking, pig oinking, mouse squeaking, goose honking, dog woofing, and horse neighing. The extra fun part is that after each page with a new animal, all the animal pictures and sounds to that point are shown, adding the new one each time. Point to the pictures and have the kids repeat all the sounds with you, or use puppets or stuffed animals to point to so the children can see better. You could also assign specific sounds to different children.

Plourde, Lynn. 1997. *Pigs in the Mud in the Middle of the Rud*. Illus., John Schoenherr. New York: Blue Sky.

Summary:
A car can't cross the road because a family of pigs is stuck in the mud.

Activity:
Use a pig puppet or picture and call the children up one at a time as the characters in the story try to move the pigs. Let the children act out the motions of shooing and the sounds of clucking, for example. Children can also repeat the rhyme, "Oh no. Won't do. Gotta shoo. But who?" Place a pig puppet or toy in the fake road or just use a picture of a pig. The characters you will need include grandma, brother, sister, mama, and papa. If you think more children will want to participate and you won't be using any other stories involving them, use them as the other animals that soon get stuck in the road with the pigs, such as hens, sheep, and bulls. Alternatively, make it a game and have half the children as animals on one side of the room and the other half as humans on the other side, bringing them to the center when it is their turn to appear in the story. Provide them with nametags that have the names or pictures of their characters so you know whom each child represents and you can better arrange them in the center.

Pollock, Penny. 2001. *When the Moon Is Full: A Lunar Year*. Illus., Mary Azarian. Boston: Little, Brown.

Summary:
Poems are provided for each month of the year.

Activity:
Have a large calendar in the front of the room and when you read each month of the year in the book, ask a child to check off that month on the calendar. Alternatively, you can use a regular-sized calendar or give each child a copy of a small calendar. For older children, play bingo by making bingo cards with all the months of the year, allowing every child to be a winner. You can also ask the children what kind of moon appears for each month by the pictures in the book. For example, January is the wolf moon. They should see the picture of the wolf and answer "wolf." You may need to do the first one yourself as an example until the children understand that the pictures match the type of moon. For example, February is the snow moon and shows snow, and March is a sap moon with buckets collecting sap from trees, etc. They may need help with some of the pictures, and you may need to point things out to them. The last two pages provide the answers to questions that you may want to share with the children as well. Or you may want to ask these questions and see what creative answers the children come up with on their own.

Pomerantz, Charlotte. 1989. *Flap Your Wings and Try.* **Illus., Nancy Tafuri. New York: Greenwillow.**

Summary:
A baby bird learns to fly and tries to encourage others.

Activity:
Simply flap your wings as if you were trying to teach the children in the class to fly. Then finish the story as all the children follow you around in a circle or every which way and pretend to flap their arms like birds.

Porter, Sue. 1989. *One Potato.* **New York: Bradbury.**

Summary:
Animals have contests to win the last potato.

Activity:
While you could let the kids perform the contest games from the stories, the stunts may be too dangerous, such as balancing on a chair, standing on your head, and running up and down to the hayloft. So instead, substitute your own activities, such as, whoever can stand on one foot the longest or run in place the fastest is the winner. You could also add other competitions at the end of the story.

Poydar, Nancy. 1994. *Busy Bea.* **New York: Margaret K. McElderry.**

Summary:
Bea always loses things and can't find them.

Activity:
Make pictures of all the objects Bea loses in the story, including her lunch box, jacket, raincoat, umbrella, a note, a sweater, and knitting needles. Tape them around the room. Ask the children periodically if they can think of where the objects might be found. Alternatively, place the lost items in a box representing the lost and found, and when Bea finds the missing objects in her school's lost and found ask children to take turns picking one of the objects out of the box and telling the group what they found.

Price, Hope Lynne. 1999. *These Hands*. Illus., Bryan Collier. New York: Hyperion.

Summary:
The book shows the many things hands can do.

Activity:
Have the children pretend to do the things mentioned in the book with their hands. First, ask the kids to hold up their hands, then read the story and act out with your hands what they should do. For example, for "These hands can touch," touch your hands or legs. For "These hands can feel," feel the floor. Stretch, reach, pat, tug, and more. Finally, ask your group what else they can do with their hands.

Price, Mathew, and Jean Claverie. 1985. *Peekaboo!* New York: Knopf.

Summary:
A family plays peekaboo with a baby in this simple pop-up book.

Activity:
Showing the pop-ups as the mother appears behind sheets and father from behind a newspaper will be exciting enough for young children. But you can also ask questions like those in the book. "Where's mommy?" Instead of just showing the pictures, make sure you wait for a response from the children. Then, when the book is finished, pass around a book, blanket, or another object for each child to play "peekaboo." As the child comes to the front or stays seated, ask the rest of the group, "Where's (insert child's name)?" Wait for them to reply.

Raschka, Chris. 1992. *Charlie Parker Played Be Bop*. New York: Orchard.

Summary:
Different sounds share the music of Charlie Parker.

Activity:
When reading the musical sounds, have children repeat them after you, such as "Fisk, Fisk," "Boomba, Boomba," and "Boppitty, bibbitty, bop. BANG!" They can sway and move around as well. You could also give them musical instruments or rhythm sticks to play along.

———. 2000. *Ring! Yo?* New York: Dorling Kindersley.

Summary:
Two young people have a telephone conversation.

Activity:
You need two telephones for this one. No one will know if you temporarily disconnect the phones in the children's department or media center. Either have a child hold the book while you go back and forth putting a phone up to each ear pretending to be the two kids in the story, or use two children and give them the phones to pretend they are having the conversation. It is simple one-word conversation. The end of the book gives two possible explanations for the conversations that took place. Two librarians or volunteers could use this as a script. Without the phone, do something similar for Raschka's *Yo! Yes?* (New York: Orchard, 1993).

Raschka, Chris, and Vladimir Radunsky. 2001. *Table Manners: The Edifying Story of Two Friends Whose Discovery of Good Manners Promises Them a Glorious Future.* Cambridge, Mass.: Candlewick.

Summary:
A silly way to present table manners.

Activity:
The book can be confusing for a storytime because the words are scattered about on each page. However, you don't have to read all the text, or at least not in any particular order. Instead of reading the text, you can ask questions. For the first scenario, for example, where a table setting is offered, ask, "Why do you need a spoon? Fork? Knife? Glass? Plate? Napkin?" See what responses you get. Or display a table setting of plastic utensils and a paper plate and see how they arrange it; then show the proper arrangement. Perhaps even mix it up and ask them if it is correct. If you ask the questions, the next page will show you silly answers, such as what would happen if you did not use a fork, etc. You can also ask how they would eat without such utensils. The following page tells you what a napkin is not. Give these examples, such as a parachute and flag, and ask the children for more. The next page shows how to fold a napkin. At this point, give each child a napkin and ask him or her to fold it in any way they like. The following pages show what happens when you do not chew your food, showing a whole watermelon in

a stomach. Ask the kids what else might happen. A few pages later there are two pages filled with questions. Ask all or some of these to get responses. For example, "What do we eat when we first get up? What do you eat when you come home from school?" Next is dessert. At the bottom of the two pages there are different objects to "check off" your selection. Instead, ask the children which they would prefer and take a vote. Choices include chocolate, gummi-bear pie, cake, Cinderella Jell-O, and pudding. Words follow that you might use in other countries; the children can repeat them. Finally, at the end, there is a four-question multiple-choice quiz that you can use to ask the children more questions. Take another poll.

Rathmann, Peggy. 1994. *Good Night, Gorilla*. New York: Putnam.

Summary:
A zookeeper says good night to all the animals as they follow him home.

Activity:
Instead of reading the animal names, pause and point at the pictures so the children can say the animal names in the story. Since there are few words, especially as the animals follow the zookeeper home, ask the children what they think is happening.

———. 1995. *Officer Buckle and Gloria*. New York: Putnam.

Summary:
Officer Buckle stops doing his safety show when he realizes the applause was all for his trick dog.

Activity:
Use a dog puppet or stuffed animal or even a picture of a dog and keep having it pop out from behind you or from behind the book. You could attach it to a string and flip it around. Pretend you don't see it even though it will most likely be in your hand. Do this during the parts of the story where Gloria does her tricks. Begin with a list of safety lessons of your own, especially for the classroom or library. In the end, make your dog do some more tricks.

Reeves, Howard W. 1998. *There Was an Old Witch*. Illus., David Catrow. New York: Hyperion.

Summary:
Like the old lady who swallowed a fly, the old witch finds scary creatures.

Activity:
This will be similar to the activities for the story *The Old Woman Who Swallowed a Fly*. Use a witch hat, and instead of putting things in the hat, pull them out of the hat. Place the following objects or pictures inside: cat, creature, mummy, skeleton, a haunt or ghost, and bat. When the witch conjures, creates, or unearths these things, pull them out of the hat at the appropriate times. Alternatively, put pictures of these objects around the room and ask the children to point to them when you read them in the story.

Regan, Lara Jo. 2001. *What Is Mr. Winkle?* New York: Random House.

Summary:
Pictures are shown of the dog Mr. Winkle in costume.

Activity:
Each page shows Mr. Winkle in a different costume. Below each photo is a question about whether Mr. Winkle is really what he represents in the photos. For example: "A Dashboard ornament?" "A Laboratory Creation?" "A Hamster with a Perm?" "An Alien?" Ask the children these questions to see what they think the dog is. According to Mr. Winkle's Web site, he is real and not a stuffed animal, as one might think, so the questions come from people who have seen him. At the end, ask the children which representation best fits Mr. Winkle. You might want to tell them at the beginning that you will be asking this so they are better prepared to answer, or show them the pictures again at the end of the book. Watch the video, too, if possible, after you have asked the children if Mr. Winkle is real or a stuffed animal or something else. Tell them the story at the beginning of the book about how the author found the dog.

Reid, Rob. 1996. *Wave Goodbye*. Illus., Lorraine Williams. New York: Lee & Low.

Summary:
Shows different ways of waving, especially with different body parts.

Activity:
Have the children act out the different waves, such as "Wave your belly and derriere." Kids can try to shake their tummies and behinds like the children in the pictures. With "Wave your elbows, wave your toes," kids can wave different body parts. In the end, everyone should get up and start shaking their bodies.

Rex, Michael. 2000. *My Race Car*. New York: Holt.

Summary:
A racecar driver prepares for a race.

Activity:
Let the kids pretend to get ready for the race as well. Have them pretend to put on their uniforms, take off for laps around the track, fill the car up with gas, lose control, and crash.

———. 2001. *The Pie Is Cherry*. New York: Holt.

Summary:
Different objects in a kitchen are described in basic detail.

Activity:
Instead of reading the many sentences, pause for responses from the children. "The sun is . . . ." The answer would be "up." "The garbage is . . . ." The answer is "smelly." "The lemon is . . . ." The answer is "yellow." There will be many guesses that are not necessarily wrong, so be sure to say that there are many possible answers. Look around the room for more ideas of ways to describe things. Let the children come up with their own situations too.

Reyes, Gregg, and Judy Hindley. 1987. *Once There Was a House: And You Can Make It!* Illus., Robert Bartelt. New York: Random House.

Summary:
Children make a house out of a box.

Activity:
Use this book if you have a large box in the library. You don't have to turn it into a house exactly as they do in the story or as in the instructions in the back. Just pre-cut or draw some windows and doors, a chimney, an antenna, gutters, pipes, shutters, a flower box, mailbox, and more out of paper. Let the children take turns putting them on the box, or do it yourself as you tell the story. You can draw very basic pictures at the last minute, or you could find the supplies shown in the book and use toilet paper tubes, hangers, egg cartons, etc.

Ringgold, Faith. 1999. *Cassie's Colorful Day*. New York: Crown.

Summary:
Cassie wears different colors and sees many colors on her day out.

Activity:
Cut out squares or circles of paper for the following colors: red, yellow, blue, white, green, black, gray, brown, purple, orange, and pink. These colors are enlarged and in capital letters in the story. Give each child a color. Several children can have the same color, or each child can have more than one color if necessary. Instruct the children to stand up when their colors are read in the story. They could hold up their colors instead if you give them a crayon or colored square or circle. They could also perform different actions as well.

Robins, Arthur. 1998. *The Teeny Tiny Woman: A Traditional Tale.* Cambridge, Mass.: Candlewick.

Summary:
A teeny tiny woman finds a bone and a voice asks for it back.

Activity:
Play a game in which the children perform an action every time a word

is spoken. Each time you say "teeny tiny" have the children do something like pinch their fingers together or pat their hands downwards to show something is tiny. Otherwise, have them stand up and sit down each time they hear the words. This has also been a great book for storytelling.

Rockwell, Anne. 1997. *Halloween Day*. Illus., Lizzy Rockwell. New York: HarperCollins.

Summary:
Kids show off their Halloween costumes.

Activity:
If you have the hats used in the story (cat, pirate, fire fighter, witch, cowboy, pumpkin, dragon, clown, robot, and super hero) or something that represents them, put one on your head or a child's head as you come to that costume in the story. You yourself can wear the princess or wizard hat and use your magic wand. End with treats like cookies or cupcakes. Alternatively, ask the children what costumes the children on each page are wearing and what they are supposed to represent.

Rodgers, Frank. 1990. *Doodle Dog*. New York: Dutton.

Summary:
A boy draws the dog he wants and it comes to life.

Activity:
Give children a piece of paper and let them draw the dog of their dreams. After the story is read or paraphrased, ask the children what they would do with their new dogs. You could also ask the children if they think Doodle was a real dog, magic, or a dream. Bring out a real dog or a dog puppet that looks real to make their dreams come true.

Rohmann, Eric. 1994. *Time Flies*. New York: Crown.

Summary:
A museum's dinosaur collection disappears as the dinosaurs come to life.

Activity:
This is one of those wordless books that encourages you to ask the children for help with the story. You could simply just show the pictures and let them think. You could also just occasionally ask what they think

is happening. For older kids, turn it into a writing assignment and they can create their own story.

Root, Phyllis. 1998. *One Duck Stuck*. Illus., Jane Chapman. Cambridge, Mass.: Candlewick.

Summary:
Different animals try to save a duck stuck in the muck.

Activity:
Every time you read the phrase, "Down by the marsh, by the sleepy, slimy marsh, one duck gets stuck in the muck, down by the deep green marsh," the children automatically repeat, "Help! Help! Who can help? We can! We can!" The story continues to show an increasing number of different animals who try to help the poor duck. Then ask the children to identify what the next animal will be who tries to help, and ask how many of each animal there are.

————. 1998. *What Baby Wants*. Illus., Jill Barton. Cambridge, Mass.: Candlewick.

Summary:
People keep bringing things to make the baby stop crying.

Activity:
Wrap a baby doll, stuffed animal, or puppet in a blanket and pretend to make it cry. Keep asking children to come up to pretend they have the items in the story that might make the baby stop crying. Start crying immediately after the child gives the baby the item. They will pretend to offer flowers, a goose, cow, sheep, tree of birds, and finally a lullaby. You could also find pictures or toy animals to give to some of the children. Alternatively, you could leave the book aside and have the children each take a turn, either after the book examples are used or in place of them, and offer their own original objects of choice to the baby, making the last one offered the one that will stop the baby from crying.

Rose, Emma. 1997. *Pumpkin Faces: A Glowing Book You Can Read in the Dark*. Illus., Judith Moffatt. New York: Scholastic.

Summary:
Shows pumpkins making different faces that glow in the dark.

Activity:
Hold up each double-page spread and ask questions such as, "Is this a jolly or happy face?" Do the same for the next pictures, including silly and mad, skinny and fat, dog and cat, and small, big, or in between.

Rosen, Michael. 1996. *Michael Rosen's ABC*. Illus., Bee Willey. Brookfield, Conn.: Millbrook.

Summary:
Poems and pictures represent the letters of the alphabet.

Activity:
It would take too much time, and be too long for a child's attention span, to read the poems for each letter. Instead, just use the book as a starting point for a discussion on the alphabet. Show the pictures for each letter and ask the children what objects or words they can think of that start with each letter. Even though the pictures are small, they will be able to see some and get some ideas. You could also put different puppets, toys, objects, or pictures around the room to give them some help. Teachers may wish to read a poem or two a day when they introduce new letters.

Roth, Carol. 1999. *Ten Dirty Pigs; Ten Clean Pigs: An Upside-Down, Turn-Around Bathtime Counting Book*. Illus., Pamela Paparone. New York: North-South.

Summary:
A counting book that flips upsidedown for two separate stories about dirty and clean pigs.

Activity:
Instead of reading the book as written, turn the statements into questions. For "One dirty pig gets into the tub," show the picture to the children and ask, "How many dirty pigs get into the tub?" This will be repeated ten times. Then flip the book over for ten clean pigs. You could also turn this into a flannel board story by copying 20 pig pictures, 10 plain and 10 with colors scribbled on them.

Rotner, Shelley, and Richard Olivo. 1997. *Close Closer Closest*. New York: Atheneum.

Summary:
Pictures of objects go from far away to close-up.

Activity:
Go backwards when showing this book to the children. Instead of showing the far away object first, show the right side of the double-page spread first, where the object is close. Fold the book to hide the left side and ask the children what they think each picture is. They are all quite difficult. Then reveal the left side, and the children will call out what the picture really represents.

Ruben, Patricia. 1978. *True or False?* Philadelphia: Lippincott.

Summary:
Photographs are used to ask true or false questions.

Activity:
The activity is already set up for you in this book. A statement will be made with an accompanying picture and the question, "True or False?" Ask the children if they think the statement is true or false from looking at the picture. If a statement reads, "John and Ben look very happy in this picture. Is this true? Or is it false?," you can follow with the question, "How do they look?"

Rylant, Cynthia. 2001. *The Great Gracie Chase: Stop That Dog!* Illus., Mark Teague. New York: Scholastic.

Summary:
Gracie the dog runs away from home and no one can catch her.

Activity:
Have the children stand up and help you chase after Gracie the dog. You can add things according to the pictures, like, "And the painter chased him, and sanitation chased him, and the hot dog vendor chased him, and the school children chased him, and the whole town chased him." Ask the children to run in place faster as Gracie continues on the run. Last of all, have the children lie down for a nap.

Saltzberg, Barney. 1996. *Phoebe and the Spelling Bee*. New York: Hyperion.

Summary:
Phoebe and her friend try to remember words for the spelling bee.

Activity:
This is definitely for older children and probably best for classroom use. As you read the story about Phoebe and Katie's practice spelling words, ask the class how they think the words should be spelled. You can write them on the board yourself or ask kids to write them. Use the hints from the book to remember the words. Give a "fun" spelling test afterwards for no credit, just to see if the book helped them remember the words. For younger children, give them letters to scramble and form words from instead.

Sampson, Michael, and Mary Beth Sampson. 1996. *Star of the Circus*. Illus., Jose Aruego and Ariane Dewey. New York: Holt.

Summary:
Animals assert that they are each the star of the circus.

Activity:
Ask the children to come up one at a time, perform a circus move, and say "I'm the star of the circus!" Then you can use the names in the story and reply back to the children, "No, you're not said Zany Zebra." You will have to make up more animal names for a larger group. In the end, have them all repeat together, "We're all stars of the circus!"

Samton, Sheila White. 1997. *Ten Tiny Monsters: A Superbly Scary Story of Subtraction*. New York: Crown.

Summary:
Ten monsters try to scare animals to make the team.

Activity:
There are two ways to approach this book. The first would be to bring ten kids up to the front of the room and have one sit down each time a monster is unsuccessful at scaring an animal. Ask the child to yell "Boo!" at another child sitting down to try to scare him or her. Naturally this will not work and the child will sit down. You could also do a basic flan-

nel board story with ten monster pictures and remove one at a time yourself or with the help of a child. Have the children remain seated and
yell "Boo!" at appropriate times when you give the signal.

**Santoro, Scott. 2001. *The Little Skyscraper*. New York: Price Stern
   Sloan.**

Summary:
A skyscraper that once was the tallest in the city starts to feel bad as
larger buildings grow around him.

Activity:
Let the children be the buildings in this story. First choose someone as
the little skyscraper, maybe giving him or her a funnel, colander, or
rolled-up paper to wear on his or her head. Have some children squat
down as smaller buildings. As larger buildings start being created in the
story it reads, "taller and taller." Have other children raise their hands
above their heads, stand next to the little skyscraper to show the bigger
buildings being built, and have the little skyscraper start to squat down.
You could even provide signs that say "Save the Little Skyscraper" at the
end of the story when people rally to stop the little skyscraper from being torn down for something bigger.

**Sawicki, Norma Jean. 1989. *The Little Red House*. Illus., Toni
   Goffe. New York: Lathrop, Lee & Shepard.**

Summary:
Different colored houses are found within one another.

Activity:
Copy or cut out shapes of different colored houses. Put them behind
one another in order of size. You could also make them all the same size.
Remove them one by one as in the story. You will need these colors in
this order to follow the story: red, green, yellow, brown, blue, gray,
purple, orange, and white. Put a picture of a bear behind the last one.
You will not need to use the book, only show it, if you tell the story in
this way.

Scamell, Ragnhild. 1998. *Toby's Doll's House*. Illus., Adrian Reynolds. London: Levinson Books.

Summary:
Toby wants a doll house, but no one believes him, so for his birthday he gets a fort, car park, and farm. He then makes his own house out of the boxes.

Activity:
Get a box, or several, and allow the children to help Toby make a house. Give them pictures of people and furniture and let them take turns taping the pictures inside. During the earlier part of the story you might also want to ask if the children think Toby is happy with the presents he received from his relatives.

Schaefer, Carole Lexa. 1996. *The Squiggle*. Illus., Pierr Morgan. New York: Crown.

Summary:
While walking with her class, a child finds a string and turns it into many things.

Activity:
Wave a piece of string, yarn, or ribbon around as you tell the story. It would be even more fun if you gave each child a piece of his or her own. Scarves, streamers, or ribbons work best. Then have them pretend it is a dragon dance, a wall, an acrobat, fireworks, a thundercloud, a pool, and a moon. At the end, let the children each have a turn at what they think the string could be. For extra fun, play music and let them dance around with the string.

Schmeltz, Susan Alton. 1982. *Pets I Wouldn't Pick*. Illus., Ellen Appleby. New York: Parents Magazine.

Summary:
A girl describes the good and bad of many pets.

Activity:
After you read each description of why the narrator believes each pet can be good or bad, ask the children if they would want that animal as a

pet. You will be asking about a frog, mice, a pig, an owl, bat, spiders, fleas, dog, goats, moles, beavers, seals, elephants, bears, alligators, crocodiles, porcupines, buffaloes, walruses, chimpanzees, wasps, bees, hippos, kangaroos, aardvarks, eels, gnus, whales, giraffes, koala bears, and hedgehogs. In the end, ask the children which they prefer. For more discussion, ask older children to name some pros and cons for some or all of the animals.

Schneider, Howie. 2000. *Chewy Louie*. Flagstaff, Ariz.: Rising Moon.

Summary:
A new dog in the family eats everything in sight until the day they are about to get rid of him.

Activity:
Use a dog puppet whose mouth opens and closes. Distribute to the children pictures of objects the dog eats or paper with the names of the objects written on them. Even if the children cannot read, you can at least see whose turn it will be next. You can also place the names of objects in a pile or tape them to a wall, board, or table, and give them out to whomever you call on next. The children will then take turns putting it in the dog's mouth as you snap the puppet's mouth over the child's object and maybe even over his or her hand. If you do not have a dog puppet, substitute a picture of a dog's head over two pieces of cardboard or poster board glued together on the edges (except for the top) with a hole for the mouth, so the children can slide the food into the dog's mouth. You will need pictures of the following items: food, bowl, trains, train station, porch, wood or a truck, guitar, and party food or supplies. If you have more children than objects, make extra food, a second bowl for when Louie gets a replacement, and multiple items from the party, such as a paper plate, cup, hat, balloon, and noisemaker. Replace the words in the story with words for which you have props.

Schwartz, Amy. 1999. *How to Catch an Elephant*. New York: Dorling Kindersley.

Summary:
A girl follows her uncle's advice on how to catch an elephant.

Activity:
Have the children pretend to be elephants stamping and stopping as the

elephant in the story does numerous times. They can also perform some of the other elephant's action such as roaring, howling, jumping, and rolling.

Scieszka, Jon. 1989. *The True Story of the 3 Little Pigs.* **Illus., Lane Smith. New York: Viking.**

Summary:
The wolf tells his story of what really happened with the three little pigs.

Activity:
Every once in a while, ask the children if they think the wolf is telling the truth. It is best to introduce this tale by first reading, telling, or acting out the original version of *The Three Little Pigs.* After both stories are told, ask the children who they believe, and which story they believe is true.

Sendak, Maurice. 1963. *Where the Wild Things Are.* **New York: Harper & Row.**

Summary:
A boy travels in his imagination to where he is king of the wild things.

Activity:
When the boy arrives in the land of the wild things, have the children in your class or storytime hold up their arms and make claw hands while stomping around, pretending to be these monstrous creatures. They can sit down when the boy sails off for home.

Serfozo, Mary. 2001. *Plumply, Dumply Pumpkin.* **Illus., Valeria Petrone. New York: Simon & Schuster.**

Summary:
A tiger looks for a pumpkin and shows what he does with it.

Activity:
Cut pumpkins out of orange paper and display them around the room. Let the children walk around the room to choose a pumpkin, as Peter does in the story. When Peter turns his into a jack-o-lantern, give the children crayons or markers to make jack-o-lanterns of their own.

————. 1988. *Who Said Red?* Illus., Keiko Narahashi. New York:
Margaret K. McElderry.

Summary:
Different colors are demonstrated with the use of colorful objects.

Activity:
Put sticky notes on the pages of the book where the color changes. Ask
the children to name some colors. After they have each had a turn, reply, "Who said red?" or "Who said blue?" as in the book, only skip around
depending on the colors you hear. Make it a game, continuing as the
book does, and repeat, "Could it be you?" Then ask that child to find
objects of that color around the room. They can be things that you have
previously placed there or things that are already present. They can be
pictures that are taped to the walls or lying about the room, or they could
be actual toys and objects you have found. Then continue with colors
not in the book, using colors of things you have displayed in the room.
Otherwise, just have the children yell, "I did!" each time you ask who
said a different color.

Seuss, Dr. 1994. *Daisy-Head Mayzie.* New York: Random House.

Summary:
A daisy pops up on Daisy-Head Mayzie's head and others try to get rid
of it.

Activity:
Don a hat or headband with a flower on top and tell the story. Use the
children as the characters who try to get rid of the flower on Daisy's head;
ask them to be a florist and doctor, etc. Let the children make headbands
with flowers before or after the story is told so they can feel like the
main character in the story.

————. 1938. *The 500 Hats of Bartholomew Cubbins.* New York:
Vanguard.

Summary:
Bartholomew has only one hat but, strangely, more keep appearing on
his head every time one falls off.

Activity:
Place many hats on a stack on your head, and continue taking them off as you tell the story. Since the story is so long, it is better for storytelling than reading or paraphrasing. You could also use the children as other characters by letting one be the king and wear a crown, give another a horse puppet so he or she can be a guard, etc.

————. 1950. *If I Ran the Zoo*. New York: Random House.

Summary:
A boy describes the animals that would be in a zoo if he were in charge.

Activity:
As you come across each new creature in the story, ask the children what they think it is. Tell them the silly animal names from the story. You will probably need to summarize most of the story and focus on the new creatures. In the end, give the children pictures of the bottom of one of the animals and the top of another so that they can come up with their own creatures for the zoo. Let them tell the rest of the group the names of their new animals.

————. 1973. *The Shape of Me and Other Stuff*. New York: Random House.

Summary:
Different objects are made of different shapes.

Activity:
Although the book does not tell you what shapes the objects are, after you read a word like a "bed" or "bicycle," ask the children what shapes are in those objects. Help them along. You could also give them an envelope of different shapes and have them hold up the one they think most represents each object.

Seymour, Jane, and James Keach. 1999. *Boing! No Bouncing on the Bed*. Illus., Geoffrey Planer. New York: Putnam.

Summary:
Two kittens keep jumping up and down on the bed.

Activity:
Instruct the children to jump if you have them stand, or bounce if you have them sit, every time you read the word "Boing!" in the story. At the end, they can jump around the room. Make sure they stay still when you pretend to be the parents telling them to stop.

Shannon, David. 1998. *A Bad Case of Stripes*. New York: Scholastic.

Summary:
Because a girl won't eat lima beans she turns different colors when they are mentioned.

Activity:
Show some of the pictures, but for the most part tell the story without the book. Stop to ask the children what colors and shapes they would like to see Camilla change to. You could also cut stripes of different colored paper, make them into bracelets and pass them out to the children while you read the story, so they can feel striped, too. After the story, they can link colored chains together as a craft.

———. 1999. *David Goes to School*. New York: Blue Sky.

Summary:
Naughty David is constantly told what to do or what not to do.

Activity:
Instruct the children to pretend that they are the teacher and repeat all the phrases you read as if they were scolding David in class. They will say such things as, "Sit down, David!" and "Don't chew gum in class!" Alternatively, if you dare, you could ask the children to behave badly. First tell them to do things like talk without raising their hands or to stare out the window so you can say, "David, raise your hand!" and "Pay attention!" Use Shannon's *No, David!* (1998, New York: Blue Sky) the same way.

Sharratt, Nick. 1997. *The Animal Orchestra*. Cambridge, Mass.: Candlewick.

Summary:
Instruments make funny sounds in this lift the flap/pop-up book, and animals are discovered inside them.

Activity:
The story tells the sounds the instruments should make, but also the sounds they actually do make. If you read, "Turtle's tuba didn't go Oompah! Oompah! It went Tu-whit Tu-whoo!" follow by asking the children what animal they think is inside the instrument. Lift the flap and show the children if they were right. In the end, make all the sounds as the animals and their instruments pop up together.

Shepard, Aaron. 2002. *Master Man: A Tall Tale of Nigeria.* Illus., David Wisniewski. New York: Lothrop, Lee & Shepard.

Summary:
A man boasts that he is "Master Man" until he meets the real thing.

Activity:
Provide an empty bucket and let the children take turns trying to lift it as Master Man's baby does in the story. The children will lift it easily and pretend to be strong. You might provide other fake objects, like a dumbbell out of a pencil and Styrofoam balls, to test the kids' strength. The last page gives the author's Web site, which has a script for readers theater. This can be fun if you have volunteers who can help you tell the story in this way. Throughout the story, children can also help you yell "roar" and "quake," etc., as the rocks shake from the strong men and their fighting.

Shields, Carol Diggory. 1998. *Day by Day a Week Goes Round.* Illus., True Kelley. New York: Dutton.

Summary:
A family does particular activities on the different days of the week.

Activity:
Provide the children with a calendar. Under each day of the week, place or draw a picture that represents something that happens in the story on that day. Give the children markers, crayons, or bingo chips and, as you read the days of the week, have them mark off the day you mention. You could also do this on a large calendar instead by letting the children take turns or demonstrating it yourself.

————. 1997. *Saturday Night at the Dinosaur Stomp*. Illus., Scott
Nash. Cambridge, Mass.: Candlewick.

Summary:
All the dinosaurs gather for a dance party.

Activity:
Before you begin, ask the children how dinosaurs dance. Have them get
up and practice and take turns showing off their moves. Then, as you
read the story and as the dance begins, allow the children to dance like
dinosaurs. After the story, you might want to play some songs about dinosaurs and dance some more.

Siddals, Mary McKenna. 1998. *Millions of Snowflakes*. Illus.,
Elizabeth Sayles. New York: Clarion.

Summary:
Simple text shows a child's fascination with the snow that falls.

Activity:
Cut out lots of snowflakes from white paper and throw them over the
children as you read this short story. First bring out one, then two, etc.
Throw the rest out at the end, when there are millions. Since the story
counts to five snowflakes before going to millions, you could also keep
adding a snowflake to a board, one at a time.

Sierra, Judy. 1995. *The House That Drac Built*. Illus., Will
Hillenbrand. San Diego, Calif.: Harcourt Brace.

Summary:
This is a Halloween version of this cumulative tale.

Activity:
Draw or copy pictures to represent the creatures and objects in this book,
including a bat, cat, werewolf, manticore, monster, coffin, mummy, zombie, fiend, and children. As one attacks or chases the next, cover the picture with the next picture. Alternatively, make masks for the children to
represent the creatures, and have one child at a time come to the front
of the room and scare away the last child, who will then sit down. Best
for older groups not easily frightened.

Silver, Jody. 1981. *Isadora*. Garden City, N.Y.: Doubleday.

Summary:
At first Isadora seems to be embarrassed with her purchase of a red boa.

Activity:
Simply wear a feather boa and dance around with it while you read or tell the story. Allow the children to take turns wearing it or dangle it over them. Change the color of the boa in the story to match whatever colored boa or feathers you have.

Silverman, Erica. 2000. *Follow the Leader*. Illus., G. Brian Karas. New York: Farrar, Straus & Giroux.

Summary:
A boy and his brother play a game of follow the leader and perform many actions.

Activity:
You be the leader, and have the children follow behind you as you circle the room holding the book and playing the actions in the story. Walk, hop, skip, trot like a pony, squat like a frog, leap like a rabbit, fly like an eagle, run around in a circle, close your eyes with your arms out and circle around, reach high, drop to the ground, crawl, march, balance on one foot, pretend to juggle, climb, jump, swim, step, and freeze. When the younger brother wants a turn, let the children each take turns performing an action that the other children can follow.

Silverstein, Shel. 1964. *The Giving Tree*. New York: Harper & Row.

Summary:
A tree gives all she has so that she and a boy can be happy.

Activity:
Draw a tree on a chalkboard, dry-erase board, or paper, and erase the parts of the tree as it gives them away in the story. Younger children may not understand the story, but they will understand the tree slowly disappearing. Make sure to include leaves and apples in the drawing.

Simon, Norma. 1967. *What Do I Say?* Illus., Joe Lasker. Chicago: Albert Whitman.

Summary:
A book that demonstrates what to say in certain situations.

Activity:
Ask the children the question "What do I say?" after every statement and see if they can respond. For example, "Oh, oh! I bump somebody. What do I say?" The answer should be "Excuse me," although you will want to accept other appropriate answers as well. You may need to prompt them with other clues or by pointing to pictures.

Siomades, Lorianne. 1999. *The Itsy Bitsy Spider.* Honesdale, Penn.: Boyds Mills.

Summary:
The nursery rhyme of the itsy bitsy spider is illustrated as a story.

Activity:
Sing the song and have the children make hand gestures as you read the story and show the picture. Or, play a version of the song and let children sing along as you turn the pages.

Sís, Peter. 1988. *Waving: A Counting Book*. New York: Greenwillow.

Summary:
More and more people keep waving until there are 15.

Activity:
As you read the story, just ask the kids to wave back at you. Otherwise, you could have only the correct number of children stand and wave each time. You might want to ask their help in deciding how many of them should stand up.

Slater, Teddy. 1996. *Stay in Line*. Illus., Gioia Fiammenghi. New York: Scholastic.

Summary:
Twelve children line up in different formations.

Activity:
This works best if you have 12 children in your group, but you can use any number. Have the children line up in pairs, and then different groupings, as the story proceeds. After marching in twos, they can then line up in threes, in a line of four and eight, single file, in a row of six, a row of twelve, and in twos and threes. Additional activities are provided at the end of the story.

Sloat, Teri. 1999. *Farmer Brown Goes Round and Round.* **Illus., Nadine Bernard Westcott. New York: Dorling Kindersley.**

Summary:
Farmer Brown's animals get all mixed up and start making the wrong sounds after a twister.

Activity:
Give children nametags to represent different animals from the story with either the word (to help you) or a picture (to help them). You will need one or more cows, pigs, sheep, cats, mares, hens, goats, hounds, and donkeys. When the twister comes, tell them to all get up and spin around in circles and land in a different place from where they were sitting. When it comes time for the animals to make different sounds, make sure the child who is the cow oinks, the pig moos, the sheep clucks, etc. In the end, they will be asked to make the correct animal sound.

———. 1999. *Patty's Pumpkin Patch.* **New York: Putnam.**

Summary:
Patty plants pumpkin seeds and watches them grow in this ABC book.

Activity:
The story itself makes no mention of the alphabet. There are letters and the mini-pictures at the bottom of each page, and these have pictures of words that begin with each letter in alphabetical order. These pictures are also found within the story pictures. Therefore, if your group can easily see, show them the small pictures. Tell the names of the letters and ask what they see in the pictures that start with these letters. They will find ants and beetles in the picture for the first two pages, for example.

Slobodkina, Esphyr. 1940. *Caps for Sale*. New York: W. R. Scott.

Summary:
A peddler loses his hats to monkeys only to get them back again.

Activity:
Many storytellers use this classic tale with children. Follow their lead, and pile hats of different types on top of your head. If there is time and you plan to use the story often, make hats to match the colors in the book—gray, brown, blue, and red. Take them off when the monkeys steal them in the story and put them back on after the monkeys toss them down. Ready-made sets are available for purchase, as well.

Slote, Elizabeth. 1991. *Nelly's Garden*. New York: Tambourine.

Summary:
Nelly Dragon plants different flowers in her garden each month.

Activity:
For this book, give each child a small calendar. Let them circle the months as you read them in the book. You could also provide them with a sheet that has the names of each month and underneath pictures of the different flowers to color. Help younger children locate the months on a larger calendar on the wall.

Small, David. 1985. *Imogene's Antlers*. New York: Crown.

Summary:
Imogene wakes up with antlers on her head.

Activity:
Make antlers out of construction paper unless you already have some, which you can purchase during the Christmas season, and put them on for the story. Start hanging different objects on the antlers as the story is told. Put feathers on your head, instead, when Imogene turns into a peacock at the end. Turn this into a drawing story, and draw the antlers, adding new objects to go with the story. Kids can do the same on individual coloring sheets or can take turns approaching the board to add on to the big picture.

Smath, Jerry. 1979. *But No Elephants*. New York: Parents Magazine.

Summary:
A woman keeps buying pets except for elephants until one won't go away.

Activity:
A simple activity would be to instruct the children to say the phrase, "But no elephants!" when you point to them at the appropriate time in the story. Another option would be to let children be the different animals the woman buys and have them come up to the front of the room as the story progresses. Then, when the elephant enters and gets stuck in the floor, have all the children walk together as the elephant carries them all to a warmer place in the house. More fun if the kids can act out and make the sounds of the animals as well. Additional activities are suggested at the end of the book. Create new animals so all the children can participate.

Soto, Gary. 1998. *Big Bushy Mustache*. Illus., Joe Cepeda. New York: Knopf.

Summary:
A boy takes a costume mustache from school so he can be like his father.

Activity:
Cut out black construction-paper mustaches and tape them on the children's faces so they feel like they are part of the story. When the boy loses his mustache, show the children samples of mustaches you have made out of yarn or paper and ask if they think the teacher will believe that any of these could be the one he lost.

———. 1993. *Too Many Tamales*. Illus., Ed Martinez. New York: Putnam.

Summary:
Maria thinks she loses her mother's diamond ring in the tamales, so she gathers her family together to eat them all.

Activity:
Hide a picture of a ring or a plastic ring around the room somewhere

or under someone's desk or mat. When the children in the story eat the tamales, let your children help find the ring. Alternatively, roll up paper as fake tamales and give one to each child when the children in the story eat the tamales. Place a ring or picture of a ring in one of them, and see who finds it. Place a real ring on your own hand, and in the end show the children that the real ring was on your hand all along. In this case, you might not want to put a ring in a tamale; just place enough pictures of rings or toy rings around the room so the children can each find one when the story ends.

Spinelli, Eileen. 1981. *The Giggle and Cry Book*. Illus., Lisa Atherton. Owings Mills, Md.: Stemmer House.

Summary:
Rhymes tell of things that make you laugh and cry.

Activity:
The beginning starts with things that make you giggle. Ask the children if these things make them giggle. For example, "Does 'Ten tickled toes, one blowing a nose' make you giggle?" If they say no, yet are laughing, make sure you point that out. Do the same if they do not laugh when they say something makes them giggle. Also, see if their actions match what they say when you ask about things that make you cry, such as "Homeless kittens, misplaced mittens." Add some of your own and ask the children what else makes them giggle and cry.

———. 2001. *In My New Yellow Shirt*. Illus., Hideko Takahashi. New York: Holt.

Summary:
A boy pretends to be many different yellow things when he wears his yellow shirt.

Activity:
Try to wear a yellow shirt when reading this story. You might even cut or copy mini-tee shirt patterns that the children can tape on themselves or attach with string after coloring. Then when the page reads, "In my new yellow shirt . . . ," turn the page to reveal what the boy feels like. Ask the children what he feels like in his shirt instead of telling them, and they can answer according to what they see in the pictures. In the story the boy feels like a duck, lion, caterpillar, and daffodil. Then go

around the room and ask children to tell you something they would like to be that matches the color shirts they are wearing.

Spohn, Kate. 1989. *Clementine's Winter Wardrobe*. New York: Orchard.

Summary:
Clementine decides what to wear to go outside in the winter.

Activity:
On each double-page spread, one page has a variety of different colors and styles of an article of clothing. When Caroline looks in her closet for something like long johns, ask the children which she should pick. It doesn't even matter if they cannot see the pictures. They can just shout out different colors or patterns. You could also have a pair already cut out and decorated to put on a board. Do the same for the shirts, jumpers, sweaters, socks, necklaces, boots, coats, scarves, hats, and mittens.

————. 2000. *Turtle and Snake and the Christmas Tree*. New York: Viking.

Summary:
Turtle and snake search for the perfect tree.

Activity:
Cut different shapes and sizes of Christmas trees out of green paper. Display them on a board and let the children help pick a tree just as the characters do in the story. You could also put more trees around the room so the children can then pick out one of their own in the end. They could even decorate it after storytime.

Steer, Dugald. 1999. *Just One More Story*. Illus., Elisabeth Moseng. New York: Dutton.

Summary:
Little mini-books inside the book help mother pig tell her child stories.

Activity:
Children will enjoy that there are mini-books within the book. You can make it more interactive, however, by giving the children choices. Turn it into a "Choose Your Own Adventure" story and flip the book around,

asking if the children want to hear *The Pig Prince, The Ugly Pigling, Piggerella,* or *The Prince and the Porker* first. If you get through all of them, ask the kids which they liked best. You could even make up some stories of your own after asking the children what kinds of stories they want to hear.

Steig, William. 1998. *Pete's a Pizza*. New York: HarperCollins.

Summary:
On a rainy day, Pete's parents turn him into a pizza.

Activity:
Ask a child to be Pete, make a poster-sized Pete and hang it on a board, use a stuffed animal or puppet, or use yourself. Then make him, her, or it—or yourself—into a pizza. Use the suggestions in the story: checkers as tomatoes, talcum powder as flour, and pieces of paper for cheese. Roll the "pizza" and pretend to put it in the oven. Follow with a pizza version of "Patty Cake Patty Cake." Use paper objects if no others can be found.

———. 1997. *Toby, Where Are You?* Illus., Teryl Euvremer. New York: HarperCollins.

Summary:
Toby hides around the house from his mother.

Activity:
This is better for small storytime groups because then the children can help you find Toby in the pictures. In each picture the parents look in one place while at the same time Toby is in another. When you read, "Is he up on the shelf?" have the kids respond "No!" and tell you where he is hiding. In this case he is under a lampshade. Before storytime or class, have one or more stuffed animals or pictures hidden around the room so kids can look for their own Toby after you read the book.

Steiner, Joan. 1999. *Look-Alikes Jr.* Photos, Thomas Lindley. Boston: Little, Brown.

Summary:
Scenes are made from everyday objects that represent new objects.

Activity:

Although this is better for small groups or individual reading, you could still hold up the book or walk around the room and ask what the children see. Ask, "What is the porch railing made of?" They may notice for the first time that it is actually made of candles. Do the same for a kitchen with a razor as a vacuum cleaner, a living room with a tambourine table, and other places or rooms in the house. Also use Steiner's *Look-Alikes* (Boston: Little, Brown, 1998), also with photography by Thomas Lindley.

Stevens, Janet. 1995. *Tops & Bottoms*. San Diego, Calif.: Harcourt Brace.

Summary:

A hare tricks a bear so that the hare gets all the good parts of the vegetables he grows.

Activity:

You will need vegetables for this story, either real, copies, or cutouts. When the hare tricks the bear by asking him to choose tops or bottoms and then plants only food that would grow on the opposite end, pull apart your vegetable to show how the trick works. Radishes, carrots, lettuce, broccoli, celery and corn are the hare's choices.

———. 1984. *The Tortoise and the Hare: An Aesop Fable*. New York: Holiday.

Summary:

A hare challenges a tortoise to a race.

Activity:

Ask the children to stand. Every time you read the word "hare" in the story, have the children run in place. Every time you read the word "tortoise" in the story, have the children tiptoe or walk very slowly. For fun, in the end have half the children running fast and half moving slowly when the tortoise wins the race. Follow with simple slow racing games, such as carrying a spoon with a ball to the finish line.

Stevenson, James. 1999. *Don't Make Me Laugh.* **New York: Farrar, Straus & Giroux.**

Summary:
Several animals tell you what not to do like laugh or hum or it will make them do something they are not supposed to do.

Activity:
This book is already set up for interaction. The characters speak to the readers and tell them not to do things. When the alligator tells you not to laugh or smile, walk around the room closely examining the children to see if they are laughing or smiling, as they inevitably will be. The waiter will ask readers not to make him laugh and especially not to touch the X on his belly. You can walk the book around and see if kids will touch the spot even after your warning, or put an X on your own belly and see if they dare. Then start laughing. When the elephant asks you not to breathe because it will make him sneeze, do exactly what he tells you not to do and ask the children to keep walking back further so they can breathe without making the elephant sneeze. When the hippo asks you not to sing, whistle, or hum, reinforce this with the kids. See if they do it anyway, which will make the hippo in the story dance and knock down the glass. The final activity brings back the alligator that asks you to put your nose to the book to see if you are smiling. Walk around and let the kids try it. You could also have another paper with an "X" marked on it and then tell the kids, as the story does, that their faces are too funny and break down in laughter.

Stickland, Paul. 1997. *One Bear, One Dog.* **New York: Dutton.**

Summary:
A different animal is added to the line on each page.

Activity:
Bring the kids up one at a time. Make each an animal: a bear, dog, mouse, frog, kitten, goose, monkey, moose, beetle, bee, and tiger. In the end when the last creature is "ME!" and there is a mirror at the back, walk around the room with the mirror so everyone can take a look at himself or herself in the book and they won't feel left out.

———. 1997. *Ten Terrible Dinosaurs.* **New York: Dutton.**

Summary:
Ten terrible dinosaurs keep losing members of their group one by one.

Activity:
Use children or dinosaur pictures for this book. You could invite ten children to the front of the room to be the dinosaurs, and send one back to his or her seat after that dinosaur leaves the scene in the story. You could also do the same with a flannel board story by cutting out ten dinosaur patterns and removing one at a time as they leave in the story. Children could also remove the dinosaurs from the board.

Stojic, Manya. 2000. *Rain.* **New York: Crown.**

Summary:
Animals warn each other of the rain that is coming.

Activity:
Use this book to play the telephone game. When each animal says it needs to warn another animal, ask a new child to whisper in the ear of someone next to him or her, "The rain is coming!" The book repeats the name of all the animals that have been told and now smell the rain. Point to the children whom you have asked to be these animals at the appropriate points in the story. It is best to put children in a circle. Alternatively, have the whole class yell, "The rain is coming," at the same time when you point to them.

Sturges, Philemon. 1999. *The Little Red Hen (Makes a Pizza).*
Illus., Amy Walrod. New York: Dutton.

Summary:
In this variation on the classic tale, Little Red Hen makes a pizza, but no one will help her.

Activity:
Have the children repeat "Not I" each time the hen asks for help. Towards the end ask the children what they think the animals say when she offers pizza and asks them to do the dishes. You could also draw a pizza on a chalkboard or poster board as you tell the story, adding different ingredients.

———. 1995. *Ten Flashing Fireflies.* **Illus., Anna Vojtech. New York: North-South.**

Summary:
Children catch ten fireflies and put them in a jar.

Activity:
There are many possibilities to make this story interactive. Get the children up and pretend to catch fireflies and put them in the jar. Give the children small circles of shiny or neon paper to represent the fireflies and they can put them in the jar. Alternatively, give them each a picture of a jar and have them draw a firefly in it as you tell the story. As a craft, give the children black or dark blue paper and have them dab white or yellow paint on it with paintbrushes or cotton swabs as you read the story and continue to add more fireflies. Make a jar out of paper for a flannel board or magnetic board and place fireflies in it or use shiny stickers. Turn out the lights and use glow-in-the-dark paint or stickers to represent the fireflies.

Szekeres, Cyndy. 1998. *I Can Count 100 Bunnies—and So Can You!* **New York: Scholastic.**

Summary:
More members of the family are added as 100 bunnies are counted.

Activity:
Each bunny is numbered. Count with the children after you read the text about the bunnies being added. Young children will not be able to count that high but they can repeat after you. Point to the bunnies as you count up to 100.

———. 1990. *Things Bunny Sees.* **New York: Golden.**

Summary:
Describes what Bunny sees.

Activity:
Instead of reading the names of all the things Bunny sees, pause to let the children answer. When the book reads, "Bunny sees little black things," ask "What does Bunny see?" or "What little black things does Bunny see?"

Taback, Simms. 1977. *Joseph Had a Little Overcoat*. New York: Random House.

Summary:
Joseph keeps using parts of his overcoat to make new things.

Activity:
Children will be interested in the cut-out pictures that show the new things Joseph makes. A simple activity would be to point to the new object and ask the children what Joseph made. After a couple times you will be able to just point and they will join in with words like scarf, tie, handkerchief, and button.

Tafuri, Nancy. 1988. *Spots, Feathers, and Curly Tails*. New York: Greenwillow.

Summary:
Questions point out the characteristics of different animals.

Activity:
Ask the questions to your children. "What has four spots?" Children will see a picture of half a cow, which will make answering easier. Flip the page and tell them "Yes, You are right. A cow has spots." Continue by using pictures or puppets of other animals and ask your own questions. You might also want to ask them what other characteristics the animals have or what color they are.

Taylor, Ann. 1999. *Baby Dance*. Illus., Marjorie van Heerden. New York: HarperCollins.

Summary:
A board book in which a dad helps a baby dance.

Activity:
Give children a stuffed animal or puppet or ask them to bring their own to class. Instruct them to pretend that the animals are their babies and have them hold them and move them to dance as in the story where the pictures show the dad lifting the baby high and low and around, etc.

Teague, Mark. 1995. *How I Spent My Summer Vacation.* **New York: Crown.**

Summary:
A boy describes his wild summer vacation as a cowboy.

Activity:
After each page or scenario stop and ask the kids if they think the boy really did all this on vacation. If they say "No," make sure you ask them if they are sure in the end when it is close to show-and-tell time and animals are peeking from the sides of the page. Use this to start a writing assignment on the same topic.

Thayer, Ernest Lawrence. 2000. *Ernest Lawrence Thayer's Casey at the Bat: A Ballad of the Republic Sung in the Year 1888.* **Illus., Christopher Bing. Brooklyn, N.Y.: Handprint.**

Summary:
The traditional story of how Casey strikes out at an important moment in the game.

Activity:
Set out storytime mats or any suitable objects as bases, give one child a ball, one a mitt, and another a plastic or inflatable bat, or anything else to resemble baseball equipment. Have them pretend to play the game as you read the story. This activity works best for older kids, but the younger ones do not have to follow exactly what is going on. Just tell them to pretend they are playing baseball, or you can urge them to copy the actions in the story. Use this idea with any sports story. Turn it into a reader's theater for older kids or when you have volunteers.

Titherington, Jeanne. 1986. *Pumpkin Pumpkin.* **New York: Greenwillow.**

Summary:
Shows how a pumpkin grows from seed to jack-o-lantern.

Activity:
Show the children pumpkin seeds or any seeds. Place them on the ground. Then cover the seeds with a sprout made out of construction paper. Cover the sprout with leaves. Then cover the leaves with a flower.

Then the flower with a pumpkin cut from paper that keeps growing and growing. If possible use poster board for the final pumpkin.

Toft, Kim Michelle, and Allan Sheather. 1997. *One Less Fish*. Illus., Kim Michelle Toft. Watertown, Mass.: Charlesbridge.

Summary:
A reverse counting book in which fish disappear from the Great Barrier Reef. Facts are included on each page.

Activity:
Better for a science lesson than storytime, this book can be depressing if children pick up on it. The idea is that the fish are disappearing because of possible environmental and human hazards. There are two ways this book can be used. The first is just to read the story with phrases like, "Twelve gracious angelfish thinking they're in heaven. Along came the divers—now there are . . ." Show the pictures and allow the children to count the fish on the pages or remember what number would come next in descending order. The second way to use it would be to create a flannel-board story or cut pictures of 11 fish and take 1 away each time. Many other creative possibilities exist in a classroom setting. For example, for older students, each individual or group could take a different page and explore the reason that the fish would disappear if what is mentioned in the story were to occur in the now protected Great Barrier Reef. For a stanza such as "Six striking tuskfish glad to be alive. Pesticides have killed one—now there are . . ." the students could explore pesticides. Other issues include fishing nets, drilling for oil, trash, feeding fish, and more. Students could study the different fish, such as Mororish idols, coral cod, fairy basslets, or surgeonfish. They could also draw the fish or other fish for an art project. The names of the fish and descriptions are listed in the back along with a glossary and a description of the silk painting technique used for the illustrations.

Tompert, Ann. 1977. *The Clever Princess*. Illus., Patricia Riley. Chapel Hill, N.C.: Lollipop Power.

Summary:
A princess does not want to choose a husband; instead she wants to rule the kingdom for herself, so she outwits them and gets her wish without magic.

Activity:
Because of the length of this story, it would be best to tell it rather than
read it. Focus on the different tasks the princess is asked to do to become ruler of the kingdom. Ask the children the riddles in the story and
see if they can get them. Ask how they would solve the problem of keeping like animals together. Then ask what the princess should do now that
she is ruler of the kingdom.

**Tunnell, Michael O. 1999. *Halloween Pie*. Illus., Kevin O'Malley.
New York: Lothrop, Lee & Shepard.**

Summary:
A witch bakes a pumpkin pie and everyone wants some.

Activity:
The best parts for interaction are the pages on which each of the creatures, the vampire, ghoul, ghost, banshee, zombie, and skeleton, say,
"Give me some pie!" Walk around the room and point to a child or tap
a child on the head and say, "Vampire, what did you say?" "Give me some
pie!" If they do not remember, you can whisper the phrase to them.

**Udry, Janice May. 1956. *A Tree Is Nice*. Illus., Marc Simont. New
York: Harper & Row.**

Summary:
There are many reasons why a tree is nice.

Activity:
The children can stand up with arms stretched out like a tree throughout the story. They can pretend to drop apples and provide shade, etc.
Afterwards, ask the children why they think trees are nice. Offer some
of your own suggestions. This could be a writing assignment for older
kids.

Vaës, Alain. 2001. *The Princess and the Pea*. Boston: Little, Brown.

Summary:
A princess uses her inheritance to win herself a husband.

Activity:
As with any version of this fairy tale, hide a small green circle beneath

one or all of the children's storytime mats or rugs or hide them around the room. Ask the children if they feel anything or if they had a good night's sleep; then ask them to look around wherever you have hidden the "peas." If you choose to have a child find the pea, let that child wear a necklace like the necklace worn by the princess in the story after he or she discovers it.

Vagin, Vladimir. 1998. *The Enormous Carrot*. New York: Scholastic.

Summary:
Many join in to pull a carrot out of the ground.

Activity:
Like other stories about enormous fruits or vegetables, use the children to help pretend to pull out the imaginary or fake carrot. Create a large carrot out of orange poster board or use bulletin board paper to roll a huge carrot and stick green paper out of the top. More simply, pretend to have an imaginary carrot or have a child either wear something orange or wear a construction-paper carrot hat to represent the carrot. Keep calling up children to be different characters in the story to help you pull the carrot out of the ground. You can change the names of the characters or use the ones in the story and add more.

Van Allsburg, Chris. 1995. *Bad Day at Riverbend*. Boston: Houghton Mifflin.

Summary:
A sheriff and the townspeople are perplexed over the strange lights and colors entering their town, which is actually a town in a coloring book.

Activity:
Give children paper and crayons to draw the actions in their own version of what is happening in the story. You could also hang a big sheet of white paper on the wall or board and color for them. Ask the children if they think someone colored in the book or if it is part of the story. Ask them if it is acceptable to color in library books or in coloring books. Older children will be better able to understand and use this story.

————. 1981. *Jumanji*. Boston: Houghton Mifflin.

Summary:
Strange things happen when children play a mysterious board game.

Activity:
Make a human board game. Just enough squares for the members of the class is fine. Or use storytime mats, carpet squares, or classroom seats or desks as the game squares. The game need be no more complicated than what is in the story. For example, when the book reads, "Lion attacks, move back two spaces," have all the children step back two spaces. Use dice, especially if you have large foam or fuzzy dice. You can have the children move the number of spaces you roll at the time. You can even let each child take a turn. Everyone is a winner in this game. Continue playing with situations you invent. Prepare a more elaborate game for an entire *Jumanji* program.

————. 1984. *The Mysteries of Harris Burdick*. Boston: Houghton Mifflin.

Summary:
Various pictures and captions give hints at stories.

Activity:
One of the purposes of these pictures, according to Van Allsburg in the "Introduction" is "the hope that other children will be inspired by them . . . ." As many have done in the past, continue to show the pictures to children and get their responses. Younger children can tell you what they think is happening in the pictures. Older kids can make up their own stories. Divide children in groups or give them each their own picture to write about, or let them choose their own if they are in a classroom. Show pictures of additional artwork to continue the exercise.

————. 1987. *The Z Was Zapped: A Play in Twenty-Six Acts*. Boston: Houghton Mifflin.

Summary:
The letters of the alphabet take the stage, then each disappears, is hidden, or is changed by something starting with the same letter.

Activity:
Show each letter picture and ask the children what is happening. They

may not answer with the exact word, as "avalanche" might not come to mind as rocks fall on the letter "A." They will, however, be able to note that rocks are falling and you can tell them it is an avalanche. Keep reminding them that the letters are mysteriously disappearing. You could also hide letters of the alphabet around the room and have children find them, or give each child a specific letter to locate. They can be from bulletin board decorations or written or printed on paper.

Vaughan, Marcia. 2001. *We're Going on a Ghost Hunt*. Illus., Ann Schweninger. San Diego, Calif.: Harcourt.

Summary:
Trick-or-treaters find scary things in their neighborhood to the rhythm of "We're Going on a Bear Hunt."

Activity:
Have the children line up behind you and walk around the room, stopping to pretend you see the scary sights in the book. You and the children will encounter a swamp, a haunted house, bats, a skeleton, a cave, and a ghost. You can also put props around the room so you actually do see what the children in the story see if you prefer. You will also keep repeating the following phrase with the children: "We're going on a ghost hunt to catch a trick-or-treat ghost. We're not afraid. No, we're not afraid. No, we're not afraid at all! Looking high. Looking low. Off on a ghost hunt. Here we go! Oh, dear. What have we here?" Then add the new scary creature or place found.

Viorst, Judith. 1972. *Alexander and the Terrible, Horrible, No Good, Very Bad Day*. Illus., Ray Cruz. New York: Atheneum.

Summary:
Alexander describes his terrible, horrible, no good, very bad day.

Activity:
Use this classic story by having the children repeat with you " . . . a terrible, horrible, no good, very bad day" after you start with "I could tell it was going to be . . ." They will catch on after a couple times. If not, you can explain to them what to repeat, or you can ask, "What kind of day is it going to be?" Follow by asking the children what would make a bad day for them.

**Von Konigslow, Andrea Wayne. 1997. *Would You Love Me?*
Toronto, Canada: Annick.**

Summary:
A child asks his parents if they would love him if he were a different
animal doing naughty things.

Activity:
Read this book in tandem with a co-worker or volunteer. One person
would read the first statement on each page, such as, "Would you love a
puppy that chewed up your sock?" and the other person would reply,
"Yes, I'd chase her down to the end of the block." If there is no one else
to read it with, ask the question of the children, having them reply with
a "yes" or "no" before reading the second statement.

**Vozar, David. 1998. *RAPunzel: A Happenin' Rap*. Illus., Betsy
Lewin. New York: Doubleday.**

Summary:
A take-off on the Rapunzel fairy tale in rap form.

Activity:
Simply rap the story. Children will follow more closely to this lengthy
tale if you move around and rap the story. Have the children get up and
dance with you. This may be better for school-aged children, although
preschoolers will be less likely to laugh at your rapping style.

**Waber, Bernard. 1966. *You Look Ridiculous, Said the Rhinoceros
to the Hippopotamus*. Boston: Houghton Mifflin.**

Summary:
Animals suggest changes to make the hippopotamus look less ridiculous.

Activity:
Although a hippopotamus can't really make all the changes the animals
suggest, and you only see the possibilities towards the end of the story
in a dream, you can make your own board story. Copy a picture of a
hippo. Then keep adding on the things the other animals suggest, such
as a horn, a mane, spots, big ears, a tail, a long neck, a shell, and a beautiful voice (music notes). Keep asking the children if they think the hippo

still looks ridiculous. Use this with *Arthur's Nose* by Marc Brown (1976, New York: Scholastic).

Waddell, Martin. 1992. *Farmer Duck*. Illus., Helen Oxenbury. Cambridge, Mass.: Candlewick.

Summary:
Animals take over a farm after the farmer makes the duck do all the work.

Activity:
When the duck does all the work at the beginning of the story, the phrase "The duck answered, 'Quack!'" is often repeated. Pause after reading, "The duck answered," and wait for the children to respond, "Quack." The other animal sounds needed in the story won't have obvious cues, so you may want to ask the children to repeat those sounds after you.

Wadsworth, Ginger. 1997. *One on a Web: Counting Animals at Home*. Illus., James M. Needham. Watertown, Mass.: Charlesbridge.

Summary:
A counting book that shares facts about different animals.

Activity:
Instead of reading the name of the next creature to the children, ask, "One what '. . . runs along the edge of her web?'" Then share with them some of the facts about each of the animals or insects, etc. Count with the children, as the numbers get higher than ten.

Wadsworth, Olive A. 1985. *Over in the Meadow: A Counting-Out Rhyme*. Illus., Mary Maki Rae. New York: Viking.

Summary:
Numbers show what the animals in a meadow might be doing that day.

Activity:
This book is fun when read really fast while making the animal noises in a high-pitched voice. It might be fun to walk around in a circle and bend your knees, along with the children, every time the words of the basic rhyme are repeated. "Over in the meadow in a nest built of sticks Lived an old mother crow and her little crows six. *Caw*, said the mother.

We *caw,* said the six. So they cawed all day in a nest built of sticks." On
the word "caw" you would bend your knees while speaking it in a higher,
screechy voice.

**Waite, Judy. 1998. *Mouse, Look Out!* Illus., Norma Burgin. New
York: Dutton.**

Summary:
A mouse searches for a hiding place from a cat.

Activity:
Ask the children to repeat the phrase, "Mouse, look out! There's a cat
about," each time it is read in the book. Point to pictures of the cat and
its shadow. You might want to say things like "Look" or "Uh-oh!"

**Wallace, Karen. 1997. *Imagine You Are a Crocodile.* Illus., Mike
Bostock. New York: Holt.**

Summary:
A crocodile does many things.

Activity:
Do just as the title suggests. Have the children crawl or slither on the
floor, pretending they are crocodiles. Most of the time they will just move
as they think a croc should, but they can also do things like duck their
head as the "crocodile sinks under water," clap their hands like a "jaw-
snapping crocodile," yawn, feign sleep, and dig, among other possibilities.

**Walsh, Ellen Stoll. 1989. *Mouse Paint.* San Diego, Calif.: Harcourt
Brace Jovanovich.**

Summary:
Mice get into some paint and mix it up to make new colors.

Activity:
For the story, have available red, yellow, blue, orange, green, and purple
markers or crayons. First draw the red, yellow, and blue. After the mice
start getting into the paint and mixing it up, ask the children what color
the mice will make when they mix yellow and red, blue and yellow, and
blue and red. Then draw that new color on the board. You can point to

the picture of the new color formed in the book. You could also hold up colors, but drawing it on paper is best since that is the canvas for the mice in the story.

Walters, Virginia. 1999. *Are We There Yet, Daddy?* Illus., S. D. Schindler. New York: Viking.

Summary:
A father teaches a boy to use a map on a trip to count the mileage when the boy keeps asking, "Are we there yet, Daddy?"

Activity:
There are two fun options for this story. One is simply to instruct the children to yell "No!" when the boy asks, "Are we there yet, Daddy?" and "Daddy says, 'No!'" Another would be to hang any road map up on the wall or a board or place it on the floor. Pretend to track the route in the story by drawing a line after every page to represent ten miles. You could also have the children draw a line to show how they interpret the mileage. Don't expect to have a usable map afterwards. You could also combine the two activities.

Walton, Rick. 1997. *Dance, Pioneer, Dance!* Illus., Brad Teare. Salt Lake City, Utah: Deseret Book.

Summary:
Animals and people dance on the pioneer trail.

Activity:
Get the children up and dancing. "Pioneer, dance. Pioneer, dance. Pick up your heels and hitch up your pants." "Pioneer, kick. Pioneer, kick. Do it high and do it quick." These are some of the phrases that can get children moving. Have them kick, bow, swing, move left and right, jump, hop, and more while telling the story. Follow with some square dancing music or play the music in the background while the story is told.

———. 2001. *How Can You Dance?* Illus., Ana López-Escrivá. New York: Putnam.

Summary:
Different obstacles to dancing can be turned into a dance.

Activity:
This makes a good follow-the-leader book. With book in hand, line up the children behind you and read the rhyming phrases. To start, "How can you dance when spring is in your shoes? Dance like the king of the kangaroos. Bounce, bounce, bounce, bounce, bounce, bounce!" and have the children bounce up and down like kangaroos behind you in a circle. This is followed by other such actions related to animals and people, such as spinning and hopping on one foot, pushing and pulling arms, waving arms wildly, stepping side to side, running, keeping in step, spinning, slowing down, wiggling, and drifting. Use all these actions as the story is read and the children continue to walk in a circle. They could also do this standing by their seats.

———. 2000. *Little Dogs Say "Rough!"* **Illus., Henry Cole. New York: Putnam.**

Summary:
Animals say words that sound like the animal sounds they make.

Activity:
Kids know a cat goes "Meow," but the book thinks they say "Me, me-you." After you read each pun on the sound, ask the children if that is really what the cats are saying. "What sound do they really make?" Kids who think that their pets talk will appreciate this game. Cows say "Moo-oon!" and doves go "Coooool!" in this story.

———. 2000. *My Two Hands/My Two Feet.* **Illus., Julia Gorton. New York: Putnam.**

Summary:
Two girls describe how they use their hands and feet.

Activity:
There are two stories here if you flip the book over. Just model for the kids what the girls in the story do and have them do it, too. With their feet they will wiggle, dance, prance, flap, stamp, twirl, move slowly, and lie still. With their hands they will stretch and yawn, wash, make a cup, hide, hold their hands, and fold them together.

————. 1995. *Once There Was a Bull . . . (Frog)*. Illus., Greg Hally. Salt Lake City, Utah: Gibbs-Smith.

Summary:
A bullfrog loses his hop as things are not as they appear to be each time you turn the page.

Activity:
Pause every time you turn the page and wait for children to finish the word. For example "He looked behind a dog . . ." Pause. The next page completes the phrase "dog house." See if the kids can guess the word. They may have different ideas and will have fun waiting to see if they are right.

————. 1997. *Pig Pigger Piggest*. Illus., Jimmy Holder. Salt Lake City, Utah: Gibbs-Smith.

Summary:
Three pigs build castles that three witches covet.

Activity:
Use a similar approach that you would use with the classic story of *The Three Little Pigs*. Three children can pretend to be pigs by wearing a pig nose you give them. Three children can pretend to be witches and wear hats, whether purchased or made out of black construction paper. Since the children will not be familiar with this version of the story, ask them to repeat the lines you read. So the witches will say "Bigger Pigger, bigger Pigger, let me come in . . . I am richer than anyone you know, and I want to buy your castle." "Not by the hair on your nosey-nose nose!" the pig will reply. "Then Huffer and Puffer will blow your house down!"

Ward, Helen. 2001. *The Tin Forest*. Illus., Wayne Anderson. New York: Dutton.

Summary:
A man sees the garbage around him and turns it into a forest of time sculptures that will attract others.

Activity:
The perfect story to start off a junk craft program or simply use this as

the craft for your storytime. Provide scraps of material, leftover craft pieces, cotton balls, craft sticks, toilet paper tubes, etc., and dump the materials on a table or on the floor. At the point in the story where the man begins to create from the scraps around him, ask the children to do the same, using the materials to create something. Then have them make a circle out of their objects and sit inside the circle, as if they had created *The Tin Forest*.

Washington, Donna. 2000. *A Big, Spooky House*. Illus., Jacqueline Rogers. New York: Hyperion.

Summary:
A big strong man thinks he is not afraid of anything, but he is wrong.

Activity:
Use storytelling for this book the way the author does according to her "Author's Note." Then when you point to the children, ask them to repeat, "He was a BIG man. He was a STRONG man!" Do this each time it appears in the story. You could even create symbols or actions, such as making a fist to represent "strong" and raising your arms to represent big.

Watanabe, Shigeo. 1979. *How Do I Put It On?: Getting Dressed*. Illus., Yasuo Ohtomo. New York: Collins.

Summary:
A bear tries to put on his clothes.

Activity:
You can do one of two things for this story. Read it and ask the questions that are part of the text. "This is my shirt. Do I put it on like this? No." Wait for the children to say no when they see the bear putting it on like pants. For the other activity, memorize the different ways bear puts on his clothes. Bring in a shirt and try pulling it over your legs. Ask the kids if you are putting it on correctly. Bring in pants and pull them over your head, put a hat on your feet and shoes on your ears. In the end, put everything on where it belongs.

Wattenberg, Jane. 2000. *Henny-Penny.* **New York: Scholastic.**

Summary:
Henny-Penny thinks the sky is falling and goes to tell the king, but the fox stops her and her friends along the way.

Activity:
Every time the animals say "shake, rattle, and roll! The sky is falling!" have the children shake and roll on the ground with you. Begin by tossing light balls, wadded-up paper, or other light objects to the children so they can experience the fake sky falling. You can also use the book *Chicken Little*, written and illustrated by Steven Kellogg (New York: Morrow, 1985) in the same way.

Weatherford, Carole Boston. 1996. *Me and the Family Tree.* **Illus., Michelle Mills. New York: Black Butterfly.**

Summary:
A boy describes the family members from whom he has received physical characteristics.

Activity:
Instruct the children to touch each part of their body as it is mentioned in the story, black wavy hair, a chin, ears, eyes, hands, cheeks, and nose. Then ask the children who they most resemble in their families. You could also hand children a piece of paper with a head shape drawn on it and have them draw the parts as you mention them in the story. For older children, follow with a family tree at the end. Even if they cannot write the names, they can draw pictures. Otherwise, just give them a family tree to take home and work on with their families. This is a simple board book.

Weeks, Sarah. 1998. *Mrs. McNosh Hangs Up Her Wash.* **Illus., Nadine Bernard Westcott. New York: HarperCollins.**

Summary:
Mrs. McNosh hangs up everything on a clothesline.

Activity:
Make a clothesline by tying the two ends of a long piece of string or yarn to two objects, such as two chairs. Purchase or use your own clothes-

pins. Give each child a clothespin with a picture of one of the objects in the story. The objects would include dresses, shirts, underwear, nightgowns, skirts, stockings, shoes, paper, news, the dog, a bone, a phone, a hat, a wedding gown, bats, a lamp, a Christmas wreath, teeth, a kite, mail, a turkey, and a chair. You can use other pictures or leave out some for which you have no pictures or which you choose not to use. Have children hang the pictures on the line.

Weiss, Nicki. 1989. *Where Does the Brown Bear Go?* New York: Greenwillow.

Summary:
Asks where animals go at night.

Activity:
The questions are already in the story. You can ask them of the children and await their responses. You will probably have to take out the word "honey" when you are reading to children who are not your own. "When the sun sinks far behind the seas, where does the seagull go, honey? Where does the seagull go?" Ask children where they think the seagulls and the other creatures in the story go.

Wellington, Monica. 1989. *All My Little Ducklings*. New York: Dutton.

Summary:
Ducklings follow their mother around.

Activity:
Get the children up and waddling like ducks in a line or in a circle while you pretend to be mamma duck. They can act out all the fun words in the story, such as "wiggle wiggle waggle" (walk funny), "scurry hurry plunk" (fall down), "wonder wander ramble roam" (leave line or circle), "pitter patter scatter" (run about), "hurry hurry quack quack" (move faster), as well as many others that involve moving and falling down.

———. 1997. *Night House Bright House*. New York: Dutton.

Summary:
In different rooms of the house objects make noise all night.

Activity:
Since this is a partial rebus story, small groups could look at the pictures

that you point to and yell them out. "'Slow down'," said the clown." Next to the word "clown" would also be a picture of a clown. If you really wanted to take the time, you could cut out patterns of all the pictures or draw them yourself and hang them around the room so older children can find matching objects. You could also do this as a bingo game and put the pictures on bingo cards for older kids to mark off when you say the words in the story. There are many pictures to choose from, 82 in all.

Wellington, Monica, and Andrew Kupfer. 1998. *Night City*. Illus., Monica Wellington. New York: Dutton.

Summary:
Things happen all through the night in a city long after bedtime.

Activity:
The story spends a page on describing what happens at each time of the night until morning when people wake up. Give children mini, store-bought paper or cardboard clocks to track the time. They could even make their own clocks out of paper plates, with cardboard hands, and brads that will enable them to move the hands. Children could take turns moving the hands of a larger clock at the front of the room. Otherwise, just give them a copied clock picture with no hands, but with numbers, and ask them to mark or point to the correct time depending on the moment in the story. You could also show the large, bright pictures and ask, "What do they do at 11:00?" Seeing the picture, the children will answer something like, "Put out a fire."

Wells, Rosemary. 1997. *Bunny Money*. New York: Dial.

Summary:
Ruby spends her money on a shopping trip for grandma's present.

Activity:
Give the children fake paper money. Every time Ruby spends a dollar or so, go around the room collecting the correct amount of money from each child. Each child will have 10 one-dollar bills and 1 five-dollar bill. This would be fun for children learning math or about money in school. The book even gives you permission to copy the bunny money on the front and back pages. It might be cute to also give each child an origami wallet, or have older kids make their own. To do this, take a square piece

of paper. Fold it into fours and unfold it. Fold two ends to the center lines. Now flip it over and fold the other long ends to the center lines. Fold this in half to make a wallet with two sections or pouches. Tape the bottom. Make a simple version by licking an envelope closed and cutting it in half. By punching holes and adding yarn or string, you can turn the two halves into purses. Put the money in the wallets ahead of time or pass it to the children during class, depending on the time.

————. 2001. *Bunny Party*. **New York: Viking**

Summary:
Ruby finds that some uninvited stuffed guests have attended her party.

Activity:
Prepare nameplates for Ruby and the ten guests, including Rapunzel, Curly Shirley, the Tooth Fairy, Mr. & Mrs. Quack, Pinocchio, Walky-Talky Teddy Bear, Max, and Grandma. Place them around a table or in a circle and sit stuffed animals or puppets in front of them. Use the children as the guests. Then sneak in more guests when Max does the same in the story.

————. 1975. *Morris's Disappearing Bag: A Christmas Story*. **New York: Dial.**

Summary:
Morris is disappointed with his Christmas present until he finds a disappearing bag under the tree.

Activity:
When the disappearing bag is found, put a blanket over yourself or another child to pretend you or the child is in the magic disappearing bag. Hide other children under the blanket when the brothers and sisters join in.

————. 2001. *Yoko's Paper Cranes*. **New York: Hyperion.**

Summary:
Yoko makes and sends paper cranes to her grandmother.

Activity:
Have a child, volunteer, or assistant hold the book as you fold paper

cranes right in front of the children's eyes. Use your volunteer or assistant for this purpose if origami is not one of your talents. You could also fold other origami objects. An extra treat for the children would be if you acted like a clown and gave each child a crane to take home rather than balloons. Older children can learn how to fold their own cranes at the end of the story, or they can fold along with you while the story is being read.

West, Colin. 1987. *The King's Toothache*. Illus., Anne Dalton. New York: Lippincott.

Summary:
A king has a toothache and Nurse Mary keeps bringing in people who cannot help him.

Activity:
When Mary brings a baker, town crier, and sailor, ask the children if they think each one will be able to help and how. They will probably not guess that it is actually the sailor who will be the one to get the king's tooth out pain free.

Whatley, Bruce, and Rosie Smith. 2000. *Captain Pajamas: Defender of the Universe*. Illus., Bruce Whatley. New York: HarperCollins.

Summary:
A boy pretends to be Captain Pajamas to save his sister from imaginary aliens.

Activity:
Put on a cape of any kind when the boy turns himself into Captain Pajamas in the story. You could also give scarves or paper towels or napkins to the children so they can pretend they are Captain Pajamas. Walk around the room with the kids as if you were sneaking around looking for aliens while you are all dressed in makeshift capes.

Whybrow, Ian. 1991. *Quacky Quack-Quack!* Illus., Russell Ayto. New York: Simon & Schuster.

Summary:
A baby boy is responsible for all the animals making sounds one day in the zoo.

Activity:
In the book's "Notes to Parents and Teachers" it reads, "Invite children to say aloud all the text in bold print, while you read the remaining words. Shared reading in this way is an ideal method to give young children confidence in themselves as readers." For a younger or larger audience, simply read the animal sounds in bold print and have the children repeat the sounds after you. They will yell "quacky quack-quack," "honk! honk!" "ee-aw! ee-aw!" "toot, toot," "woof! woof!" "sss-ssss!" "snap! snap!" "r-o-a-r!" "scream!" (the child's sound), "threw!" (the child throwing bread), and "YUM! YUM!" (the bird's eating the bread).

Wiesner, David. 1988. *Free Fall*. New York: Lothrop, Lee & Shepard.

Summary:
A boy's dreams are shown in pictures.

Activity:
Since there are no words to this book, use the activity parents have been using forever. Show the pictures and let the children tell you what is happening in the story. You might want to have a different child continue the story on each page so the story progresses with different ideas. End with the game where you start a story (different from the book) and let the children take turns adding to it.

———. 1992. *June 29, 1999*. New York: Clarion.

Summary:
Coincidentally, large vegetables fall from the sky after a girl launches her science-experiment seedlings into the sky.

Activity:
This is best if you have both volunteers and time. If possible make large poster board vegetables. Have the volunteers each hold one and emerge from their hiding place one by one as the vegetables are mentioned in the story. You would need turnips, spinach, cucumbers, lima beans, artichokes, parsnips, broccoli, peppers, eggplant, avocados, potatoes, and rutabagas. You could also just cut out or draw patterns of these vegetables. Make a large white cloud out of poster board with an envelope taped to the back and pull out the vegetables and drop them to the floor as mentioned in the story. You could also make several and toss them out to your audience.

Wild, Margaret. 2001. *Nighty Night!* Illus., Kerry Argent. Atlanta, Ga.: Peachtree.

Summary:
Baby animals keep tricking their parents by hiding where they shouldn't.

Activity:
Using different animals each time, the book has a mother or father say good night to his or her children. Only when they look closer, it is another animal. On the page where this is revealed, point to the pictures of the baby animals, look shocked, and turn back to the page of the parent. Ask the children if these are this animal's children. For example, "Do the pigs belong to this duck?" Then read the text. For example, "'Oink! Oink! Surprise!' said the piglets. 'You sassy scalawags! You're not my darling ducklings!' said Father Duck." You can repeat this for the sheep and chicks, hen and lambs, and pig and ducklings.

Williams, Linda. 1986. *The Little Old Lady Who Was Not Afraid of Anything*. Illus., Megan Lloyd. New York: Thomas Y. Crowell.

Summary:
A woman is followed by pieces of clothing until they form a scarecrow.

Activity:
Use this book for storytelling. In the story, when the shoes go "CLOMP, CLOMP," wiggle your feet. When the pants go "WIGGLE WIGGLE," shake your legs. When the shirt goes "SHAKE, SHAKE," move your torso. When the gloves go "CLAP, CLAP," clap your hands. When the hat goes "NOD, NOD," nod your head. When the pumpkin head comes and the full body appears at the door, do all the actions all at once. Kids can join in with you if you ask them to stand up. You could also turn this into a flannel board story and use patterns to add the parts of the pumpkin-head scarecrow together one by one, but the first option is more fun.

Wilson, Karma. 2001. *Bear Snores On*. Illus., Jane Chapman. New York: Margaret K. McElderry.

Summary:
Animals decide to have a party in the cave where a bear remains sleeping.

Activity:

There are several options with this book. The first would be to use stuffed animals or puppets to represent the animals in the story, a mouse, rabbit, badger, gopher, mole and, of course, the bear. Cover the bear in a blanket to show that it is sleeping and then bring out the animals one at a time. You could also do this with children as well. Another option is to just repeat words. Instruct the children that when you point to them, they simply repeat, "But the bear snores on." A final option is to instruct the children to snore every time you point to them at the appropriate point in the story. Towards the end of the story, the children can also act out and make the sounds the bear does when he is awakened.

Winthrop, Elizabeth. 2001. *Dumpy La Rue*. **Illus., Betsy Lewin. New York: Holt.**

Summary:

Dumpy La Rue is a pig that wants to dance despite her parents' warnings.

Activity:

Dance! Have the kids get up and start dancing during the story, just as Dumpy La Rue does. For more organized fun, let each child be an animal in the story. Some will be pigs, some turkeys, some cows, horses, mules, goats, and foxes. When you read that animal name in the story, have the children pretending to be those animals stand up and join Dumpy and her friends. Use pictures or make sure you remind children what characters they are.

Wisniewski, David. 1998. *The Secret Knowledge of Grown-Ups*. **New York: Lothrop, Lee & Shepard.**

Summary:

The "real" reasons grown-ups tell kids why they should do or not do certain things is revealed.

Activity:

First read a rule to the children, such as "Eat your vegetables." Ask the children why grown-ups want them to eat vegetables. If they do not give the "Official Reason" from the book, tell them what it is. Then, read them the truth according to the author. It is a long book for a storytime, so you may want to pick and choose a few rules to share. Then ask the kids to share some of the rules they have at home. A writing assignment might be to have the children make up their own rules and real reasons they exist.

Wong, Olive. 1995. *From My Window*. Illus., Anna Rich. Parsippany, N.J.: Silver.

Summary:
A boy describes the things he sees out his window.

Activity:
One double-page spread will read, "Looking down on the street." The text on the following spread will tell what can be seen and illustrate it as well. Instead of reading these words, point to the objects and have the children respond with what they see, such as snow, trees, tracks, people, trucks, and a friend. Children may respond with different objects as well, but keep pointing to pictures until their answer matches that of the books. Follow with questions about what the children see out their own windows or out the window in the classroom or storytime room.

Wood, Audrey. 2001. *Alphabet Adventure*. Illus., Bruce Wood. New York: Blue Sky.

Summary:
The little alphabet goes to school, but the little "i" loses his dot.

Activity:
For smaller groups the children could help look for the little "i" in the book. There are several other options for larger groups. You could provide an alphabet chart for children and allow them to touch or put a mark on each letter you mention in the story every time you say that letter. You could also provide them with only the letters mentioned by name in the story and have them hold up the correct letter each time. Alternatively, give each child in the group a different letter and have him/her stand each time you say that letter. The book indicates that in some scenes, particularly the party scene, all the letters big and small can be found. Smaller groups can locate all the letters. Use this with *Chicka Chicka Boom Boom* by Bill Martin, Jr. and John Archambault with illustrations by Lois Ehlert (New York: Simon & Schuster, 1989).

————. 1985. *King Bidgood's in the Bathtub*. Illus., Don Wood. San Diego, Calif.: Harcourt Brace.

Summary:
A king will not get out of the bathtub no matter what people do to make him get out.

Activity:
Put two pieces of poster board together or use two laundry baskets to pretend they are a single bathtub. You sit in or on one. Keep inviting children up to sit in the other as different people in the story try to get the king out of the tub. You could also make a circle with the children and make the center of the circle the bathtub.

————. 1984. *The Napping House*. Illus., Don Wood. San Diego, Calif.: Harcourt Brace.

Summary:
Several animals and a boy and his granny fall asleep on the same bed.

Activity:
Get a large pillow, cushion, or beanbag chair. Bring children up from your audience to place their heads on the pillow as different characters enter the story and sleep on the bed. You could cut out pictures and make this a flannel-board story, adding the characters to a drawn or copied picture of a bed. Alternatively, use stuffed animals or puppets to place on a toy bed or one you made yourself. Children can also sit on a blanket as an alternative to lying on a pillow. When everyone leaves the bed, have the children do so one at a time, as in the story.

Yektai, Niki. 1988. *Crazy Clothes*. Illus., Suçie Stevenson. New York: Bradbury.

Summary:
A boy puts his clothes on all wrong.

Activity:
Have the kids laughing with this book while you mimic the boy in the story and put clothes on you, a toy, or another child in all the wrong places. Put pants on your head; a sweater on your legs; a shirt over the

pants on your head, and then around your neck without your arms in the sleeves; socks on your hands; and a jacket over it all.

———. 1989. *What's Silly?* Illus., Susannah Ryan. New York: Clarion.

Summary:
Pictures are shown first of a silly way to do something, and then illustrating the correct way.

Activity:
The book keeps asking what is silly. You can ask children in a smaller group or walk around the room and see if they can tell. Take turns asking children, or show everyone and ask them to stay silent until you show everyone and wait for a group response. A picture might show a woman with a dog on her head and a hat on a leash.

Yorinks, Arthur. 1999. *Tomatoes from Mars.* Illus., Mort Drucker. New York: HarperCollins.

Summary:
Giant tomatoes from Mars fall to the Earth.

Activity:
It would be fun if you could inflate a bunch of red balloons, keep them hidden, and then continue to toss them out to the kids while reading the story every time tomatoes land on the pages of the book. When a concoction of oil and such is sprayed on the tomatoes in the end of the story, use a water bottle to spray. You could also cut tomatoes out of red paper, or use red beanbags, balls, or tomato pincushions to toss out.

Young, Ed. 1997. *Mouse Match: A Chinese Folktale.* San Diego, Calif.: Harcourt Brace.

Summary:
Papa and Mama Mouse want to find the best suitor for their daughter, so they aim high, finally deciding that another mouse is the best match.

Activity:
The most fun part of this book is that all the pages unfold to make one extremely long page. Use a few children to come up and help you hold

the book as you tell the story. If that isn't enough fun, you can use the children to help figure out whom (or what) the mice will choose next as a suitor for their daughter. Instead of revealing right away that the first choice is the sun, ask, "They looked out the window and saw rays. What do you think they want as their daughter's husband?" If they do not immediately guess that it is the sun from what is provided in the book, add your own hints. "It is yellow and bright and comes out during the day way up in the sky." Other suitors include a cloud, wind, mountain, and finally a mouse.

————. 1992. *Seven Blind Mice*. New York: Philomel.

Summary:
Mice come across an elephant and take turns guessing what it is in this classic story.

Activity:
This is a perfect example of using questions. Ask the kids if they think the guesses of the mice are correct. "Is it a great cliff?" "A pillar?" "A snake?" "Spear?" "Fan?" "Rope?" No. They will probably know right away that it is an elephant, but that's okay. Pretend like you are not sure if it is, and in the end tell them they were right all along.

Zelinsky, Paul. 1990. *The Wheels on the Bus*. New York: Dutton.

Summary:
A version of the song in which the different motions from the bus are repeated, such as people going in and out and wipers going swish swish swish.

Activity:
Locate a recording of "The Wheels on the Bus" and play it while turning back and forth to find the right point in the story. You might want to mark the pages so you remember which to flip to for each action. Otherwise, sing the song with the children as you turn the pages. Have the children make the motions as well, such as arms moving back and forth for wipers, hands opening and closing for doors, hands in a steering wheel position moving back and forth for wheels going round, leaning forwards and backwards for people moving in and out, a thumb behind the shoulder for the bus driver telling people to move back, lifting arms up like pumping weights for the windows going up and down, bouncing up and

down for the riders going "bumpety-bump," crying for babies crying, and a finger to the mouth for a mother shushing.

Zemke, Deborah. 1988. *The Way It Happened*. Boston: Houghton Mifflin.

Summary:
Sarah falls from her bicycle, but the story changes as it is repeated from person to person.

Activity:
Play the telephone game with this story. Pretend to whisper, but do it in a normal voice to one child. Keep moving from child to child to "whisper" the next part of the story. You could also have the children pretend to whisper to one another, taking turns as you reach a new page. End with a real game of telephone, whispering a phrase in one child's ear to see what the result is in the end.

Ziefert, Harriet. 1998. *I Swapped My Dog*. Illus., Emily Bolam. Boston: Houghton Mifflin.

Summary:
A man swaps his dog, and then keeps swapping, until he gets it back in the end.

Activity:
There are many ways you can involve the children in this story. One of the most fun ways is to give each child an animal from the story, whether on paper or a stuffed animal or puppet, including a horse, mule, goat, sheep, cow, pig, hen, and a cat. Put down the book and use different animals avoiding rhyme if this works better for you. Then each time the man (librarian) swaps one animal for another, you can walk up to different children and swap it for their animals in the same order as the story. You could also have the animals on a table or have children come to the front of the room or remove them from a flannel board.

———. 1988. *Me Too! Me Too!* Illus., Karen Gundersheimer. New York: Harper & Row.

Summary:
A girl copies what her sister does.

Activity:
Every time the sister says "Me too! Me too!" point to the children and have them say these words. You could prompt them with, "What does she say?" Follow with a game of follow the leader in which the children respond "Me too! Me too!" before copying you.

———. 2001. *Squarehead*. Illus., Todd McKie. Boston: Houghton Mifflin.

Summary:
George does not like anything that is not shaped like a square because that is the shape of his own head—until a dream makes him think differently.

Activity:
Take pieces of paper or construction paper. Even scrap paper will do. Make sure they are the shape of a square. Have enough for each child in the classroom or storytime group. Now cut two holes in each square so that they can become squarehead masks, and the children can peek through the holes and all become squareheads. Have them hold the squares to their faces and ask them to stand up each time you say the word "square" or "squarehead." Follow by asking the children to identify objects that are square shaped in the room or name other things that are square shaped. Then do the same for circles since at the end of the book George begins to mention many circular objects that he likes.

———. 1995. *The Three Little Pigs*. Illus., Laura Rader. New York: Puffin.

Summary:
Pigs leave home to build houses of their own only to be disturbed by a big bad wolf.

Activity:
Use storytelling for this tale. Copy pig-head patterns and put them on sticks, or just give the pictures to three children to hold over their faces. Do the same with a picture of a wolf. Bring up three more children to be the houses. Have the children repeat the traditional lines of "Little Pig, Little Pig, let me in," "Not by the hair on my chinny chin chin," and "Then I'll huff and I'll puff and I'll blow your house in." You might want to add humor for parents who may be listening by saying the pigs

were like 40 years old and the mom kicked them out. You can add compassion by saying the wolf landed in the hot pot and went flying out of the chimney never to be seen again instead of telling the children that he died.

Zimmerman, Andrea, and David Clemesha. 1999. *Trashy Town*. Illus., Dan Yaccarino. New York: HarperCollins.

Summary:
A trash man collects trash cans from around town and fills his trash truck.

Activity:
There are several options for this story. Choose one, or do them all at once. The book is divided, with a text box on the side of each page. The left tells where Mr. Gilly gets his trash and the right almost always reads, "Dump it in, smash it down, drive around the Trashy Town!" Children can repeat this with you while making the motions of dumping an invisible trash can, smashing it, and then pretending to drive. Turn it into a dance. Ask them if the trash truck is full, and wait for them to yell, "No!" They can pretend to drive. You could also have some garbage cans and fill them with wadded-up pieces of scrap paper. Have the children take turns picking some out and dumping it into another basket, or into something that will be designated as the trash truck, until all the paper is gone. You could even crinkle up paper and throw it around the room and either have the children pick it up as they repeat the rhyme or take turns putting some into the designated trash truck.

Zion, Gene. 1956. *Harry the Dirty Dog*. Illus., Margaret Bloy Graham. New York: Harper & Row.

Summary:
A dog that hates baths runs away and gets unrecognizably dirty.

Activity:
Copy a dog picture that looks similar to Harry and place it on a board. Each time Harry gets dirtier by playing at the railroad or down a coal chute, etc., keep adding black marks to the picture. Use charcoal, pencils, markers, crayons, or black dot stickers. You could also provide a picture for each of the children and ask them to do the same on their own pictures. Take the picture off to reveal a clean one underneath when Harry gets a bath, or give the children each a clean picture to take home.

Theme Index

If you choose to use themes or want to use this book to enhance your themes, what follows are topics represented in the picture books included in this book. Most are included in more than one category. Not every book is listed under every possible theme.

Accidents

Colliding with Chris (Harder), 69
Oops! (Kline), 93
Scratches and Scrapes (Linn), 98

Adjectives

Hairy, Scary, Ordinary: What Is an Adjective? (Cleary), 45

Adventures

Captain Pajamas (Whatley), 207
Colliding with Chris (Harder), 69
Daring Dog and Captain Cat (Adoff), 15
Harold and the Purple Crayon (Johnson, Crockett), 84
Sally the Sky Diver (Noakes), 137
Scaredy Mouse (MacDonald, Alan), 102

Africa

Master Man (Shepard), 175
Nanta's Lion (MacDonald, Suse), 105

Ailments

Arthur's Nose (Brown, Marc), 35
Bad Case of Stripes, A (Shannon), 174
Bark, George (Feiffer), 56
Dog Breath (Pilkey), 152
Giant Hiccups (Farley), 56
Glerp, The (McPhail), 121
Goldie Locks Has Chicken Pox (Dealey), 49

Airplanes

Aliens/Outer Space

Alphabet

America

Animals/Birds/Reptiles/Amphibians/Insects

Animal Sounds

Appearances

Art

Babies

What the Baby Hears (Goodwin), 66

Balloons

Can You See the Red Balloon? (Blackstone), 31

Balls

Yellow Ball (Bang), 25

Bands

Animal Orchestra (Sharratt), 174
Froggy Plays in the Band (London), 100
Max Found Two Sticks (Pinkney), 153
Our Marching Band (Moss, Lloyd), 127

Baseball

Ernest Lawrence Thayer's Casey at the Bat (Thayer), 190
Mouse Practice (McCully), 116

Basketball

Allie's Basketball Dream (Barber), 26
Swish! (Martin), 112

Bath

King Bidgood's in the Bathtub (Wood), 212
Take Me Out to the Bathtub (Katz, Alan), 88

Bats

Bat Jamboree (Appelt), 18

Bears

Bear Snores On (Wilson), 209
Bearobics (Parker), 146
Bear's Picture (Pinkwater), 153
Brown Bear, Brown Bear, What Do You See? (Martin), 111
Gotcha! (Jorgensen), 85
How Do I Put It On? (Watanabe), 202
Jump! (Lavis), 96
Milo's Hat Trick (Agee), 16
One Bear, One Dog (Stickland), 186
10 Bears in My Bed (Mack), 105
Tops & Bottoms (Stevens), 185
We're Going on a Bear Hunt (Oxenbury), 21
Where Does the Brown Bear Go? (Weiss), 204

Bedtime

Bicycles

Biography

Birds

Birthdays/Parties

Boats

Body

Clowns/Mimes

Coloring

See Art

Colors

Communication/Miscommunication

Competition/Contests

Construction

Cookies

Cooperation

Copying

Costumes

Counting

See Numbers

Cowboys/Cowgirls

Bad Day at Riverbend (Van Allsburg), 193
How I Spent My Summer Vacation (Teague), 190

Cows

Click, Clack, Moo: Cows That Type (Cronin), 48
When Cows Come Home (Harrison), 70

Crayons

Bad Day at Riverbend (Van Allsburg), 193
Crayon Box That Talked, The (DeRolf), 51

Creation

Head, Body, Legs (Paye and Lippert), 148

Crime

Cecil Bunions and the Midnight Train (Paraskevas), 145
Dog Breath (Pilkey), 152
Hallo-Wiener, The (Pilkey), 152
Nursery Crimes (Geisert), 63
Officer Buckle and Gloria (Rathmann), 159
Socksnatchers, The (Balian), 23
Web Files, The (Palatini), 144
Who Took the Cookies from the Cookie Jar (Lass and Sturges), 96

Crocodiles

Imagine You Are a Crocodile (Wallace), 198

Crying

Giggle and Cry Book, The (Spinelli), 182
What Baby Wants (Root), 164

Cumulative Tales

House That Drac Built, The (Sierra), 176
Mike's Kite (MacDonald, Elizabeth), 103
My Little Sister Ate One Hare (Grossman), 68
Sitting Down to Eat (Harley), 69

Dads

Dancing/Gymnastics/Aerobics

Days

Dinosaurs

Saturday Night at the Dinosaur Stomp (Shields), 176
Ten Terrible Dinosaurs (Stickland), 187
Time Flies (Rohmann), 163

Dirty

See Clean

Disabilities

Moses Goes to a Concert (Millman), 124

Disobedience/Obedience

And to Think That I Thought That We'd Never Be Friends (Hoberman), 77
Boing! (Seymour and Keach), 173
Daring Dog and Captain Cat (Adoff), 15
David Goes to School (Shannon), 174
I'm Not Bobby (Feiffer), 57
Lilly's Purple Plastic Purse (Henkes), 73
Little Blue and Little Yellow (Lionni), 99
Mmm, Cookies! (Munsch), 132
No, David! (Shannon), 174
Not Yet, Yvette (Ketteman), 91
Quiet, Wyatt! (Maynard), 114
She Did It! (Ericsson), 55
Ten Furry Monsters (Calmenson), 39
Ten Terrible Dinosaurs (Stickland), 187
Where the Wild Things Are (Sendak), 171

Doctors/Dentists

See Ailments

Dogs

Bark, George (Feiffer), 56
Black and White (Crisp), 47
Can You Find Sadie? (Ohanesian), 142
Chewy Louie (Schneider), 170
Daring Dog and Captain Cat (Adoff), 15
Dog Breath (Pilkey), 152
Dog's Colorful Day (Dodd), 53
Doodle Dog (Rodgers), 163
Great Gracie Chase: Stop That Dog! (Rylant), 166
Hallo-Wiener (Pilkey), 152

Dolls

Donkeys

Dragons

Drawing/Coloring

See Art, Crayons

Dreams

Drums

Ducks

Environment

Exercise

Eyes

Faces

Fairs

Fairy Tales

Family

Flowers

Daisy-Head Mayzie (Seuss), 172
Flower Garden (Bunting), 38

Flying

Bat Jamboree (Appelt), 18
Flap Your Wings and Try (Pomeranz), 156

Folktales/Folklore

Chicken Little (Kellogg), 203
Enormous Potato, The (Davis), 48
Fox Tale Soup (Bonning), 33
Girl Who Wore Too Much, The (MacDonald and Vathanaprida), 104
Greedy Old Fat Man, The (Galdone), 60
Hatseller and the Monkeys, The (Diatke), 52
Head, Body, Legs (Paye and Lippert), 148
Henny-Penny (Wattenberg), 203
Little Red Hen, The (Galdone), 60
Mouse Match (Young), 213
Pied Piper of Hamelin, The (Holden), 78
Story of Chopsticks, The (Compestine), 45
Teeny Tiny Woman, The (Robins), 162
Three Billy Goats Gruff, The (Carpenter), 42
Three Little Pigs, The (Ziefert), 216
Tikki Tikki Tembo (Mosel), 127
Turnip, The (Domanska), 53
What's in Fox's Sack? (Galdoe), 61

Following/Leading

Follow the Leader (Silverman), 177
Monkey See, Monkey Do (Holsonback), 78
Pied Piper of Hamelin, The (Holden), 78
Remainder of One, A (Pinczes), 153
Stay in Line (Slater), 178

Food

Bad Case of Stripes, A (Shannon), 174
Bark, George (Feiffer), 56
Bon Appetit, Mr. Rabbit! (Boujon), 34
Boom, Baby, Boom, Boom! (Mahy), 108
Bunny Party (Wells), 206

Footprints

Forests

Found

See Missing

Foxes

Friends

Garden

Gender Roles

Ghosts

Giants

Goats

Grammar/English/Spelling

Grandparents

Humbug Potion: An A B Cipher (Balian), 22
Little Old Lady Who Was Not Afraid of Anything, The (Williams), 209
Little Scarecrow Boy, The (Brown, Margaret Wise), 36
One Hungry Monster (O'Keefe), 143
Patty's Pumpkin Patch (Sloat), 179
Perky Little Pumpkin, The (Friskey), 58
Plumply, Dumply Pumpkin (Serfozo), 171
Pumpkin Faces (Rose), 164
Pumpkin Pumpkin (Titherington), 190
Room on the Broom (Donaldson), 54
Shake Dem Halloween Bones (Nikola-Lisa), 136
Ten Furry Monsters (Calmenson), 39
There Was an Old Witch (Reeves), 160
Very Busy Spider, The (Carle), 41
We're Going on a Ghost Hunt (Vaughan), 195
Why a Disguise? (Numeroff), 141

Hands

Eyes, Nose, Fingers and Toes (Hindley), 75
Missing Mitten Mystery, The (Kellogg), 90
Mitten Tree, The (Christiansen), 44
My Two Hands/My Two Feet (Walton), 200
These Hands (Price), 157

Hats

Caps for Sale (Slobodkina), 180
Catch That Hat! (Clark), 45
500 Hats of Bartholomew Cubbins, The (Seuss), 172
Hatseller and the Monkeys, The (Diakite), 52
If I Were a Halloween Monster (Moler), 126
Jennie's Hat (Keats), 89
Martin's Hats (Blos), 33
Milo's Hat Trick (Agee), 16
What's on My Head? (Miller), 123
Whose Hat? (Miller), 124

Hens

Little Red Hen, The (Galdone), 60
Pig's Eggs (Partridge), 147

Heroism

Ducks Disappearing (Naylor), 134

Library

Book! Book! Book! (Bruss), 37

Lift the Flap/Pop-Up Books

Animal Orchestra (Sharratt), 174
Billy's Boots (MacKinnon), 106
Peekaboo! (Price), 157
Vroom! Vroom! (Augarde), 20
Wheels on the Bus, The (Zelinsky), 214

Lights

Flashlight (James), 83
Very Lonely Firefly, The (Carle), 42

Lions

Nanta's Lion (MacDonald, Suse), 105
We're Going on a Lion Hunt (Axtell), 20

Lost

See Missing

Magic

Clever Princess, The (Tompert), 191
James Marshall's Cinderella (Marshall), 87
Mad about Plaid (McElmurry), 118
Magic Moonberry Jump Ropes, The (Hru), 80
Magical, Mystical, Marvelous Coat, The (Cullen), 48
Milo and the Magical Stones (Pfister), 151
Milo's Hat Trick (Agee), 16
Molly and the Magic Wishbone (McClintock), 115
Morris's Disappearing Bag (Wells), 206
9 Magic Wishes (Jackson), 82
Poof! (O'Brien), 142
Sweet Touch (Balian), 23

Manners

I Don't Eat Toothpaste Anymore! (King), 92
One of Each (Hoberman), 77
Pass the Fritters, Critters (Chapman), 43
Rules, The (Kelley), 89
Story of Chopsticks, The (Compestine), 45
Table Manners (Raschka and Radunsky), 158

What Do I Say? (Simon), 178

Masks

If I Were a Halloween Monster (Moler), 126
Why a Disguise? (Numeroff), 141

Matching

Missing Mitten Mystery, The (Kellogg), 90
One of Each (Hoberman), 77
Socksnatchers, The (Balian), 23

Math

See Numbers

Messes

See Clean/Dirty

Mice/Rats

Dark at the Top of the Stairs, The (McBratney), 115
If You Give a Mouse a Cookie (Numeroff), 139
Lilly's Purple Plastic Purse (Henkes), 73
Lunch (Fleming, Denise), 58
Milo and the Magical Stones (Pfister), 151
Monk Camps Out (McCully), 116
Mouse, Look Out! (Waite), 198
Mouse Match (Young), 213
Mouse Paint (Walsh), 198
Mouse Practice (McCully), 116
Pied Piper of Hamelin, The (Holden), 78
Scaredy Mouse (MacDonald, Alan), 102
Seven Blind Mice (Young), 214

Missing/Lost/Found

Alphabet Adventure (Wood), 211
Black and White (Crisp), 47
Busy Bea (Poydar), 156
Cousin Ruth's Tooth (MacDonald, Amy), 102
Ducks Disappearing (Naylor), 134
Great Pig Search, The (Christelow), 44
His Mother's Nose (Maloney), 110
Louella Mae, She's Run Away (Alarcon), 16
Max Found Two Sticks (Pinkney), 153

Mystery/Detectives

Names

News Reports

Night

Noses

Numbers/Counting/Math

Nursery Rhymes

Opposites

Origami

Outdoors

Owls

Pancakes

Parades

Parties

Patience

Peddlers

Pets

Photographs

Picnics

Pigs

Pillows

Pillow Pup (Ochiltree), 142
Pillow War, The (Novak), 138

Pizza

Little Red Hen (Makes a Pizza), The (Sturges), 187
Pete's a Pizza (Steig), 184

Poetry

Michael Rosen's ABC (Rosen), 165
Now What Can I Do? (Bridges), 35
Up in the Air (Livingston), 99
You Read to Me, I'll Read to You (Hoberman), 78

Police

Officer Buckle and Gloria (Rathmann), 159

Princesses

Clever Princess, The (Tompert), 191
James Marshall's Cinderella (Marshall), 87
Princess and the Pea, The (Vaës), 192

Pumpkins

Little Old Lady Who Was Not Afraid of Anything, The (Williams), 209
Nursery Crimes (Geisert), 63
Patty's Pumpkin Patch (Sloat), 179
Perky Little Pumpkin, The (Friskey), 58
Plumply, Dumply, Pumpkin (Serfozo), 171
Pumpkin Faces (Rose), 164
Pumpkin Pumpkin (Titherington), 190

Puzzles

Humbug Potion: An A B Cipher (Balian), 22
Jigsaw (Moss, Miriam), 128
Nursery Crimes (Geisert), 63

Questions

Are We There Yet, Daddy? (Walters), 199
Bear on a Bike (Blackstone), 31
Brown Bear, Brown Bear, What Do You See? (Martin), 111
Can You Find Sadie? (Obanesian), 142
Have You Ever Done That? (Larios), 95

Rabbits/Bunnies

Raccoons

Rain

Reading/Books/Stories

School/Teachers

Science

Search and Find

Seasons

Signs

Silly

Sisters

Size

Soup

Space

Spiders

Sports

Stars

States

Stores/Shopping

Tightropes

Mirette on the High Wire (McCully), 116

Time

Around the Clock with Harriet (Maestro), 106
Day by Day a Week Goes Round (Shields), 175
Night City (Wellington and Kupfer), 205
Time to . . . (McMillan), 120
Web Files, The (Palatini), 144

Topiaries

Nursery Crimes (Geisert), 63

Towns

See Cities

Toys/Play

Bad Day at Riverbend (Van Allsburg), 193
Bunny Party (Wells), 206
Crayon Box That Talked, The (DeRolf), 51
I Spy: A Picture Book of Riddles (Marzollo and Wick), 113
Jumanji (Van Allsburg), 194
Jump! (Lavis), 96
Kipper's Toybox (Inkpen), 82
Little Red House, The (Sawicki), 168
Mmm, Cookies! (Munsch), 132
Morris's Disappearing Bag (Wells), 206
Toby's Doll's House (Scamell), 169
Two Little Trains (Brown, Margaret Wise), 37
What Shall We Play? (Heap), 72

Trains

Cecil Bunion and the Midnight Train (Paraskevas), 145
Down by the Station (Hillenbrand), 74
Engine, Engine, Number Nine (Calmenson), 39
Two Little Trains (Brown, Margaret Wise), 37

Transportation/Travel

Are We There Yet, Daddy? (Walters), 199
Bear on a Bike (Blackstone), 31
Bus for Us, The (Bloom), 32
Cecil Bunion and the Midnight Train (Paraskevas), 145

Travel

Trees

Trickery

Title Index

C

About the Author

Jennifer Bromann is currently the library media specialist at Lincoln-Way Central High School in New Lenox, Illinois. Her last position was head of youth services at Prairie Trails Public Library in Burbank, Illinois. She received her BA in Rhetoric with a minor in the Teaching of English from the University of Illinois-Champaign/Urbana, her MLIS from the University of Wisconsin-Milwaukee, and her school media certification from Dominican University in River Forest, Illinois. Bromann is currently working towards her doctorate in Reading and Literacy at Northern Illinois University. She is also the author of *Booktalking That Works* (Neal-Schuman, 2001), as well as several articles for *School Library Journal* and many book reviews for *VOYA*. She can be reached at bromannj@hotmail.com.